THE **DOCTOR,**
THE **HITMAN,** AND
THE **MOTORCYCLE**
GANG

The True Story of One of New Jersey's
Most Notorious Murder for Hire Plots

ANNIE McCORMICK

Camino Books, Inc.
Philadelphia

Manufactured in the United States of America

1 2 3 4   24 23 22 21 20

Library of Congress Cataloging-in-Publication Data

Names: McCormick, Annie, author.
Title: The doctor, the hitman & the motorcycle gang : the true story of one
   of New Jersey's most notorious murder for hire plots / by Annie
   McCormick.
Other titles: Doctor, the hitman and the motorcycle gang
Description: Philadelphia, PA : Camino Books Inc., [2019]
Identifiers: LCCN 2019030679 (print) | LCCN 2019030680 (ebook) | ISBN
   9781680980295 (paperback) | ISBN 9781680980301 (ebook)
Subjects: LCSH: Kauffman, April, -2012. | Kauffman, James, -2018. | Murder
   for hire--New Jersey--Case studies. | Motorcycle gangs--New Jersey--Case
   studies. | Medication abuse--New Jersey--Case studies.
Classification: LCC HV6533.N3 M38 2019 (print) | LCC HV6533.N3 (ebook) |
   DDC 364.152/3092--dc23
LC record available at https://lccn.loc.gov/2019030679
LC ebook record available at https://lccn.loc.gov/2019030680

ISBN 978-1-68098-029-5
ISBN 978-1-68098-030-1 (ebook)

Interior and Cover design: Jerilyn DiCarlo
Cover Photo: April Kauffman and Dr. Jim Kauffman. Photo courtesy of Kim Pack.

This book is available at a special discount on bulk purchases for educational, business, and promotional purposes. For information write:

Publisher
Camino Books, Inc.
P.O. Box 59026
Philadelphia, PA 19102
www.caminobooks.com

CONTENTS

PROLOGUE

When 35-year-old Kimberly Pack received the phone call from the Atlantic County Prosecutor's Office asking her and her husband to clear their schedules for the following Tuesday, January 9, 2018, she said, "We will be there." But the mother of two young boys did not get overly excited, or for that matter, excited at all. When asked later exactly how she felt on the day she received this call, Kim answered: "Numb."

Kim had been down this road many times before, and she was not expecting much. It was now 2018, and she assumed this was just another meeting about her mother's unsolved murder in 2012.

A newly appointed Atlantic County Prosecutor named Damon Tyner had taken office in the spring of 2017, and one of the first people he called was Kimberly Pack.

The new prosecutor promised to put new resources into the dormant investigation of the murder of her mother, April Kauffman, who was 47 at the time of her death. Tyner also promised to give frequent updates, and to share whatever information he could along the way. For the first time Kim felt that someone in a position of authority was on her side, really putting forth a major effort. Still, she felt cautiously optimistic at best, as false hopes had also become a normal part of her life. The mere fact that Prosecutor Tyner had reached out when he took office felt significant; for years, she'd received few updates and met resistance whenever she made an inquiry regarding the investigation.

The very day of April's murder it took detectives hours to tell Kim that they were investigating a homicide and that her mother had not died a natural death. Kim had already figured as much by the presence of the yellow crime scene tape and the news helicopters hovering above.

When the day arrived for the meeting with the Prosecutor's Office, Kim's husband Randy had taken off work and was in the shower getting ready for their 1 p.m. meeting when the phone rang around 11 a.m.

The location of the meeting had changed from the Prosecutor's Office in Mays Landing to the FBI field office in Northfield. The couple was asked to come as soon as possible.

Kim knew this was not just another meeting.

When the Packs walked into the FBI's second floor office, they were greeted by FBI Special Agent Dan Garrabrant.

Garrabrant, a twenty-year veteran of the FBI, had promised Kim that he would find the person or persons responsible for her death and see to it that they were brought to justice, no matter who they were or how long it took.

That day had arrived.

Garrabrant ushered Kim and Randy into a spacious conference room, where the team of people responsible for untangling one of the most notorious murder-for-hire plots in New Jersey history stood.

Detective Jim Scoppa from the Atlantic County Prosecutor's Office, flanked by Chief Assistant Prosecutor Seth Levy and First Assistant Prosecutor Cary Shill, stood next to the team's new leader, Prosecutor Damon Tyner. Tyner placed a hand on Kim's shoulder, looked her in the eye and said softly, "We got 'em, we got all of them."

Every person in the room then proceeded to hug Kim, who was overcome with emotion, and shake hands with Randy, before sitting them down and sharing some of the gruesome details.

Dr. James Kauffman, Kim's stepfather, and the man she had long suspected of killing her mother, had been arrested and charged with murder. In an unforeseen twist, investigators had found that Jim, the fidgety, nervous, physically unprepossessing doctor, was heavily involved with an outlaw South Jersey biker gang in what prosecutors described as an elaborate and lucrative drug dealing scheme. Kim knew that leading up to her mother's death, her mother had uncovered some of the truth about some of Jim's dirty deals and his labyrinth of lies. Prosecutors say that when she found out and threatened to expose the illicit pill mill he was running out of his medical office, a contract on her life was set in motion.

The months following the meeting at the FBI office in Northfield would begin what Kim hoped would be the final chapter of her years-long journey in fighting for and ultimately finding justice for her mother.

But the case was far from over, and was still to bring many new and disturbing details to light.

The tangled web involving the doctor, the hitman, and the motorcycle gang was about to unravel.

Chapter 1

PREMONITIONS

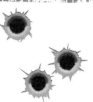

"I feel like I'm on borrowed time here...."

April Kauffman's familiar throaty laugh filled listeners' ears when she spoke those words on May 9th, 2012. She was live on her radio program, *The King Arthur Show*, in the Ocean City, New Jersey studio of WIBG-FM with her co-host, King Arthur Gropper. Kauffman was in the midst of thanking politicians—including New Jersey Governor Chris Christie, New Jersey Congressman Frank LoBiondo, and the Secretary of Veterans' Affairs General Eric Shinseki—who had helped with her philanthropic work on behalf of local veterans. Her comment followed a joking remark about thinking that her microphone was cut off.

But April Kauffman really was on borrowed time.

That day was a high point for her, marking a moment of great affirmation. April, a staunch advocate for the men and women of the military, had just received the distinguished New Jersey State Governor's Jefferson Award for her work on veterans' behalf. April was a force. She could get things done thanks to her out-sized gifts of tenacity, passion, and charm. And it didn't hurt that she was gorgeous. At 47 years old, with her tall curvy body, blonde hair, and stunning looks, she was both sexy and smart. When she walked into a room, she was captivating. Today had brought the satisfaction of knowing that her years of hard work, on an issue she cared about so much, had been recognized.

Two guests had joined April and King Arthur today: Bob Greco and Sam Fiocchi. They were both active in the political life of nearby Cumberland County, Greco as Republican Party Chairman and Fiocchi as a county Freeholder. The microphone went hot, the "On Air" sign lit up in red. Today's topic would be the good news about TRICARE, an insurer for military veterans. Shore Medical was now accepting it, and veterans across the area had April to thank. She had successfully advocated for this while juggling her other volunteer work with the Wounded Warriors Project, the United States Coast Guard, the Southern Shore Chapter of the American Red Cross, and the Atlantic County Toys for Kids program.

"I did the work," April went on. "I put my boots on the ground, and lobbied using my own money, time, and airfare." You could hear the emotion in her voice. April was savoring her accomplishment; at the same time, she was deeply affected by the hard fight to win. Her comments then took a more personal turn.

"My bottom line, if nothing else, is to leave my legacy on this planet to my beautiful daughter and grandchildren." April paused and gave another throaty laugh, then jokingly proposed that she might be eligible for a military honor given to some fallen veterans: "Hey, I could get a flyover at my funeral now?" She mused that people could really say, "Here was an American citizen who really stood up and dug her heels in and… yelled fire and expected it to be put out."

To understand how emotional April was during this broadcast, you have to understand the enormity of what she had just accomplished as a civilian volunteer. TRICARE, which is paid for by the Pentagon, provides health care to more than five million Americans. Shore Medical is one of the main hospitals serving the Jersey Shore area. The plan provides health care services for active duty United States military and retirees with 20 or more years of service as well as to their dependents.

April took on the cause after hearing about the long treks that veterans living in Atlantic County had to make in order to undergo dialysis, radiation, and chemotherapy treatments. No local medical facility providing these types of care accepted TRICARE.

School buses would take more than a dozen patients from Atlantic County to the VA Hospital in Delaware, more than a two-hour drive. Then the radiation patients would transfer to a second bus and ride another hour and a half to the Veterans Hospital in Philadelphia. Some of the radiation patients could opt to stay in a hotel room overnight if they felt too sick from their treatment. The dialysis patients in Delaware did not have that option. The school buses shuttling the veterans had no bathrooms, uncomfortable seats, and no air conditioning. Many of the veterans were elderly, some in their eighties. No family members were allowed on the bus.

The bathroom stops were limited. Side effects from some of the treatments include frequent urination and an inability to control bowels. After several accidents on the bus, the group dubbed themselves "The Coffee Can Gang," since coffee cans were often their only option to relieve themselves. Some who had accidents were too embarrassed to return. Hearing that story would appall anyone, but April Kauffman went beyond being appalled.

Bob Frolow, head of Veterans Services for Atlantic County and a veteran himself, already had the issue on his radar. He had begun a petition-signing campaign to push for improvements. Frolow had also reached out to Shore Medical Center and was working closely with Shore's CEO at the time, Rick Pittman. He had already run into walls at Veterans Affairs, and he needed all the help and support he could garner. Rick Pittman recalls how when April entered the picture, she brought a burst of energy to bear on solving the problem. The first time he met April, he was struck by her beauty, her enthusiasm, and her passion for the people she affectionately called her "military heroes."

April had been joined in this cause by her husband, Dr. James Kauffman, an endocrinologist who treated many veterans in his practice. Dr. Kauffman had a working relationship with the hospital and had a good reputation. Since 1990, he served at the hospital as their Director of Metabolic Care. The Kauffmans worked together to bring TRICARE coverage to local veterans. As part of the campaign, Congressman Frank LoBiondo, whose district included parts of South Jersey, sent a letter jointly with Senator Bob Menendez to General Eric Shinseki, the Secretary of Veterans Affairs, explaining the need for improved healthcare in the region.

April wanted to meet Shinseki, to make sure he got the message. As was her style, she made it happen.

The National Association for Uniformed Services (NAUS) had scheduled its annual conference at Fort Belvoir in Virginia on Saturday, November 6th, 2010. April discovered that you do not have to have a military background to attend the NAUS event—so she signed up. She called Rep. LoBiondo's office for help in arranging to speak with General Shinseki, one-on-one. LoBiondo's office was on board.

Rick Pittman remembers arriving to pick up the couple early that Saturday morning, at 5 a.m. The Kauffmans lived in a large house in Linwood, NJ, an affluent town in Atlantic County just over the bridge from the beaches of the New Jersey Shore. Jim stood at the end of the driveway ready to go, then April came out and the three headed on their road trip. They planned to drive to Virginia and head back the same day.

For Pittman, finding a solution to this problem was personal. He comes from a military family. In 1966, the day he graduated from the University of Scranton, he went into the Army. Pittman landed in Vietnam, and served in the 313th Signal Company and 199th light infantry brigade from 1969 to 1970, eventually retiring as a First Lieutenant. Pittman assumed the Kauffmans had military ties as well because they were so passionate about this issue.

During the long drive south he brought up his time in Vietnam, and Dr. Kauffman said that he too served in Vietnam, in the Special Forces. The conversation, however, was brief and vague. All the doctor would say was that he had been sent "all around." Pittman found this strange. Most Vietnam veterans remember very clearly where they served in Vietnam. However, Pittman also knew that many had suffered life-altering, traumatic events. Veterans witnessed tremendous suffering and loss of life, and the images they took home were too much for some to want to recall. Maybe, Pittman thought, Jim had one of those experiences in Vietnam. He didn't bring it up again.

The trio arrived at the conference, and waited for the question and answer portion of the meeting to begin. April did ask a few questions, but they still felt they needed one-on-one face time with General Shinseki. Jim decided he would corner Shinseki in the men's room and ask his questions. Pittman was impressed at the couple's relentlessness. The trio returned home happy with what they'd done, and hopeful about a response. Sources inside the NAUS told Pittman that the paperwork outlining a deal to contract military dialysis services had sat on the Secretary's desk for months. But, shortly after their visit, Shinseki signed the papers.

Soon after that, Rick Pittman retired from Shore Medical, and Ron Johnson took over as CEO. He too was willing to accept TRICARE, but the change in coverage inched along on a bureaucratic timeline. In December of 2011, over a year after attending the NAUS conference, April was finally able to make the exciting announcement. In May, Ron Johnson announced that the hospital would accept TRICARE starting in June.

Dr. Kauffman had already announced the previous December that he would accept TRICARE at his offices. Yet a few months before the announcement, in the fall of 2011, April had felt frustrated with her husband. The paperwork that would allow his practice to accept TRICARE still sat on her husband's pile of paperwork on his desk. Why wasn't he as eager as she was on this issue they had been pushing so hard for? Jim was a veteran himself—there was even an article mentioning his service hanging on the wall in the office. Wasn't he proud as a veteran to provide his services to the men and women of the military? "I'll get to it…," he kept saying.

Jim's military service had played a large part in kindling April's passion for helping veterans. April and Jim had hosted dinners for men and women serving in the Coast Guard during "Operation Fireside," a Red Cross project placing cadets in homes for holiday dinners. Every year April cooked a massive Thanksgiving dinner and opened her home for the cadets. The couple ordered stretch limos to shuttle the cadets in lavish style to and from the local Coast Guard base.

A few years earlier, April had told her best friend, Peg O'Boyle, that Jim had received his Purple Heart in the mail. Apparently he had lost his medal, and ordered a replacement on eBay to replace the one he was awarded. Peg's antennae went up. but she could not figure out why he would lie. She had seen him multiple times wearing his Green Beret with the military insignia.

Even as April became more enmeshed in assisting veterans with their issues, her own "veteran's issue" came to a head. Around December of 2011, April learned for sure that Jim had lied about serving in the military. "If I tell everyone, it looks like I knew it," she confided to one of her closest friends, Lee Darby. When April first confronted Jim about this, his response, according to close friends was disturbing: "If you tell, I will put a bullet in your head and in your face."

April was not going to let her secret knowledge about her husband ruin the broadcast on May 9th. She even spoke about learning the news about TRICARE with her husband. "I said to my husband last night while having dinner at the Northfield Diner, looking right at him and it was a little bittersweet... and I was emotional. I did cry a little and I didn't think I would. I looked at him last night and said, 'I'm out of a job.'" She laughed while contemplating what was next. "So you guys are going to have to give me a new crusade. I'm thinking homelessness and veterans are big issues, and I think I might just slide over there."

When the broadcast was over, April said to Gropper, "We're going to go out and have a bite and have a drink." Gropper had work to do and declined to join them. Around 4:15 April, Fiocchi and Greco headed to Yesterday's Bar, a beach shack-style bar in the small community of Marmora. April had a Stoli vodka on the rocks, and according to the bartender she was upbeat and chatty. The three friends left around 5:50 p.m. April paid cash for the tab and headed home. While she was still at the bar Jim sent her a text around 5:00 pm saying, "I'm home."

What happened the rest of the night is mostly from Jim's perspective. The accounts of what he said transpired that evening would change years later.

Late that night April and Jim were playing with April's new iPhone, transitioning from her Blackberry to the phone. The couple were trying to figure out how to work Siri, and the new apps and features, including talk to text. While they tried to figure out the phone, Suzanne Devito, April's close friend and a pharmaceutical representative who frequented Jim's office, texted her about plans later that week. April, Jim, Suzanne and three others were going to attend a show at The Comedy Stop, and Suzanne wanted to change their dinner reservations. April and Suzanne went back and forth about where to go for dinner. Suzanne, as a drug representative, had held breakfasts at Jim's practice for years. Jim had never instructed Suzanne before about how to enter his office, but tonight he wrote: "When you get there, if no one is available to open the door use my cell phone."

Suzanne texted April she was able to get a reservation at Cafe 2825, a popular Atlantic City restaurant. The two said goodnight.

Overnight, others received strange messages from April's phone. A handful of people received forwarded emails from April, some dated months before. They arrived in batches.

Gropper, her radio co-host, said his was a political joke. He wasn't the only one to get flooded with forwarded emails dated back days to months earlier, all from April's new phone. They began coming in around 1:45 in the morning and ended around 4 a.m.—a surprising time for them to receive a message from April. People who worked with her on veterans' issues, like her good friends, Donna Clementoni and Bob Frolow, woke up with their inboxes full of the forwarded messages and noticed more recipients cc'd. All were months-old emails that she had previously sent.

Donna was perplexed when she sorted through them the next morning. April had already responded to these emails months earlier. Then she noticed they were not all forwards, there were several responses from April to the emails dated months before. April's responses appeared to have been typed at 1:30 in the morning.

Re: INVITATION TO A TOUR...
February 24, 2012 5:54:35 PM   1:35 AM

I would love to do a tour some time and feature this on my show.

The tour referenced in the email was on March 15th, and Donna and April had already moved on to other projects. Why was April responding to her about it again?

Re: employer support of the guard...
January 23,2012 8:51 PM   1:33 AM

These type of stories happen too much.

Another email about a subject that Donna and April had already discussed, the email April responded to was sent months prior. In the coming days, more people would come forward and say they received forwards of old emails too.

The last text message from April's phone was sent at 3:27 on the morning of May 10th, to Billy Gonzalez. Billy was a young man April had employed for years to do odd jobs around her home. One of those jobs was to take care of her pet birds and clean their cages.

It read, "See you in the morning."

Billy had never received a reminder text from April in the five years he'd worked for her.

Chapter 2

MOM'S DEAD

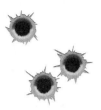

As Kim Pack drove to her morning appointments on May 10, 2012, she looked up to blue skies and puffy white clouds, and took in the distinct scent in the air. It was the subtle, comforting and familiar bouquet of springtime in Atlantic City: a mix of ocean breezes with the earthy aroma from temperatures rising over 70 degrees. Memorial Day weekend, the unofficial start of summer, was just around the corner. After that the summer season would begin. That would bring masses of weekend shore-goers, mostly from the Philadelphia suburbs, Southeast Pennsylvania, and Southern New Jersey, descending on Atlantic City, Margate, Ventnor, Longport and Ocean City. The tourists would shatter the local residents' peace and calm, filling the lonely beaches, and cramming the normally traffic-free roadways for the next five months.

Normally Kim would have enjoyed the lulling warm air for at least a moment. On this Thursday morning, her mind was elsewhere, and she was worried.

By mid-morning, Kim still had not heard back from her mother, April Kauffman. Kim's morning had been its usual routine, rushing her two boys, ages five and eighteen months, to daycare. Kim, a successful pharmaceutical sales representative, had a busy day ahead which included meetings and lunches with medical offices in her coverage area on the Jersey Shore. She had scheduled time this morning to take a call with her good friend and business partner, Suzanne DeVito, about a timeshare she was thinking of purchasing. Kim, her boys, and her husband Randy traveled with April several times a year to Disney World in Orlando, Florida. and a timeshare there would make sense. Kim wanted to speak with her mom before she arrived at her 11:45 lunch meeting at a physician's office in Ocean City. Pharmaceutical representatives often host lunches to pitch their drugs to doctors' offices. Once inside, she could not take personal calls since she had to focus on explaining the products. It's a high-pressure job; every rep has a quota to meet each month.

Kim and April usually spoke every morning. Kim mentally replayed the past few hours. Could she have missed a call from her mom? She scrolled through her phone, checking her call history. She had first tried April's home phone around eight a.m. and again shortly after that. Then, she called twice to her mom's cell phone, sent a text but never received a response.

Her mother was an early riser—usually she was dressed by five or six a.m. You could expect to see April's platinum blonde hair perfectly in place. With years of cosmetology experience, she applied her makeup with professional precision, using eyeshadow and eyeliner to make her captivating green eyes pop even more; pink lip gloss completed her look with a frosty pout.

Kim shared her mother's beauty. They were almost lookalikes, except for Kim being petite and several inches shorter. Kim's smile, like her mom's, lights up a room, and her skin always had a sun-kissed glow as if she'd just stepped off the beach. Mother and daughter had a close, sisterly bond since April had Kim when she was just seventeen. Kim had taken on the traits of a mini-adult: a worrier, always doing the right thing, excelling in school and completing college early. In contrast, April had graduated from the school of hard knocks; nothing slowed her down. A committed, diligent worker, April made her business ideas and later her philanthropic efforts, especially for veterans, come to fruition. As her friends would say, "April always shot for the stars, and never missed." April loved to work a room and hold court on the radio. Kim had an engaging personality, but she avoided the limelight her mom was drawn to.

Kim thought of reasons why April hadn't responded to her calls. Maybe April had the TV on loud in her kitchen with the coffee machine brewing. With her philanthropy projects, the beauty salon she owned, and her radio host duties, April was known to have a phone to each ear while texting on her Blackberry. Most mornings Kim would bring Starbucks over after dropping off the boys. Often, April would pull out their Disney mugs and have Kim try different teas she was always collecting. Sometimes, the two would meet up for breakfast at the Northfield Diner. Every single morning, the mother and daughter either spoke to each other or saw each other.

Kim had texted April again around nine a.m.: "Hi. Where are you?" In Kim's rush, she could have sworn her mom wrote back just after ten a.m. with a vague response to Kim's request to meet for a late lunch. But now, as Kim scrolled through her phone, she saw nothing.

Before eleven a.m., she texted her mom again. As Kim hit send, the call she'd expected from her friend Suzanne came through. Kim pulled over into a parking lot near the doctor's office where she was going for lunch. She figured she'd talk to April after Suzanne's call ended, but while still speaking to Suzanne, another call began beeping through. The name "Jim Kauffman" appeared on her phone.

Suzanne was a close, long-time friend of Kim and April's, and she knew about Kim's shaky relationship with her step-dad. After ten years of marriage to April, Jim's relationship with April's family and friends was so tense that Kim refused to spend holidays with him. Just a week before, April had sat in her daughter's house crying, knowing her marriage was all but over. April's family and close friends had heard before about her allegations of abuse.

"Suz, I gotta go. Jim's calling me," Kim said.

"What, why would he be calling you?" Suzanne asked, knowing how strained things were between them. Kim replied nervously, "I don't know. I gotta go..."

Kim flipped to Jim's call; she answered, "Hello."

Jim's words came fast and frantic on a repeat: "Mom's dead, Mom's dead, Mom's dead ..."

"What, what do you mean?" said Kim. Jim replied, "What? Didn't you hear me? Mom's dead."

Kim's shock, rage, and panic began to build as she tried to process the news.

"What did you do to her?" she replied without thinking to her stepfather. Then she hung up.

Kim sat in the car shaking. She had no idea how she was going to get to her mom's house in Linwood, but she put her car in drive. Jim hadn't said that April was in Linwood, but Kim headed on instinct toward the home her mom shared with Jim at 2 Woodstock Drive.

Just as she was about to go over the Ninth Street Bridge that connects Ocean City with Somers Point, Jim called back. When Kim answered, Jim began yelling, "Did you hear me? Mom's dead."

Kim responded, "I heard you, and if you had anything to do with this, I swear to God you're going to have major problems." She ended the phone call. Tears filled her eyes.

Chapter 3

TWO WOODSTOCK

Kim must have gone into shock; the next twenty or so minutes were blocked out of her memory. In a catatonic state, Kim arrived in Linwood. Everything was going in slow motion, with the chaotic sounds and actions around her slow and muted. She pulled into Woodstock Drive, threw on her hazard lights, and pulled up to the house that was the anchor of the cul-de-sac. Two Woodstock Drive, the beautiful 7,000 square-foot home full of her Mom's cooking, laughter, and love, was now filling with police and emergency crews. Neighbors were gathering, looking around confused and concerned.

At least two cop cars were parked outside when Kim arrived. Randy, Kim's husband and a driver for UPS, had left the brown delivery truck haphazardly parked. He must have been closer to the house when Kim hysterically called him. Then she saw Jim's Ford Explorer parked in the driveway. It looked like it was running and overheating. A thick green puddle formed on the driveway underneath his SUV and trickled down into the street, staining the roadway.

Kim thrust the gearshift into park and jumped out, ripping off her heels and tossing them in the street. She ran towards the front door, but turned her head when she saw Billy Gonzales, her mother's handyman, sitting in the driver's seat of Jim's car, smoking a cigarette.

"What Happened.....what happened?" she screamed. The handyman shook his head and raised his hands as if to say, "I don't know." Just then a police officer came out of the house. "No, you can't talk to him." Kim looked into Billy's eyes. He looked scared and confused, but he wasn't in a cop car so he must not be in trouble, she thought. Kim pushed the cop out of her way, saying, "Where is my mom?" The cop said nothing, but pointed her to the left. She heard muffled voices; her heart began to pound again. Kim was terrified about what she would find to the left when she walked inside. She didn't know if she could handle seeing her mother's dead body.

Jim stood inside the house, surrounded by some of the staff from his medical practice—they had dropped everything to be there for him when he called the office with the news. Nurse Practitioner Barb Greenling, Terry Warner, and Mary Welcer were there; Lydia Argus had gone to get Jim's mother, Ruth. Jim had called the office shortly after he left for a doctor's appointment around eleven a.m. to tell them April was dead. The scene was tense. Randy stayed close to April's best friends, Lee Darby and Peg O'Boyle, whom Jim had also called. Jim's best friend Ron Welcer, a former Linwood police sergeant, was there. His wife Mary Welcer had called to tell him. Kim was half relieved she hadn't walked in on the sight of her mother's body right away, but at the same time, it was very hard for her to see Jim there.

Jim sat in a chair in front of the fireplace, his legs spread apart, his head down and his arms dangling. When he brought his head up, his face wore a look of shock. Kim couldn't help herself. Rage flooded through her and she began screaming in his face.

" ...You're never nice! You are a scumbag! " Her gut and her heart told her he was responsible. How? She didn't know. Linwood police officers swooped in, pulled Kim back and told her to calm down. Paramedics grabbed hold of her, asking if she wanted to go to the hospital. Terry Warner, whom Kim knew from working in the office occasionally, brought her water. Kim took deep breaths.

"I just want to see my Mom… I just want to see my mom…," she kept repeating. Then she collapsed on the floor.

When she got up, she saw several detectives upstairs. Their eyes met; the detectives kept their faces blank. Kim thought, This can't be good. The detectives ordered her and everyone out of the house and into the backyard.

Kim stood by the pool in the backyard, watching as leaves floated in the water; the moment was surreal. Settling on a seat next to a picnic table, knowing her mother's body still lay inside, she thought about how Jim had come into their life, all the times he tried to drive them apart, and how Kim always wanted to like him. Kim's stomach sank, remembering her mother's fears of what Jim might do as their marriage had begun to come apart. thought he was going to kill her as the option of divorce soon appeared inevitable.

With Jim standing there, Kim began to feel a little crazy.

"So what happens, what happens?" She asked him, not sure what she even meant. "Does this really happen? How do you know she's dead?" Kim hoped to hear words of comfort from her stepfather. Instead, Jim answered with zero emotion.

"You've seen one dead body, you've seen 'em all."

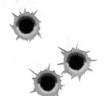

Chapter 4

THE MAD BOMBER AND THE BLOND BOMBSHELL

Kim Pack had first met Jim Kauffman on a snowy day in the winter of her sophomore year in high school. The teenager was waiting patiently for her mom at a popular and bustling local hair salon where April worked. Kim, who attended Mainland High School, came by after school that day and planned to go to her mom's house. Kim had been living with her father in Linwood so she could go to the high school there, since her Mom lived in Absecon, which was not in the same district. April, then April Sagransky, was living then in her childhood home with her second husband, a local doctor, but the marriage was crumbling and divorce was on the horizon.

April was even in the process of changing her name to April Christine, using her middle name as her surname. Dr. Jim Kauffman, who was fifteen years April's senior, had been paying a lot of visits to April's salon. He was also going through a separation; at least that's what April thought, and what she told her daughter and friends. He was cold—that was Kim's impression when she first met Jim. His personality was the total opposite of her mother's. April had asked Dr. Kauffman if he could give both her and her daughter a ride home in his SUV. It had snowed, and April only had her Corvette, a car not designed for severe weather. The doctor had his own successful endocrinology practice in nearby Egg Harbor Township. April was a blond bombshell who turned heads when she walked into a room. April and Jim had run in the same social circles for years. April had even been to the Bat Mitzvah of one of Jim's two daughters, at his beautiful home on 2 Woodstock Drive.

The two reconnected and quietly began a courtship. On one of their first dates, they took a motorcycle ride to the Vietnam Veterans Memorial in Washington, D.C. Jim told April that he had served there as a Green Beret, something that really impressed April. "It was like he came in on a white horse," one of April's friend's recalled. They loved long motorcycle rides and going away on beautiful vacations. Jim made her laugh. The tall, beautiful blonde with the great figure and the straight-shooter attitude had met her Prince Charming.

April had an affinity for anything that moved fast; she loved the speed of Corvettes, motorcycles. Some might interpret her attraction to speed as a sign of wanting to live on the edge. But those closest to April say it was like meditation for her: the only time her mind could be at ease, and stop moving. April's mind moved 100 miles an hour faster than most. She was a survivor, always staying above water, always helping, and constantly in a search for love, making up for what she hadn't had as a child.

Jim and April's courtship came to a halt after only a few months, when April discovered that Jim was in fact still married, and confronted him about it. Jim moved out of his Linwood home and rented an apartment in Ocean City. After some time passed, the two got back together. They were married on Valentine's Day of 2002 on a cruise ship, with no family or friends present. April lost some friends over their relationship. That didn't stop the two from forging their new life. Eventually, April moved into 2 Woodstock Drive but she wanted that to be temporary. She wanted a fresh start for their marriage. She wanted a fresh chance to get her life right. The two had met on the Linwood doctor's party circuit, after having circulated in the small radius of Jersey Shore towns virtually their whole lives.

April Fovozzo was born in Absecon to a mother who entertained a revolving door of male callers; some of them treated April horribly, and some were abusive. April knew at a young age that she was a "chosen one." Some children would carry that description with pride, as destining them for greater things. But April was the "chosen one" because her mother kept her while placing her brothers and sisters into the foster system, leaving April with devastating guilt. April's grandmother had helped to raise her.

April gave birth to her daughter, Kimberly Connor, in 1982, when she was seventeen. Like many teenage relationships, the relationship with Kim's dad did not last long, but they did remain friends her whole life. April raised Kim essentially on her own. After she got her cosmetology license, she worked in salons and did hair and nails in people's homes. When casinos arrived in Atlantic City, she worked with McCullough Models, a modeling agency catering to the Miss America hopefuls. The agency also hired cocktail waitresses for the casinos and special events. April was fun, vivacious, and always brought her hardworking, positive attitude to photo shoots or the casino floor. It was a flashy, sexy time, with big hair, glossy lips, bright lights, and fortunes to be won.

Although her life in this boardwalk fast lane might sound exciting, April struggled to make ends meet. Kim remembers standing in the check-out line when she was a little girl, watching her mom with holes in her Keds sneakers, doing the math in her head to decide what they could afford to keep, and what they had to put back in the shelves. Those life lessons, and April's strict approach to parenting, taught Kim that nothing is handed to you.

Even with everything on her plate, April still found time to volunteer for others in need. She would offer her nail services as a pick-me-up to senior citizens at a local retirement home, or dress up as silly characters for kids' charity functions.

Jim Kauffman presented a diametric opposite to April's magnetic personality. He was quiet and reserved, and his upbringing was much different than hers. Growing up in Margate, Jimmy Kauffman's nickname was "The Mad Bomber." The precocious little boy taught himself how to make explosives and then showed his friends. Jimmy bought saltpeter and a chemistry set at the local Rexall drugstore. He already had charcoal and sulfur, and soon learned to combine them in the proper ratios. From the local toy store, he bought a Jetex fuse, usually used to ignite model airplane engines. The result was a big, satisfying BOOM.

At the time it seemed innocent; back then you could buy bullets at the hardware store and the kids wouldn't think anything was amiss. After all, it wasn't like he was blowing up a car. But those who gave him that nickname say they wouldn't have done it if the other boys hadn't thought there was something "off" about him. One fellow student recalls, "He was unusual in the sense that he wasn't someone you could feel comfortable around completely. He didn't have a lot of friends. He didn't hang with a certain crowd; he seemed like a loner."

However, Jim's prowess with chemistry did align with his lifelong dream to become a physician, as well as his fascination with guns. In high school Jim was 5 foot 9, handsome with an easy smile, dimples, and thick hair with a slight widows peak, and wore black-rimmed glasses. But he was still quiet and didn't fit in the popular crowd. Jim struggled at Franklin and Marshall College after graduating with Atlantic City High School's Class of 1967. He entered college in the fall of 1967 but left the then all-male college in the spring of 1969, blaming his departure on the looming possibility of the draft and horrible grades. He had either failed or barely passed his courses in both his freshman and sophomore years; ultimately it was the Committee on Academic Standing that told him he had to withdraw.

Jim was readmitted to Franklin and Marshall in January of 1971. This time he worked hard and blossomed, earning As, Bs, and Cs. in summer school at Rutgers, he made solid Bs. In his senior year at Franklin and Marshall, he made the Dean's List. The following year with a major in biology, Jim improved his GPA and scored well on his MCATS.

In the fall of 1972, Jim began applying to medical school with his bolstered grades and a letter meant to pull on the heartstrings of admissions boards. In the letter, Jim blamed his nearly two-year absence from school on his issues trying to conquer a tough childhood in Margate City. Jim's mother, Ruth, had come to New Jersey from England, during a time when Jews were being persecuted in Germany. Jim's father, Jack, had fought in World War II, and Jim related that his father was the only man in his platoon to survive an attack during the war; he was a hero. But Jim added that his father didn't see himself that way.

Kauffman grew up in a well-kept home on a nice block in Margate City. Friends don't remember visiting the Kauffman house too often, in part because Jim did not want to spend a lot of time there. His girlfriend from that time later said that "he grew up in a very difficult and sad household," and that Jim's relationship with his parents was cold. Jim's upbringing was so traumatic that he would later say he struggled with the thought that he was psychotic.

In the letter to Philadelphia College of Osteopathic Medicine, Jim wrote about how he used his time away from college to understand himself better:

I decided to go to a psychiatrist. That decision was one of the hardest I have ever made and also a turning point in my life. I went almost a year, trying to put back the pieces of a shattered life. I learned I was not psychotic, but had an emotional maladjustment due to my environment at home. I learned how to face this problem and any others that may arise... I can state with certainty I have more compassion and understanding for other people than do most people, because I know what it's like to have problems.

On Jim's application form for PCOM, in the section asking the applicant's "selective service classification," Jim wrote 4-F. This military classification indicated men who were incapable of serving due to medical or psychological unfitness.

The Philadelphia College of Osteopathic Medicine accepted him, to begin classes in the fall of 1973. In his own words, Jim set out at PCOM to be a "white knight" and "eliminate cancer and heart disease with one blow only pausing to cure the common cold during a brief respite."

On PCOM's campus, Jim ran into Arthur Nahas, an Atlantic City High School classmate from his graduating class. Nahas was two years ahead of Jim at PCOM. Jim revealed that he had left Franklin and Marshall for two years because of mental health struggles. Dr. Nahas always remembered that, even thirty years later when he was at a party at 2 Woodstock. During that party, Jim was wearing a green beret and showing off his massive collection of guns, and his handmade bullets. Just like when he was a little boy, he was still fascinated with explosives. At the party that night, his old classmate heard Jim telling a story about serving in Vietnam. Jim said he had served in Special Forces, and related a story about being ambushed, the only one who got away and crawled to safety.

Nahas knew this was impossible; he knew that Jim couldn't have served in Vietnam. "Why would he lie?" Nahas thought. Their friendship was more of a professional acquaintance—both were physicians, and they saw each other at pharmaceutical dinners. He didn't bother to challenge Jim's story—a story that bore similarities to the one he told about his father.

Yet Jim told the same stories to other close friends. One of Jim's best friends, Ron Welcer, was a police officer for Pleasantville and Linwood who retired after 25 years. One of the first times that Ron spent time with Jim, they went to a gun range. Jim wore his green beret, but he struggled to open a GI ammo can. Ron laughed, and busted Jim's chops over it: "If you're going to wear a beret, you should at least be able to open an ammo can." Another one of Jim's best friends, a doctor, had been a medic in Vietnam. Jim told this friend that he'd been bayonetted in the abdomen and left for dead; other times he would act evasive about the topic. Jim also wore medals. When Kim had to do a college project on someone in the military, she turned to Jim. She felt no suspicion of her stepfather's memories, and in fact felt a new sense of compassion for him. In Kim's paper, she wrote, "The Vietcong ambushed his camp, stabbed him, and left all comrades for dead. His sole mission was to grab the dog tags and bring them to their families so they knew what happened to their boys...."

But Jim had given Kim had strict instructions: she must destroy the tape she had used to record the interview, and never speak about his time in the military with Ruth, his mother.

When Jim graduated from PCOM, he returned to the Jersey Shore area to work. By 1990, he became the Director of the Metabolic Care Unit at Shore Memorial. He gained a loyal following in his Internal Medicine-Endocrinology practice. He treated patients for diabetes, hormone issues, thyroid concerns, glandular issues, and Cushing's Disease. A number of his older clients said Dr. Kauffman would often waive fees if they were struggling financially, and that instead of costly prescriptions, he would give them samples which the pharmaceutical companies often left behind in handfuls. Jim also became a regular on the pharmaceutical speaking circuit, giving talks about different drugs for treating diabetes and other medical issues he covered.

When Jim started seeing April, he had the trappings of success, and she was at one of the most vulnerable points in her life. From the outside looking in, April and Jim Kauffman's lifestyle appeared lavish and full. There were big parties, gatherings, and fundraisers at 2 Woodstock—sometimes resulting in excessive-noise complaints from neighbors far down the block. Even though April wanted to plant roots with Jim in a new home, when he resisted, she made the house distinctive and showcased her hosting abilities. April's childhood had been so void of any semblance of a loving home that she desperately tried to create a nest, a safe place in her adult years.

Guests entering 2 Woodstock walked into a huge foyer. On the wall of the foyer hung a double caricature from Jim's sixtieth birthday. It depicted April as a busty blonde, holding hairdressing scissors, and Jim with an eye patch and a tattoo signifying military experience, with the letters USMC, for United States Marine Corps.

Jim and April held their parties in the massive, 1,200-square-foot sunroom, where dozens of skylights lined the ceiling. The room had a bar, pool table, and big couches, and outside there was an in-ground pool. Jim, an avid gun collector and shooter, had his own gun room with an area dedicated to making his own bullets.

Upstairs, one of the guest rooms, which she called the magnolia room, was yellow with a chandelier of yellow-tinted glass and wrought iron details, and yellow walls with floral painted decorations. The window dressings matched and a fireplace added a coziness to the room. The red room, or master bedroom, had walls painted red with white piping on the door frames; floral curtains complemented the color scheme. The opulent master bathroom featured marble countertops, a marble shower, wood fixtures, built-in wood cabinets, and a Jacuzzi with a stained-glass chandelier overhead.

Early into their marriage, there were problems. Neighbors and close friends had stories about Jim's dark side. When April had a cancer scare, he told her that if she had the disease, she deserved it. He would say cruel things, often around money. When he saw her planting flowers in the yard one day as he drove by, he screamed, "What's wrong with this picture? You're planting flowers and I'm working." April's friends reported that in order to keep April on a tight financial leash, Jim only allowed her to use one credit card, which he monitored closely. April did write checks; Jim would give her large amounts of cash to make money orders or to hand-deliver for construction payments on their home in Arizona. Jim asked her not to work anymore when they married, but April couldn't imagine giving up her hustling.

She and Jim bought a hair salon called Artistic Signature in Northfield, and asked the previous owner, a man named Bob Avellino, to stay on as manager. A little over five years later and just a few months before April's murder, the Kauffmans closed the doors to the salon and attempted to sell it. In 2008 The Kauffmans also opened a restaurant in Northfield, The Cherry Café and Catering Company. The restaurant closed, but April continued the catering business from their home. Jim blamed April for the failure of both businesses, saying they had lost hundreds of thousands of dollars on them. April had turned her attention away from both businesses as her involvement in radio and her philanthropic interests grew—and neither of these made money.

April was on the airwaves with "King Arthur" Gropper for three years. He first heard her while she co-hosted another show and was impressed. "I was on WIBG," he remembered. "I left to go onto WOND, she came with me there, then I went back to WIBG. We were really good friends. She wanted to do veterans stuff. So for one hour once a week I let her do what she wanted, she could bring guests, do whatever she wanted to do for that hour."

Through the years, Jim and April's fighting intensified. April told friends that Jim fired a gun during one fight, and she reacted in self-defense, breaking at least one of his ribs. Years later, that bullet hole remained in the couple's hardwood floor. She never contacted the police. One neighbor regretted not calling 911 when they watched through a window as Jim wrapped his hand around April's neck. The neighbor had seen the couple acting amorously through the same window, but said they could tell that this was different. This was a domestic fight.

Over the course of their marriage, there were affairs alleged on both sides. When Jim learned that April had fooled around with a close family friend, he threatened to put a bullet in both the man's head and in April's. That time, police reports were filed. Another alleged lover later told police April had said to him that if she was killed, "Jim did it." After her death, police identified several of April's alleged lovers and interviewed them. One relationship appeared to have become very serious. April liked the man's stature as a powerful businessman. But she ended the relationship in the spring of 2012.

In October of 2011, while the Kauffmans were in Arizona with their friends Ron and Mary Welcer to celebrate April's birthday, the Kauffmans had an awful fight. That weekend, Kim had gotten a frantic call from her mom—April had found a stockpile of multiple prescriptions for antipsychotic medications in her name. Jim would later say it was simply a mistake on his part, a "bad habit" he had when calling in prescriptions for other people; sometimes he would mistakenly give April's name. Over the Christmas holidays, Jim threatened to "go nuclear" on Kim and the kids. Jim, April said, was waving a gun. By this time, Kim and Randy already told her mother that Jim was not welcome at holidays— he had too many outbursts and tantrums, and made people uncomfortable, seemingly on purpose.

The Christmastime fight stemmed from April's discovery that Jim was definitely not a veteran. She was mortified. All the work they'd done together with other vets, with her thinking he was one of them! She demanded a divorce; his saying no was a final straw. April threatened Jim with the one thing she knew he was obsessed with—money. She was going to bankrupt him. April's best friend, Lee Darby, witnessed Jim deny April a divorce around Christmastime, after he had promised her paperwork of the couple's financials. In February, April went to a lawyer. She told friends she was also seeking a forensic accountant. She had questions about how Jim was making his money.

In the final months of her life, Jim's moods swung between extremes. He started agreeing to buy things, planned to remodel the kitchen, furnish the Arizona home. In March he agreed to pay for April to have her breasts redone, her nose fixed, and a mini-facelift. She planned either to stay overnight at the hospital in the city or have a nurse stay with her at home. Kim waited anxiously to hear how the surgery went, expecting a call from the nurse, the doctor, or Jim. Instead, April called.

Kim strained to hear her mother's muffled voice. April sounded drowsy and delirious. Finally, Kim heard her mom say, "I'm coming home."

"Put Jim on," Kim demanded, concerned.

"What do you want?" Jim barked into the phone. "We're coming home." Kim waited the hour it should take them to arrive home from Philadelphia, then headed over to 2 Woodstock. When she came inside, her mother was in her bed and Jim was putting fentanyl patches on her. Kim was convinced he was trying to kill her. Not long before this happened, April had mentioned to Kim that her eyebrows were falling out, and she wondered aloud if Jim was trying to poison her. Yet just a few weeks later, the couple hosted a close friend and his daughter in Arizona, and everything seemed fine.

Toward the end of her life, April began speaking more openly to others, and details about the fissures in their marriage began to seep out beyond her close circle. In her final weeks, April was honored at several functions for her volunteer work with veterans. It was humiliating for April to go through these public events knowing that Jim had been posing as a veteran. She didn't invite him, but he still showed up. A flier was later found on April's desk, accusing Jim of lying about his service. Other people were starting to realize Jim's lie just as April's profile was rising.

In her last weeks, April told one of her best friends that besides the issue of his posing as a veteran, she had just learned about something with Jim's finances she thought she could hold over his head. But she didn't reveal to any of her friends or family what that was. The last week of her life friends say that April was hitting Jim hard about getting a divorce.

The weekend before her death, April seemed to come to terms with the end of her marriage to Jim. He was acting so strange; more nervous than she had ever seen him. He was obsessively scratching his skin and arms, blaming it on a medical condition. That final weekend, April went to her daughter's house, despondent. She didn't know how to start over, she said. She was nearing fifty. April was not just worried about how she would sustain herself financially; she felt sad, thinking that by this time in her life, she thought she would be with the person with whom she would grow old. But she could no longer keep trying to look past their problems. Kim couldn't seem to find anything to say that would comfort her mother.

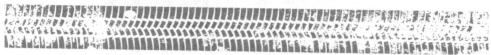

Chapter 5

MAY 10, 2012

The morning that April's body was found, Jim called his friend Ron Welcer at 6:24 a.m. Almost every morning, Jim would talk on the phone to his friends and fellow early risers, Bob Avellino and Ron Welcer. That morning, Jim complained to Ron about a broken Glock handgun, and to talk about the Phillies. The call lasted longer than normal. According to statements gathered by police, normally Ron would initiate the morning call, but this time Jim had called him. At 7:21 a.m., Bob called Jim; he later told police his friend seemed fine. The two discussed the award April just received and the couple's plans to redo their kitchen.

Nor did most of Jim's office staff notice anything wrong with their boss that morning. The day began with a catered breakfast hosted by April's friend Suzanne and her pharmaceutical company's team around 7:30 a.m. Jim was eating eggs from the breakfast spread and preparing for the day. But one staff member told investigators that he smelled like "low tide" when she entered his office—that putrid sulfur-like smell that rolled onto the beach early, sometimes before dawn. The same co-worker later told police she thought Jim had been wearing the same clothes from the day before. When she caught him staring off into space while sitting in his office and asked if he had a long night, he didn't reply. Jim saw at least one patient that morning who later told police the doctor appeared pale and withdrawn.

Dr. Kauffman called Billy Gonzalez twice that morning, first at 9:30 a.m. asking if April was up. Billy thought she might be sleeping, but didn't want to bother her; the door to her bedroom was closed. Billy went about feeding the exotic birds downstairs in the front room. April normally got up around 6 or 7 a.m., and she was constantly on the phone with her husband throughout the day. The second call from Jim to Billy came after 11. Jim had left his office and was on the way to a doctor's appointment. Jim told Billy to check on her. With Dr. Kauffman still on the phone, Billy found April lying on the floor face down. She was wearing a black short-sleeved nightshirt. He noticed a cut on her arm and shook her to wake up, but she didn't move. Billy hung up and called 911. But Dr. Kauffman also called police as soon as he hung up the phone with Billy. The dispatchers heard both men calling at the same time as they sent an ambulance to 2 Woodstock. Jim arrived home in just a matter of minutes.

Jim ran inside 2 Woodstock, sprinting through the front door and up the stairs. He stopped dead in his tracks at the doorway at the sight of his wife's body. A physician for thirty-plus years, he didn't touch her or try to resuscitate her. He later said that was because he saw "lividity," a sign that someone is dead. Instead, he ran outside. No one told Jim that April was dead. Billy just thought his boss had a cut on her arm and was unconscious.

The medics arrived and went upstairs, and Billy followed Jim outside. Dr. Kauffman fell on his hands and knees on the front lawn, yelling over and over, "She's dead, She's dead!" and "Why now?" Upstairs, the medics pronounced April dead at 11:45 AM.

Detective Sergeant John Hamilton of Linwood Police and Detective Sergeant Michael Mattioli of the Atlantic County Prosecutors Office Major Crimes division arrived and began asking the doctor questions. Jim told them he'd gotten home about 5:15 the night before. April came home around 6, and he opened a bottle of wine; they cooked steaks on the grill. They chatted after dinner about remodeling the kitchen, went upstairs and spent time in the hot tub, and had sex. Then Jim went into a guest bedroom—the Magnolia Room—where he often slept because of his snoring. He told police he watched the eighth inning of the Phillies game, but couldn't remember when the game ended. He said he then went back into the master bedroom to kiss April goodnight. She was still up, texting and checking Facebook on her phone. He said he went back to bed in the Magnolia Room, watched the news and fell asleep.

The next morning, Jim told the police, he followed his usual routine: up before 5 a.m., changing in the master bedroom because his clothes were there. He said he saw April stirring in her sleep around 5:10 a.m., with a pillow over her head. He went to the garage and drove his Ford Explorer to work. He told police the front door had been locked when he left—that the doors to their house were always locked, specifically the front door. He went to buy the newspaper at the Wawa, a chain convenience store, at Shore Road in Somers Point, but the paper had sold out, so he headed to the hospital to do his rounds. Then he drove to a second Wawa at six, and was at his practice at 6:15 to make coffee for "the girls" in his office.

Detective Hamilton noted that just a half-hour after April was found, Kauffman was notably matter-of-fact and precise with investigators about his movements that morning. He told Det. Sgt. Mattioli, "I'll be on video there...," when mentioning his trip to the first Wawa. Although Hamilton had noted how calm the doctor seemed, Kauffman was thrown off when Mattioli and Hamilton asked about specific details.

"Was your wife cold when you touched her?" Mattioli asked Jim. "Detective, I never touched her." Kauffman apparently noticed a reaction from both lawmen. He said to Mattioli, "Detective, I am a doctor, and have seen enough dead bodies to know when someone is dead." Kauffman asked the investigators how April died.

"The Medical Examiner suggests there was a small gunshot wound," Mattioli answered. Kauffman threw his head back, crying out, then held his hands to his head. Hamilton wrote in his notes, "At no point were any tears observed when Kauffman appeared to be crying."

Upstairs, April lay on the floral area rug face down, her head towards the doorway, her feet by the nightstand, her blonde hair covering her face and neck. Her left arm, tucked under her body, was smeared with blood. The medics had tried to revive her, and the telemetry electrodes were still attached to the backs of her arms and legs.

The medical examiner, Dr. Hydow Park, went to the scene and later conducted an autopsy, describing April's wounds in his report. She sustained three gunshot wounds to her body, from two bullets. One of the bullets hit the posterior side of her left upper arm above the elbow, fracturing her humerus bone. The other bullet hit the front, or dorsal side, of her left forearm, then re-entered just below her left breast, piercing her lung and causing significant internal bleeding. One to two liters of blood filled her chest cavity. She did not die instantly, and could have been alive for twenty seconds or even up to a minute or two. Investigators believe once she was shot in her arm, she got out of bed and took a few steps, then was shot again, fell and died. Park was able to recover the bullets from April's breast and her arm, and investigators took a portion of plaster from the bedroom where the third bullet was lodged. A loaded shotgun, which April kept under the bed for protection, appeared untouched.

Hamilton and Mattioli asked Jim if they kept any cash or jewelry in the house, and if he thought anything had been stolen. He answered that he didn't keep cash in the house. Jim went back outside to the group of friends and family waiting in the yard.

"Yes, she was shot," he told the group. "It was a .22." Kim looked at him.

"How do you know it was a .22?" she asked. At this point, investigators still had not told Kim her mother's death was suspicious, but news choppers were flying overhead.

Looking around at the people gathered there, he said, "The police told me." The truth was the police had not told him. They hadn't told anyone what type of weapon they thought was used. More friends arrived, including Jim's friend Bob Avellino. Jim started walking around, joking about getting his Tom Collins mixer out of the house. He asked Mattioli if he could retrieve his bottle of Canadian Club Whiskey and a bottle of sweet vermouth located in the first-floor bar area. His friend, Ron Welcer, would later get Jim a bottle of whiskey and make sure he had a hotel room to stay in. When police finally put yellow tape around the home and told everyone to leave the backyard, Kim spoke up.

"What the hell is going on here?" Just as the words left her mouth, a news chopper flew overhead. She confronted one of the investigators at the scene. "You've gotta be kidding me. They know, but I don't! Why would they be here if my Mom died a natural death?" The detective answered, "Well, um, we are here because we have reason to believe that your mom didn't die a natural death."

Kim looked at the investigator and pointed her finger towards her stepfather, who stood behind the yellow tape in the street, "Well, you can look right over there because that man... is responsible for the death of my mom."

Jim never spoke to the police again. The next morning at 9 a.m., he contacted one of the most powerful defense attorneys in the state, Ed Jacobs, and retained him days later. That night when Mattioli called Jim to tell him the house was still a crime scene and he could not return, Jim apologized for inconveniencing police with his requests for alcohol and later his heart medication. Mattioli assured him it wasn't a problem. The doctor said, "If I had been [a problem], I'd be in handcuffs already." Then he added, "By the way, Detective, if you ever have to put handcuffs on me, be careful, I have a very bad shoulder."

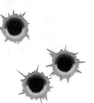

Chapter 6

MOTHER'S DAY

Kim stood by her mother's coffin. In her hand sat a ceramic Tinkerbell figurine, a keepsake of one of their trips to Disneyworld. The tiny fairy wore a green strapless dress and two perfect green slippers. Two delicate white wings floated out from her back. The sassy fairy from the animated Disney film of Peter Pan spread pixie dust to help humans fly; she was a bright light, a helper. Maybe that's why Tinkerbell had been April's favorite Disney character. After all, April spent her last years trying to help everyone in her path, not just veterans, but people she came across who suffered various hardships. April would give them food or odd jobs, trying to sprinkle a little hope through her small acts of kindness. "Tink" was also April's nickname for Kim, her beloved daughter who was like her in so many ways.

Kim held the doll close, then placed it in her mother's coffin. She had already put a doll of Captain Jack Sparrow from Disney's *Pirates of the Caribbean* inside. Kim smiled, remembering her Mom's running joke about the hunky pirate: "I'd give anything for Johnny Depp dressed up as Jack Sparrow for one day." Kim carefully added a few small blocks from her childhood that her mother had made into keychain fobs, along with pictures of Kim and her boys, and notes from both Kim and Randy.

It was Mother's Day, Sunday, May 13th. Just a few minutes before, Kim and Randy arrived at Roth-Goldstein's Funeral home to see her mother for the last time. It wasn't typical for the Jewish funeral home to hold a viewing—that was not part of Jewish traditions. In the Jewish faith, the body is supposed to decompose naturally, so embalming is not employed. Raised Catholic, Kim wanted to respect her mother's adopted Jewish faith, and planned her final goodbye in accordance with Jewish rituals. She had chosen this funeral home because the owners specialized in arranging Jewish funerals. The viewing, however, was a must for Kim. She was thankful the funeral director obliged.

April had converted to Judaism when she married her second husband, Dr. David Sagransky. She took her new faith seriously, and continued to practice after marrying Jim—in fact, she was more observant than Jim. Jim often said that he hadn't been religious since serving in Vietnam, and that harrowing experience made him lose faith. April hosted dinners for the high holidays, making sure that Jim's mom, Ruth, had a place to celebrate her faith.

The day before she viewed her mother's body, Kim had gone to the funeral home with Randy, her mother's best friend, Lee Darby, Jim, and his mother Ruth to begin making preparations for April's farewell. Together, they worked to come up with an obituary using the computer at the funeral home. Then they had to pick plots, since the couple did not have one, and a coffin.

For Kim, the grieving hadn't really begun. She was still functioning, but she was in shock. And she quickly realized she needed to keep up her guard. It was as if she had to be a double agent—mourning daughter, and suspicious step-daughter, all at the same time. Jim, she decided, could not be trusted. But yelling at him, openly blaming him and ostracizing him could impede the most important thing: helping the police to catch April's killer.

As they went into the room displaying a full array of coffins and caskets to choose from, Kim watched as Jim appeared to grow emotional. It sounded like he was crying. Each time Kim looked at him, Jim's hands covered his face, muffling his sobs. But his fingers would periodically slide away from at least one eye, almost as if he was peeking at the price tags of the caskets. Jim stopped short in front of a beautiful rectangular cherry-wood casket with a glossy sheen and a beautiful white satin lining. "It has to be this one," he dramatically proclaimed. He continued, "because of the Cherry Café..." And he looked up to Kim and Randy for approval. That was the restaurant she had owned. Jim had hated it; Kim later told investigators that her mom believed he was sabotaging it on purpose.

Settling on the cherry coffin, Jim went to pay. Kim overheard as he handed not one but two credit cards to the funeral employee, telling him one of the cards might be maxed out. "Are you having financial problems?" Kim asked Jim soon after. He denied having any problems. Other people, however, began reporting back to Kim that Jim was telling them a different story.

When Kim and Randy came back on Sunday for the private viewing, they met Jim inside. Right away, Kim felt that Jim was again putting on a show. When they got to the room with the coffin, Kim stayed behind to let Jim view her mother's body first.

"Let me get this over with," Kim remembers him saying. She didn't want to be in the same room with him, and definitely not during her final moments with her mother.

Kim waited behind a partition that blocked her view, which she preferred. She heard Jim exclaim, "Why now??!!" and then drop down to his knees, alternating between heaving sobs and exclamations to his wife. Then, in what felt like just a few seconds, he walked away. As he passed Kim, he said, "Okay, your turn." The anguish from moments before had disappeared.

Kim and Randy walked up next. Kim took a deep breath and squeezed Randy's hand.

"Oh my God, Oh my God, Oh my God," she kept saying. She fought her body's reactions, telling her either to vomit or pass out. The reality that this was the end, the end of her mother's life—that the woman who had been the larger-than-life mainstay of her existence now lay in this small cherry-wood box—was too much to take in.

The funeral director had given careful attention to April's face, but Kim could see that it had been swollen and bruised, and her nose looked like it had been broken. This must have happened when April fell, and then lay face-down for so long. In that moment, Kim realized that what had made April a beauty was her personality, her mannerisms, her smile. True, she was a knockout, but it was really her life, her spirit, that made her inner beauty shine through. If April had been in this room alive, everyone, even strangers, would feel her warmth, her presence.

So Kim focused her attention on her mother's hands. Ever the manicurist, April's nails were always filed, buffed and painted; her skin beautiful and soft. Today they were painted her signature red. Growing up, Kim had begged her mom to give her back scratches with those long nails. Even in recent years, when Kim was worried or anxious, April would sometimes soothe her with a back scratch.

"That's not her," Randy said to Kim.

"It is her," Kim responded, even though she felt the person in front of her was some sort of imposter. She did not want this to be real.

Kim had wanted her Mom to be buried in the mother-of-the-bride gown she had worn for Kim and Randy's wedding, which was held on a week-long cruise with family and friends. Somehow, Jim had made a happy family moment into a tense and uncomfortable event. A number of family and friends all boarded a cruise ship to celebrate the union between Randy and Kim, who had been high school sweethearts. Jim began berating April over the cost of the cruise, and wouldn't let it go.

April's special dress would have looked lovely. But the funeral director explained that the scars on April's chest from the autopsy would show.

"We're sorry… it's impossible for us to put her in that dress," the funeral directors told Kim. She understood. When the police had let Kim back into 2 Woodstock Drive after the scene had been cleared, she selected two dresses with her aunt, Julie Loftus (her biological father's sister). Now April lay in the casket wearing the other dress, which was black, high-cut and conservative.

Kim stood in front of the casket in the silence of the old funeral home, the creaks of doors and the shuffles of employees walking on floorboards in the distance. She grabbed her mom's hand, torn between hating to see her in the coffin, and feeling she could not leave her behind. She held onto her hand and silently asked her for strength.

The funeral was the next morning. Those family members who were to ride in the limousine parked their cars at Sandy Point, a restaurant in Somers Point, where a reception would be held afterward. Kim got into the limo and sat next to Jim. He wore mirrored sunglasses and a navy striped suit, and spent the ride lamenting that no one from Shore Memorial had offered their condolences. Arriving at the Beth El Synagogue in Margate, they were joined by thousands of mourners, including the Legion Riders, veterans who are also motorcycle enthusiasts, making up part of the motorcade. It was a spectacle that April would have loved. The funeral director juggled members of the media, even some from national news outlets. Kim greeted every person who came to show their respects. They included a congressman, several mayors and county freeholders, scores of other local politicians, and people from the veterans' community. The line was so long it stretched outside of Beth El Synagogue and onto Margate's busy Jerome Avenue. The sanctuary filled, and funeral directors had to limit mourners as the ceremony began.

Kim was seated two seats away from Jim. She was relieved not to be sitting next to him—she needed a buffer. She watched him closely, searching for a tear on his cheek, but his eyes were hidden behind his sunglasses, which he wore through the service. She heard him sniffling the entire time, sounding like his nose was running. She remembered how her mom used to make fun of him and call him "Allergic Lou" because of his constant runny nose.

When he took his turn at the podium, she thought he would take off his sunglasses. Wasn't it disrespectful to keep them on, and in your own house of worship? Maybe, she thought, it was his way of keeping people from looking into his soul. She thought back to his explanation about hiring an attorney: "Everyone always frames the husband," he had told her. He even said he had a plan in place in case he got arrested, with a million dollars set aside for bail.

As Jim spoke, he called April "the most generous, giving person in the world." He ended the eulogy by saying, "I love and miss you so much. I don't know what to do without you."

Many mourners left that day calling his eulogy heartfelt. The local media noted how he praised his wife. Out of the entire speech he gave about his wife, two phrases stuck out to those closest to April: Jim said, "I'm going to miss her berating me," and, "I hope to be with you soon."

With such a large turnout, the funeral directors kept everything on a tight timetable. The day was exhausting. As they pulled up in the limo to Rodef Shalom

Cemetery, Kim looked out the window. Several men dressed in military uniforms stood in a line. Jim got out of the car, along with his mother Ruth. Then Kim heard Ruth say, "Jim, why are there so many police here?" Jim started fumbling with his phone, and Kim nearly tripped over him as she watched Jim dial. She thought she heard him on the phone with his attorney, as Jim eyed the five or six police officers and detectives standing in the cemetery. But the moment passed without incident. They sat next to each other on folding chairs by the graveside. Kim clutched her stomach and leaned forward, away from Jim. She looked again for a sign of tears, but saw none.

As they sat Shiva—the week-long Jewish observance after a funeral—over the next three days at Ruth's home in Margate, Kim continued to search for the tears. Instead, Jim seemed to hold court. He smiled, he invited people to come with him on trips to Arizona. On the third night, Wednesday, Randy looked at Kim.

"I can't take this shit," he said to her. "Your mom was murdered, and no one is saying a word, or questioning anything. What the hell is going on here?"

Randy and Jim had never been close. They met back when Randy and Kim began dating in high school, and Randy would come to parties and family gatherings at 2 Woodstock Drive. For April's sake, her dutiful son-in-law tried to become friendly with Jim. He had gone to the shooting range with him six years before, but it was forced and awkward. Jim had worn his green beret to the range, as he had with his friend Ron Welcer. But since April's death, Jim had begun treating Randy like a confidant. Unbeknownst to Jim, police overheard his call to Randy when they stopped in at Kim and Randy's home just hours after discovering April's body. The phone volume was loud enough that investigators heard Jim tell Randy that he'd spoken to his attorney, Ed Jacobs, who told him that the prosecutors "don't have shit." Randy replied that the police had just been there and that they seemed "confident" about the investigation. Jim responded, "They can kiss my ass."

Jim kept that narrative going to anyone who would listen at shiva. He told people the autopsy performed on April had been compromised, and that police had nothing on him. Jim told Randy that the police had not found any shell casings and that they had no other evidence. He went on to comment that in their large home, one wouldn't hear a small-caliber gun like a .22, and that low-caliber guns don't make a big mess. At this point, investigators had still not said what type of weapon was used, and the media had only reported that April died of multiple gunshot wounds, although the police had told Jim at the scene that the medical examiner thought it was a small wound. Ballistics test run in the days immediately after the murder confirmed the bullets recovered from April and the bedroom all came from the same .22 caliber handgun. But authorities had not found the weapon and had not revealed to the public any information about what caliber gun had been used. Jim, however, had told people the day April was discovered that the murder weapon was a .22 caliber handgun.

When police served a search warrant on 2 Woodstock immediately after the murder, they recovered more than a dozen guns and an abundance of ammunition in two separate gun cases. Jim had an entire room just to house his small arsenal, including a section where he made his own bullets. Around five p.m. on the Monday after the murder, detectives removed the large tan Waste Management dumpster from behind Jim's medical offices and searched it looking for a weapon, but found nothing.

On that Wednesday, May 16th, the last night of shiva, Linwood Police and the Atlantic County Prosecutors Office made a call to the Pima County Sheriff's Department in Arizona. The New Jersey investigators told the Arizona authorities that they were inquiring about 8135 East Cloud Road in Tucson, Arizona, April and Jim's second home, and "looking into specific weapons that could have been used in the homicide; specifically .22 caliber weapons." The investigators would be delivering a search warrant to Arizona, requesting seizure of any .22 caliber weapons as well as .22 caliber accessories and ammunition. The warrant stated that "Mr. Kauffman had two .22 caliber pistols registered to him in New Jersey." Detectives told Pima County that they had already recovered one .22 caliber pistol and at least a dozen other registered weapons from a room in 2 Woodstock, but they had some information indicating that another might be in Arizona.

Five days later, on May 21st, investigators made the trek to Arizona with a search warrant in hand. Inside a gun safe in the garage, they found more weapons. They left with a Ruger SP101 .22 caliber revolver, a Ruger Mark III .22 caliber handgun with a magazine, a box of 100 unfired cartridges of Remington .22LR subsonic ammunition, and a box of 50 unfired cartridges of Thunderbolt .22LR ammunition.

Chapter 7

PAGAN BROTHERS

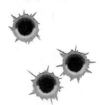

"I need to speak to you right now."

Andrew Glick tried to keep his voice calm and quiet as he spoke into his cell phone; he didn't want his wife Vicki to hear him. Glick had just walked in the door of his Northfield home two minutes before, expecting to change out of his chef uniform, kick back and relax. Now he was walking out again. As soon as he came in, to news blaring from the television, Vicki had rushed over to tell him his doctor's wife had been killed. Her body had been discovered around 11:30 that morning. Glick hadn't heard anything about it, as he'd been preoccupied at work all day.

Vicki quickly filled her husband in on the news. All of Linwood was in shock. The police said no one was in danger, and the school wasn't put on lockdown. It must be because they knew the identity of the murderer; many thought that meant April's husband.

As Vicki rattled off the details from the news, Glick couldn't pay attention; he felt numb. He kept struggling to keep his composure while watching the helicopter aerial shots of the Kauffman home on the TV.

"I gotta go," he told her, but Vicki kept talking.

"Do you think he did it?" she asked. Vicki had never met her husband's physician. "I'll be back... I gotta go," he responded, heading toward his pickup truck.

The person Glick had dialed on his phone was Glenn "Slasher" Seeler, the sergeant at arms of the Cape May County chapter of the Pagans. Glick had been sworn in as president of the Pagans just two months before. The hulking biker was more than six feet tall. His strawberry blonde hair and light blue eyes softened the intimidating look he conveyed when he wore his biker gear and showed off his tattoos. His nickname was Chef, because of his day job—currently he worked as a chef at Our Lady's Residence in Pleasantville, New Jersey, a home for senior citizens. The president of a chapter is also called a Diamond, and any order given by a diamond or president to a member had to be obeyed. Glick had to report only to the Mother Chapter, and he didn't want them to get wind of the Cape May

County Chapter's involvement in a murder, especially if the victim was a woman and the wife of a non-Pagan.

Minutes after speaking on the phone with each other, both men were in the parking lot of a local shopping center. Glick was beside himself. "Please tell me you have no involvement in this…" he said to Seeler. The other Pagan denied he was responsible.

"Dude, look at the condition I'm in. What the hell are you kidding me?"

At thirty-one years old, Seeler looked years beyond his age. He was heavily overweight, with severe back problems from numerous bike accidents. At one point, he had been paralyzed; now he walked with a limp. But both men already feared they could be implicated in April's murder, and they both knew that the list of people who knew that Dr. Kauffman had been looking for someone to kill his wife was a long one. At that moment, however, Seeler wasn't telling Glick that two weeks ago he had floated the hit job on Mrs. Kauffman to a neighbor of his when they met at the Ramada Inn. That neighbor, as it turns out, was a sometime confidential informant for the Atlantic County Prosecutor's Office.

That afternoon after the news hit, Seeler had bragged to that neighbor that he had something to do with it. However, both Seeler and Glick told each other their versions of how Fred Augello approached them to carry out the crime. Fifty-six-year-old Ferdinand "Freddy" Augello, a.k.a. "Miserable," was the former president of the Cape May County Chapter of the Pagans Motorcycle Club, having been ousted and forced into retirement. Besides his association with The Pagans, he was also a local musician and business owner. Fred owned a sign and graphics shop in nearby Ocean View, and he also made custom guitars.

Glick told Seeler he had declined Fred's offer right away. Seeler said he was offered $20,000 for the job, and that Fred told him he would get a separate finder's fee from the doctor.

Both Glick and Seeler were familiar with how Fred had been forced to leave the club. The former President had "lost his diamond" being accused of stealing money from his chapter during the annual "Roar to the Shore" gathering in Wildwood, New Jersey. The "Roar to the Shore" is a free public event held annually in Wildwood, which is solidly in Pagans territory; even local business and law enforcement take part. It's held at the end of the riding season, usually during the first weeks in September. The Pagans normally take over several motels and hotels, and use the event as an opportunity to raise money for their chapters. Authorities maintain a heavy presence to make sure things don't get out of hand. Fred had been in charge of raising money for his chapter, but he denies stealing from them. He claimed to have left because the younger generation wanted the Old Heads out. Either way, Fred wasn't considered "out bad," meaning he would be banned from wearing colors and hanging out at Pagan events.

Glick and Augello didn't have any bad blood, and they had stayed friends after Fred retired. Today, however, Glick was seething: "I can't believe that motherfucker went through with this; what the fuck? We're in a world of fucking shit, this is super bad, what are we going to do, Glenn?" Seeler assured Glick they would be fine.

Forty-seven-year-old Andrew Glick did not have the background you might expect for someone leading a notorious biker club. He had grown up in Delaware, attending parochial school until ninth grade, then the vo-tech school through his high school graduation. He boasted to friends about his high SAT scores, and was accepted to the Culinary School at Johnson and Wales University. He attended the Rhode Island school until his mother passed away. In 1998, needing a new start, he moved to Somers Point, New Jersey to be closer to his sister.

He stayed for a while with his sister and her husband, a police officer. Then he found his own place on Cooper Avenue in Somers Point, which he called The Barracks. Glick bought a motorcycle, but considered himself only an enthusiast. He quickly found Uncle Mike's Bar in Mays Landing, and made that his second home. There he started networking among the other motorcycle riders, and soon was asked by members of the Longriders Motorcycle Club if he was interested in prospecting for them. Six months later, in 2001, he became a member and got his "patch." After about a year with the Longriders, he started to drift towards another local motorcycle club, the Tribe; sixteen months after that, he was patched over and immediately became a full member of the Tribe. At that time in South Jersey, the Tribe was one of the top support clubs to the Pagans.

Members of the motorcycle clubs, or MCs, maintain that they are just clubs. But the FBI deems some of the clubs to be gangs. The Department of Justice officially lists seven major motorcycle gangs (MCs) as "criminal enterprises" nationwide. Those are the clubs running drugs, guns, or women for prostitution. American Motorcycle Association (AMA) has stated that "99% of the motorcycling public are law-abiding; there are 1% who are not." Pagans and other outlaw clubs now proudly call themselves one-percenters. Whatever the actual proportion, the FBI considers the Pagans to be an outlaw motorcycle gang, specifically concentrated in the Northeast and Mid-Atlantic regions of the country.

In Southern New Jersey and the Philadelphia region, the Pagans dominate along with the Warlocks, Outlaws, and Wheels of Soul. Each of these self-styled "1% Clubs" has one or more support clubs, also called "duck clubs." The outlaw gangs use the support clubs as a kind of membership farm team. Support club members get a taste of the action, and the one-percenters see how they handle it. According to law enforcement sources, in 2010-2011 the Pagans in the Philadelphia area were considered weaker, while the South Jersey chapters were thriving. The FBI reported the South Jersey Pagans had the largest membership and most significant presence of any Outlaw Motor Gang in the region, and if anyone tried to move in on their territory, they saw a violent response from the gang. In 2009, Philadelphia Pagans caught the attention of the United States Attorney General, who wrote in a report to Congress on the growth of illegal street gangs that the Pagans not only distributed methamphetamines, PCP, cocaine, and marijuana, but they actually created laboratories to produce retail quantities of meth.

The Pagans are divided into regions with different leadership, and the organization operates somewhat like a company. The Mother Chapter acts as the CEO or boss overseeing all the chapter presidents. The Pagans have no national headquarters, so the Mother Chapter president operates from wherever they already live. Below the Mother Chapter or Mother Club president are chapter presidents who operate like a COO or chief operating officer. Each chapter has a president, vice president, sergeant at arms or SAA, and an enforcer. The Pagans are often aligned with other organized crime syndicates like La Cosa Nostra. This is the case in both Philadelphia and New York, where Pagans work as enforcers and often share or establish drug territories so no one steps on each other's toes.

In 2010 and 2011, there were rumblings from longtime members complaining that under current leadership, anyone could be a Pagan. The Mother Chapter president continued to receive tithes from the club members regardless of the business they were bringing in, so he was making money. Some members complained that lax recruiting and screening led to what some call "dime-store Pagans;" they just had to pay dues upwards of $1,000 -$1500 a year plus monthly dues around fifty bucks, depending on the chapter, and own a bike in order to be a member; if someone had a trade useful to the club, such as bike repair, they could join and use a loaner bike.

Around this time, local law enforcement had eased up a bit on following the clubs, since violence and illegal activity had slowed down in comparison to much of the previous decade. In the late nineties and early 2000's, law enforcement had their hands full with biker gangs. The Hells Angels had tried to move in on Pagans' turf. In 1999 there was an assassination attempt on the reputed president of the South Philadelphia Pagans, Steven "Gorilla" Mondevergine, a former Philadelphia cop. Then, in Lancaster, Pennsylvania, sixty miles west of Philadelphia, the Sons of Satans' clubhouse was firebombed. Because they were a support club of the Pagans, the outcome saw the Pagans, Sons of Satan, Bandidos, Outlaws, Vagos, and Mongols pitted against the Hell's Angels.

In Long Island in 2002, the Pagans stormed the Hells Angels' "Hellraiser Ball" as part of an attempt to stop the Hells Angels from taking over Long Island territory. Ten vanloads of Pagans and Pagan associates stormed the event, and according to *The New York Times*, one Pagan was killed and ten others at the event were injured. A February 25, 2002 article in the Times reported that seventy-five bikers in all were charged, seventy-three of them Pagans.

Those familiar with the world of motorcycle gangs said the explosion of violence was the first such confrontation between the two gangs at a public exposition since the 1970's, and could signal a dangerous new phase in their rivalry in the United States.

A month after the Long Island showdown, a South Philadelphia tattoo parlor was firebombed. The owner of the shop was an alleged Pagan and one of the 75 bikers arrested on Long Island. To law enforcement, it looked like the Pagans were losing their grip. Mondevergine was jailed on assault and racketeering charges. Also in 2002, another onetime Pagan leader, Thomas James "Tom Thumb" Campbell, was charged in the killing of an Upper Darby police officer. That Delaware County town, on the Philadelphia border, has long had a heavy Pagan presence.

Authorities feared another outbreak in the biker wars after a fatal incident in South Philadelphia in 2005. Reputed Hells Angels member Byron Evans was the target of a pair of gunmen in a white Suburban. Tom Wood, reputed Acting Hells Angel President at the time, had been his pickup truck next to Evans on his motorcycle after the two had just left a local gentleman's club. Philadelphia Police think Wood was trying to stop the gunmen from shooting Evans when he was shot and killed. The case was never solved.

By 2011, some club insiders said, the Pagans in Philadelphia "had no balls or heart." South Jersey, on the other hand, had never suffered a decline in power or influence. Law enforcement sources say the chapters they had to watch closely during that period were in Newark, New Jersey, and Pennsylvania chapters in Lehigh County, Chambersburg, and Lancaster.

The Pagans had established chapters in Cape May County, Atlantic County, Cumberland County and Salem County. (Later, the club decided to simply designate clubs by regions.) Many members were guys who liked to ride, and wanted to feel like part of the community. In South Jersey, Pagans and support clubs used the big open roadways to drive through the beautiful farm country in Salem, Cumberland and Gloucester Counties. and down the Garden State Parkway and New Jersey Turnpike. On weekends, they traveled in groups on less-traveled side roads that looped around the bays, and over the bridges and roads that connected the islands following the coastline of the New Jersey Shore.

Law enforcement kept their eye on these club activities. New Jersey State Troopers would pull over groups of bikers riding together if they were wearing their "colors"—clothing that showed their club affiliation. Police would ask for identification and write down names, addresses, and bike registration, as part of a strategy to keep track of who was in the club and individual chapter. This information would then be available to the FBI and other law enforcement. The members did not protest much; there wasn't much they could do. In 2011, turf wars had simmered. But conversations about new opportunities had begun among

Pagans, at least in South Jersey, Florida and Bucks County, Pennsylvania. There was talk about getting involved with prescription pain pills which were becoming the hottest drug to deal on the street.

Andrew Glick liked the camaraderie of being in the Tribe. Eventually, members of the Tribe started to migrate toward becoming full-blown Pagans—like the big league team in the region. When Stephen "Big Stevie" Wittenwiler, a.k.a. Misfit, the reputed Tribe president at the time, became a Pagan, Glick followed. This decision was helped along by Glick's failure to become the Tribe's president when Big Stevie left. In December of 2006 at the Pagans' Christmas party, Glick began prospecting for the Pagans. In April of 2007 in Charleston, West Virginia, he became official.

Glick was proud to put on his "colors." A true "three-piece rocker," found on the back of a cutoff vest, advertises a club member's affiliation. The top rocker is a patch with the club's name, while the middle rocker is an image called the club patch. The Pagans' patch depicts the Norse fire-giant, Surtyr, sitting on the sun, wielding a sword under the word Pagans in red, white, and blue. The bottom rocker or patch states their origin; for the Pagans, that's now simply East Coast.

Below the bottom rocker, a member can add personal patches with acronyms such as PFFP (Pagans Forever, Forever Pagans), and sayings like NUNYA (short for "Nunya business," a common response to questions from police), or ARGO (short for "ARGO fuck yourself"). A chapter president might wear a diamond patch, and there are 1% patches to signify a one percent club. If the member is with the Mother Chapter there is usually a black leather band at the top. Some chapters allow members to wear a Nomad patch if they are not with a specific chapter.

Wearing the vest and colors is believed to come with a great responsibility. The colors are not the property of the rider, but the club. The vest is never allowed to touch anything else. That's not a problem on a motorcycle, but if a member is riding in a "cage"—a truck or car—the colors cannot touch the seat. When in a "cage," For a member to show respect, he should wear them inside-out so they touch the member's heart.

Glick expected to join the Atlantic County Chapter. But to become a member of a chapter, the vote had to be unanimous, and he received one "no" vote out of nine. So Glick went to the Cape May County Chapter instead. That's how Glick met Fred Augello. In Cape May, Fred Augello was president. Glick always held down a steady job as a chef, first in the casinos, then eventually working for a company that provided kitchen staff for retirement homes in the area. Because Glick had steady employment and a bank account, he immediately became treasurer. The position didn't carry much juice in the club, but it still made him an officer. As Glick would say, he had money, and people with money are better treasurers than "broke asses." But Glick was well organized and good with his finances. By the time he had become president, he looked the part more. He added some new tattoos, including a diamond with 1% on his arm.

Glenn Seeler always looked like a villainous member of a motorcycle gang. Seeler was six feet tall and about 240 pounds, with earrings and a goatee. He became a member of the local chapter and received his Pagan colors in 2008 at the annual Christmas party. His body was covered in tattoos: a Chinese symbol on his right hand, a skull on his right middle finger, a she-devil on the inside of one arm and the Nazi SS double-lightning-bolt symbol on the inside of his left arm. "PAGANS" was tattooed across his chest.

Glick and Seeler both had side hustles going. If you're in the club, every hustle you have should benefit the club. The Mother Club and the national president would have to know and agree to whatever that hustle was, and get a piece of the action. This rule also applied to those retired from the club.

Six months earlier, in December of 2011, Seeler had told Glick about a new way several members were making extra cash. "How the hell did you get that?" Glick asked Seeler when his friend produced a prescription bottle of 120 30mg oxycodone hydrochloride tablets. The brand name for the pills is Roxicodone, and on the street they were known as roxies. This was a legitimate prescription, not off-the-street prescription meds: Seeler's name and address were listed on the bottle. The prescribing doctor listed on the bottle was Dr. James Kauffman. With a legitimate prescription from a real doctor, you knew that you were getting the real thing. There was no threat of a street-level dealer cutting the drug with baby laxatives, and using a stolen pill press machine to press it all together.

Glick presented a potential solution to Seeler's problem: he had too many pills. He asked if Glick would buy some off of him. Glick says his friend tantalized him with the simple question, "Do you want to get in on that?" To which Glick replied, "Hell yeah, what do I got to do?"

Once Glick agreed, Seeler got back to him with a set of instructions. He was to meet Dr. Kauffman at his Egg Harbor Township office on a Saturday morning with three things: his driver's license, insurance card, and a business card from Freddymade Guitars with Fred Augello's name on it. Fred, according to Seeler, was in charge of the hook-up with Kauffman. The doctor would know Andrew was coming, but Fred's business card would be his all-access VIP pass to get the drugs.

Glick arrived the Saturday after New Year's Day for an 8 a.m. appointment. He was a few minutes early, and the office hadn't opened yet. When Dr. Kauffman arrived, Glick dwarfed the small doctor, who unlocked the office door and told Glick to come inside. The two men were alone. Kauffman gave Glick paperwork to fill out, and once inside the examination room, conducted a brief exam. Glick legitimately had type 2 diabetes and needed to be seen by an endocrinologist. Kauffman prescribed him medications for his diabetes. Glick was the perfect cover patient. They both knew he was really there for pain meds, and the doctor obliged, giving him the script for 120 30mg oxycodone hydrochloride pills.

Kauffman seemed curious about Glick. "Nice tattoo," he told him during the exam admiring Glick's artwork on his arm. Kauffman asked him how long he'd been in the club. Did he hold any rank? Throughout the visit, Kauffman made idle chitchat about the club, bike enthusiast to bike enthusiast.

Kauffman never mentioned the fact that, minus the smoke and mirrors of the exams and medical questions, the entire point of the visit was a planned drug transaction. Then, just as if they were a normal doctor and patient the visit was over. Glick left thinking he was 120 pills richer.

Several days later, Fred and Joe "Irish" Mulholland, a member of another Pagan support club called the Herd, met Glick at his house in Northfield. They immediately asked where the pills were. That was when Glick learned how this arrangement would work, he would later say. "Irish" was not a Pagan, but he was friends with Fred.

Glick was given a choice of how to move the pills. Glick could give Fred half of the prescription—sixty pills at the time—and Fred and Mulholland would move them and keep all of that money. Or he could give them the entire prescription and they would give him a cut. If not, Glick could pay them the street amount for the sixty pills, which at the time was around $1,000. The entire bottle could go for $2400 to $3600 on the street, depending on whether they were sold for $20 or $30 a pill. Glick says Fred and "Irish" told him that if Glick had people he trusted, they were looking for more people to get in on the drug ring.

It didn't sound like the doctor was benefitting much from this—just the $100 payment in cash to Kauffman at each visit. Fred and "Irish" did not mention if the doctor was also getting a cut from sales. However, it was then, Glick said later, that Augello revealed another element that could make it so "the sky was the limit" on the pill-sale arrangement. The doctor wanted a job done, and was growing impatient.

The job was to kill his wife April.

"Do you know of anybody?" Glick says Augello asked him. Glick blew off the proposition. Murder was not his forte, and he was not comfortable with the idea of harming a woman. However, he told Joe and Fred he would think about it.

Glick and Seeler didn't know it at the time, but they were already being watched by law enforcement. And not just local cops: The DEA and the FBI were watching most of their moves. This was because they were already in deep on another ongoing illegal drug operation. In July of 2011, the FBI had caught wind of a prescription pill pipeline. They believed that Glick and Seeler were shuttling opioids from Miami, Florida to Egg Harbor Township in New Jersey. The DEA had learned of the distribution ring a few months earlier, after Glick met with a confidential informant in Miami in February of 2011, near Glick's second home in Port St. Lucie, Florida. In an effort to close the deal, Glick wrote the informant a letter setting down his illegal plan in writing:

[Let] me know if anyone down there is interested in moving those things Two-Tone is getting from the doctor. Lots of money to be made on them more than the other stuff. Could make the chapter rich if 8 or 10 members got that script, I could move them all of the time.

Two-Tone was another Pagan from a Florida chapter. The chapter was Glick's Cape May County chapter of the Pagans. If eight or ten members got that "script," it would mean they had a legitimate prescription of oxycodone they could sell. The confidential source set the plan in motion; however, rather than going to Glick's New Jersey residence, they were sent by Federal Express to a friend's home in Egg Harbor Township. That friend was a Pagan associate, and heavily involved in selling drugs. Glick helped to finance the operation. At one point he wrote a check for $5,900, and at another time, for $11,000. Besides pills, the team was also moving cocaine.

In October of 2011, Seeler and Glick had met with some Florida Pagans at a bar in Stuart, Florida. The FBI had a surveillance team surrounding them. A week or so later, Seeler and his wife met with Pagans again in Florida.

By February of 2012, the FBI and DEA considered this operation a drug ring. They had cameras set up on utility poles around the center of the ring, at the Pagan associate's home in Egg Harbor Township. During the surveillance, agents saw Glick arrive in his Chevrolet Silverado pickup truck almost daily. In April of 2012, the confidential informant from Florida came to visit Seeler. First he stopped at Seeler's temporary residence at the Ramada Inn on the Blackhorse Pike, and then he continued on to Glick's Northfield home to talk more about the drug trafficking operation.

At that point, Seeler and Glick now had Kauffman wrapped into their expanding drug network. But Kauffman and Fred seemed to be unaware of the New Jersey–Florida connection that Glick and Seeler were running simultaneously. The Kauffman connection appeared to be a bonus operation. The authorities watching Seeler and Glick, however, had no idea that alongside the drug-business talk between the men, there was also some gossip regarding a plot to kill a doctor's wife at the doctor's request.

Little Stevie Wittenwiler, known as Billboard, was a Pagan legacy. His dad was in with Glick, and even though father and son were in different chapters, Little Stevie got in on Seeler and Glick's New Jersey-to-Florida ring. The pagan associate running the organization was his best friend from growing up in Margate. In the fall of 2011, Little Stevie allegedly asked his old childhood friend if he was interested in making some extra money; he then mentioned the plot to kill the doctor's wife. Little Stevie's friend would later tell authorities about the offer, and said that he declined the job.

On the day of April's murder, after leaving his home so quickly, Glick sat at the bar with Seeler, still in shock. Then Seeler told Glick that he was supposed to pick up an envelope that day from Dr. Kauffman—containing, he assumed, part of the cash payment for the murder. Those plans were changed when, at the last minute, Fred decided to have his ex-wife, Beverly, pick it up.

Glick couldn't stop worrying. April was now dead, and police were calling it a suspicious death. Glick feared the Pagans were an obvious connection, since several Pagans had been sailing in and out of Kauffman's office, making it their private pill mill. On the paperwork Glick filled out for his first doctor's visit, under "Who referred you," he had written Glenn Seeler.

If the mother club learned that Pagans were involved in a murder-for-hire plot for a non-Pagan, and it involved a drug ring that the mother club wasn't seeing a dime from, it would be very bad news for Glick. As president, he could not only lose his diamond; they could actually burn his diamond tattoo off of his arm, and kill him.

"They're going to see Pagans, they're going to be here in the next day," Glick said to Seeler. "We better come up with something..." Both men agreed they needed to talk to Fred.

But Fred was nowhere to be found.

Chapter 8

HARRY JOHNSON AND THE HITMAN

Jim Kauffman gained a new best friend in August of 2011; his name was Harry Johnson. No one can recall ever meeting Harry. He wasn't listed as one of Jim's patients, nor was he one of Jim's buddies. Harry's contact information wasn't even saved in Jim's phone. But Harry's phone number called Jim Kauffman's cell phone number *three hundred twenty-two times* from August 2011 through May of 2012.

For the most part, their phone calls were brief. But on May 2nd, 2012, there were ten calls back and forth. On May 7th and 8th they spoke twice each day, with one call lasting four minutes, and another at least ten minutes. But the last time Harry ever called Jim Kauffman was May 9th, 2012. On that day, he made a 39-second call at 4:46 p.m. Within 24 hours, April was dead; Harry never called Jim Kauffman again.

In the months after April's death, authorities began to see connections emerging between Jim Kauffman and the Pagans. Authorities got zero cooperation from Dr. Kauffman, but April's friends came to police with anything they thought could help.

In the summer of 2012, as part of a flurry of search warrants, Jim's 9550 Blackberry Storm was among the items searched. Three years later, the case was still not solved. Investigators wanted to take a second look at the Blackberry and since the Atlantic County Prosecutor's Office was still in possession of the phone, they did a new analysis. That's when they found out about the phone calls between Harry and Jim, and the chilling coincidence of the phone call between the two on the day before April's murder.

Harry's number had been attached to a "burner" phone. Prepaid throwaway cell phones like this are often used for illegal activities like selling drugs, or for indiscretions a husband may not want his wife to know about. To activate one of those phones after you buy one, you have to register a name and address online. In reality, there was no Harry Johnson, and the address listed for the phone—153 Atlantic Avenue, Atlantic City—was bogus. Harry Johnson's name was a vulgar moniker—the kind of name a porn star might adopt. Investigators were left wondering who this Harry Johnson really was. What they didn't know was that Fred Augello's wife, Beverly Augello, was the person who registered the burner phone, and the name was just her idea of a joke, a pornographic "play on words."

Beverly and Fred Augello were divorced, but she still worked with him at their sign company. There was a 15-year age gap between Beverly and Fred. He had been married before he met Beverly; when they started dating in 1996, Beverly was blonde and tall and pretty, and she liked to party. Fred had long hair and tattoos on his arm. He was an artist at heart. He had attended art school for two years, and he loved music. Fred had played the guitar ever since he could hold one, and began performing in gigs around the shore.

He also loved motorcycles. Shortly after Fred and Beverly began dating, he became a Pagan. The couple fell in love and were married, and in true Pagan style, Beverly became his "property." In Pagan club tradition, wives or serious girlfriends are "old ladies." They are not privy to club business, do not discuss it, and do as they are told. Beverly even had a jacket that said "property of Miserable," Fred's club nickname. However, Beverly broke Fred's heart when she fell in love with another man. Because of their age gap, Fred felt Beverly looked up to him as her protector in many ways, and after the divorce she still considered him her best friend. They separated in 2003 and divorced in 2008, but the former couple remained in business together. Beverly did the graphic arts and kept the books. They split the business fifty-fifty, but Beverly was the owner.

The business took a dive in 2008. When they started, they had been making about $70,000 a year, but after 2008 they averaged only $30,000 a year. Fred also built custom guitars on the side, and played a lot of local bars and venues with his band, "Who Dat." In 2011, Beverly started seeing Dr. Kauffman as a patient. She also began noticing more of Fred's friends and former Pagan brothers coming into the shop. Even though she was no longer Fred's old lady and he was retired from the club, she was conditioned to remove herself from a conversation that sounded like club business. When Joe "Irish" Mulholland, the member of the support club the Herd, and Fred's close friend, would walk into their shop, she would go downstairs; lately he'd been coming around a lot, as was Andrew Glick and Glenn Seeler, along with his wife Cheryl. Cheryl, a loyal "old lady," had "Property of Seeler" tattooed on her back.

In August of 2011, Beverly remembers Fred handing her a burner phone. He wasn't savvy with computers, and he asked Beverly to register the phone online so he could activate it. At the time, he was dating someone pretty seriously, but he told Beverly he wanted a separate cell phone for privacy, "to call other women." Beverly registered the phone in the name of Harry Johnson, handed it to Fred and didn't think about it again. The cell phone never made a call to anyone after

May 9, 2012, but the timing of the phone's activation would later pique the interest of authorities, revealing a strand in a growing web of connections between Jim Kauffman and Pagan associates. The day before the phone was activated, Kauffman had called a phone number listed to a known Pagan associate. In 2015 law enforcement tracked several calls and texts between that associate and Glenn Seeler, Fred Augello, Beverly Augello and another Pagan associate who was also receiving prescriptions from Kauffman.

In the months after April's death, authorities hadn't yet made the connection between Harry Johnson and Jim Kauffman; but they did see connections emerging between Jim Kauffman and the Pagans. Authorities got zero cooperation from Dr. Kauffman, but April's friends came to police with anything they thought could help.

There was something fascinating about April and her ability to immediately befriend someone she just met. Regardless of whether she was talking to someone at the dry cleaner's or a waitress in a restaurant, or if she thought someone needed her help, whoever met April was her friend. April had a habit of putting the names and contact information of everyone she met and places she visited into her phone, and there they would stay, unless you did something to cross her.

Among those many contacts, there was one contact police overlooked: "Motor P." April's phone never received or made a call to Motor P. Whoever that was, they eerily shared the same cell phone number as Harry Johnson.

Three days after April's murder, a friend approached Linwood Police and reported that earlier that year, as April was describing Jim's threats to harm her, she told her friend not to worry. April disclosed that the president of the Pagans, an acquaintance of hers, said that if anything ever happened to her, he was going to kill Jim. If she was referring to Fred Augello, she may not have known that Fred had been ousted from the Pagans. Her family and friends never heard April refer to Fred as a close friend. But the staff of April's restaurant, the Cherry Cafe, remembered him frequenting the restaurant around 2011. Linwood was a small town, and Augello and April had actually met when they were children. Fred's mother had been friends with April's grandmother, who had raised her; more recently, April had gotten to know Fred's uncle, a veteran, through her charitable work.

She met Beverly through that connection. Beverly suffered from chronic bronchitis and had no health insurance, and April asked Jim to help her. Beverly began seeing Jim regularly, as a charity case. Beverly said that eventually she began receiving the 120-pill Oxy scripts, and like the others, she gave half of the pills to Fred. Beverly told investigators she was just doing as her ex-husband told her. She admitted she had a problem—she was addicted to prescription pain pills.

April made that introduction and then moved on. She had no significant connection with Jim's practice; her only regular activity involved managing Jim's social calendar and his speaking engagements. Jim's staff later told police that they only remember April bringing lunch to the office, or meeting up with Jim and staff for happy hours after work.

April had also met Glenn Seeler in passing when she and Jim had gone to a bike event in Smithville, a small historic town north of Atlantic City, shortly before she was killed. Fred was at the event and had introduced Glenn. Seeler remembered April as having a pink motorcycle, although April's family maintains she never owned a pink bike. Even at a non-Pagan event like this one, it wasn't unusual for law-abiding bikers to run into Pagans or members or their support clubs.

No one knows what conversation April may have exchanged with Fred, or someone else whom she may have believed was the president of the Pagans. When she spoke with her friend, she didn't identify by name the Pagans president who had told her she would be protected. It's also possible that April, forever the caretaker, was just trying to reassure her friends and family during a time when her domestic life was growing increasingly unsafe. And it may have made April feel better, as if someone had her back.

After April's murder, talk of whom Fred Augello had approached to kill April Kauffman continued to grow within in the Pagan's circle. Speculation on the number of people who the doctor himself had approached also grew. But Andrew Glick maintained that he still did not know who had done the hit, and that he didn't try to find out. However, about a year and a half after April's murder, in late 2013, Glick says that Fred started opening up to him about it for the first time. This may have been because Fred's confidant and close friend, Joseph "Irish" Mulholland, was no longer available: he had checked himself into a drug rehab center in Florida, to kick an addiction to painkillers like the ones Dr. Kauffman prescribed.

One day when Glick brought Fred money from sales of the pills from the doctor's office, he reported that business was doing well.

"This is a really good deal; everyone is making money," Glick said to Augello. It was then that Glick remembers Augello starting to talk to him about the hitman.

"Ya know one of the key people is no longer able to say anything," Augello said, and Glick watched as Augello made a trigger-pulling motion with one hand. Glick took that to mean he was talking about the hitman.

"You know, Mulholland?" Glick says his former club president asked him.

"Joe!?" Glick responded.

"No, no, no, another guy," Fred replied. Glick says he was baffled—he didn't know another Mulholland. But Fred explained that their mutual friend, Joe Mulholland, happened to have the same last name as the hitman, Francis Mulholland. Glick was curious but let it drop—he knew he'd be seeing Fred more, with Joe Mulholland in rehab and Seeler down in North Carolina. It was Fred who brought it up again a few months later, telling Glick the gunman had been found with a needle in his arm and that he was "no longer with us." Glick asked again "You mean Irish?"

"No...," Fred responded. Glick had no idea who Francis Mulholland was.

On October 8, 2013, Francis Mulholland was found dead in his home in the 100 block of Jacksonville Avenue West in the small community of Villas. Francis went by Fran to family, and Frank to friends. Francis had a history of drug problems, and police were familiar with the address, having been called to his house for various issues over a period of several years. Some neighbors described him as horrible to live next to, because of his often public drunken fights and antics. But a killer? No, he didn't seem like a murderer; just a drug addict with a tendency for drama and violence.

From the outside, the three-bedroom, two-bathroom ranch with white siding looked every bit the delightful, cozy summer cottage. Built in 1936, the house sat only a few steps from the Delaware Bay. Striped awnings on the front windows gave it a quaint, period feel. Several manicured shrubs lined the front lawn just a few short feet from the street.

Villas is a part of Lower Township, Cape May County. It is located on the west-facing side of the tip that juts out of the bottom of the state and faces the Delaware Bay. On the other side of the tiny peninsula lies Wildwoods, about a ten-mile drive away. With its wide sandy beaches, it is of New Jersey's biggest tourist destinations.

When police entered Francis Mulholland's home, there was nothing quaint or charming inside. The kelly-green rug was littered with mail, clothes, and shoes. They found empty plastic bags with traces of heroin inside, holding smaller folds of blue wax paper labeled "pitbull," along with a tin containing a syringe. Heroin users often use a lighter to heat the heroin in a tin can or a spoon, which liquefies it, and then use the syringe to draw it in so they can inject it. There were two empty bottles of a prescription for 30 mg. Oxycodone prescribed by Dr. James Kauffman, but they were prescribed to Joseph Mulholland. Francis was found in his boxers, shirtless, and with his face down on the carpet in a pool of foamy fluid. His body lay at the foot of an opened-up sleeper sofa. It looked as if he had been frozen in place while trying to crawl across the floor, with his right side stretched straight out and his left knee bent almost to his left elbow. There was a bloody mark over his left eyebrow, possibly from him lying on his face for hours. Near the pill bottles the police found $200 in cash, reading glasses, and an ashtray, and the remote control for the TV lay beside him on the floor.

On an end table sat a pink snow globe, a knocked-over holiday candle, and a copy of an Alcoholics Anonymous book. Above that, a prayer card of the Virgin Mary was stuck into the edge of a picture frame, next to pictures of someone's baby. The house was a mess, yet it didn't seem to have been burglarized or ransacked.

Francis was a Northeast Philly guy, originally from the working-class Port Richmond neighborhood. He followed his parents to Villas after they moved there, taking Francis's son along with them to raise. Francis had served some time and had run-ins with Philadelphia Police in the nineties. But he cleaned himself up, and at Villas he started coaching football—not only his own kid's team, but others as well.

Francis would meet one of his best friends while coaching: Joseph Mulholland. Joseph had kids of his own who played football and wrestled. The two shared the same last name, but weren't related. In appearance, they were like Mutt and Jeff. Fran was a small guy, only about 5'7", and heavy-set. He preferred to wear leather jackets and acid-washed jeans or jean shorts. His son remembered that even though his dad was often at sporting events, he hated sweatpants, and never wore them. Francis had the fair Irish look: fair skin, light-brown hair, and blue eyes.

Joseph, on the other hand, towered over Francis at 6 feet tall, and weighed a trim 175. Also Irish, he was red-faced, with light blue eyes. His hair was dark with white in his sideburns, and combed to the side or straight back. Both arms were tattooed down to his wrists. Joseph was a house painter by trade. He'd been married a long time and had a family; yet those close to Francis didn't get a good vibe from him, and thought he was a freeloader. The two men got a kick out of having the same last name, and Joseph started calling him "'cuz." Both men struggled with alcohol and drug addiction. Francis had suffered a shoulder accident years before when he worked at a local manufacturing plant, beginning a dependency on pain medications he was prescribed which led to heroin.

Villas resident Henry Von Colln began hanging out with both Mulhollands when he decided to get sober in the fall of 2013. Von Colln already knew Joseph through his wife, a nurse. Von Colln said Joseph was dedicated to helping others get sober, and took Von Colln under his wing when they met. Von Colln was fresh out of rehab and attending several AA meetings a day, morning, midday, and evening, and by October, the three men were attending the meetings together regularly.

According to Von Colln, Joseph picked him up on the morning of October 8, 2013 for the 7:30 a.m. AA meeting. Joseph had first gone to pick up Francis, but told Henry there was no answer when he knocked on Francis's door, although he heard the TV blaring. Joseph dropped Von Colln off at his house after the meeting, just after 8:30 a.m., and promised to pick him up in time for the 1 p.m. meeting. Joseph later called Henry and said he was worried about Francis. He went to Francis's home again. The TV still blared, and again no one answered.

Joe came to get Henry and they headed over to Francis's house together. Henry, smaller than Joe, went through an open window that Joseph couldn't fit through. He saw Francis lying on the floor. His skin was blue and he didn't seem to be breathing. Henry immediately called 911 and ran to open the locked front door. He hadn't known Francis or Joseph for very long, but understood that they were close, and tried to keep Joseph back so he wouldn't see his friend this way. Joseph collapsed on the front porch, bawling like a baby. The police arrived. A Lower Township police officer later noted that he had made contact with a "relative" at the scene, a man who told police he was Francis's cousin. As the police hustled inside with a defibrillator and oxygen, "Mr. Mulholland stated to me that the patient was inside and cold and that I didn't need my equipment...."

Two women showed up at the scene: Joseph's wife, and Francis's date from the night before, whom Joseph had set him up with. Joseph had called them both that morning to ask if Francis had been in touch with either of them.

The Lower Township Police Department doesn't handle death investigations, so they called for the detectives from the Cape May County Prosecutors office to respond. Officers at the scene spoke to both Joseph and Henry. When investigators saw the pill bottles, they called Dr. Kauffman's office and were connected with nurse-practitioner Barb Greenling. She acknowledged that they had a patient named Joseph Mulholland (the name on the bottles). The officers asked Greenling to come down and make the death pronouncement. Lynne Rybicki, the Forensic Nurse Examiner Coordinator with Cape May County, was also called to the scene. She made the pronouncement at 2:35 PM.

When Greenling arrived on the scene, she said she had no idea who the man was lying on the floor. She couldn't identify him. Detective Ashlee Mariner spoke to Joseph about the bottles found with his name. Joseph explained by saying that he'd been staying at the house off and on, and that the pill bottles must have been in a box he had given to Francis, a box that also held a paint sprayer he used in his house-painting work. Joseph then went through the day's chronology with the police, from his first visit at 6:30 that morning until he and Von Colln discovered the body.

One thing investigators found at the scene might have made them pause: a blue ax handle wrapped in plastic, with "PFFP"—short for Pagans Forever, Forever Pagans— and "ICEMAN" written in black marker. The other side of the ax handle, which was found on Francis's bed, bore the markings "Mulholland" and "PFFP."

Eleven years earlier, the Pagans had shown their preference for hand weapons like this. When the Pagan OMG (Outlaw Motorcycle Gang) East Coast had stormed the Hells Angels Hellraiser Ball in 2002, only one biker out of the seventy-five bikers charged was arraigned for using a gun, and he was a Hells Angel. The Pagans had come armed for hand to hand combat, and afterward law enforcement confiscated "knives, bats, axe handles and other exotic weapons...." The fight sounded more Game of Thrones than Scarface. The Pagans' "little friend" is often an ax handle with the metal ax head removed, and nicknames are often engraved.

But Francis was never a Pagan. His family says he never rode nor owned a motorcycle. To their knowledge, no one in the family was connected to a motorcycle club. Nor did the family know him to have ever owned a gun, let alone to have known how to shoot one. The Northeast Philly boy primarily used a baseball bat as his home protection system, usually at the ready next to his bed or behind the front door. The detectives never heard Francis's name in the course of any other investigation. They did know who Dr. Kauffman was, but never followed up with him or his office after that day, according to the reports.

Francis's son was notified by other relatives. In the midst of his shock and grief, he found it strange that police told him Joseph claimed to be a cousin. They had kept Francis's belongings at headquarters until his son, now in his twenties, could get there. His son instructed them not to give them to Joseph, as he was not family. The family cremated Francis's body and held a memorial for him a few days later. Between twenty-five and thirty people attended, including people he had coached over the years. People from Alcoholics Anonymous and Narcotics Anonymous also came to pay their respects; they told his son stories about his dad helping them get sober. Henry Von Colln had a similar story—although he barely knew Francis, he had been a huge support in Henry's early stage of sobriety.

Francis's family, and especially his son, had many unanswered questions about his death. Joseph Mulholland told Francis's son, "Do yourself a favor and don't go after nobody." It was an odd thing to say. Did he know that Francis's son had been known to call out the drug dealers feeding his dad's habit? Or was it a warning that there was something bigger behind how his father died?

Detective Ashlee Marriner, from The Cape May County prosecutor's office, took over the case from Lower Township police the day Francis was found dead in his home. She would later testify that at the time, she had handled less than ten overdose cases. In April of 2014, six months after Francis's death, Marriner interviewed the woman Francis had gone out with the night before his body was discovered. She gave Marriner more information then she had offered to the responding officer that day. Earlier, she had said that Francis had not complained of any pain or medical problems that evening. This time, she related that Francis had felt dizzy during dinner and didn't like the taste of his food. Francis's son says his dad called him around one a.m. that night—the same time his date reported dropping him off—to tell him about the date he'd been on. His dad had been on a long stretch of sobriety. Through the ups and downs of his addiction, the father and son had only talked when Francis was sober. In that last phone call, his son felt that his dad was clean.

A few months later in September of 2014, nearly a year after his death, Francis's phone was analyzed. There had been some interest in his phone by investigators on the day they discovered Francis. In the report, they included a photograph of the screen on his flip phone, specifically a call that came in at 1:24 p.m.

on October 8th from a caller identified as "Dimingo." Glick often mentioned a Pagan named Domingo in conversation. Most of Francis's other contacts were people from Alcoholics Anonymous and some family. There were no numbers saved in his contacts from Glick, Augello, "Harry Johnson," or Dr. Kauffman. The case was closed. Francis's official cause of death: Toxic Effects of Heroin.

On January 9, 2018, Francis's son called his cousin Tim. Had his cousin seen what police were saying about his dad on the news—that he was the hitman who had killed the beautiful blonde radio show host?

Hearing this, Tim got chills. He remembered his uncle taking him fishing in the summer of 2012, in June or July. Before they headed out, they stopped at a Wawa. Francis left the store with a magazine and pulled it out to show his nephew. Tim didn't remember the name of the publication, but an investigator later knew it was the "Boardwalk Journal," which had run April Kauffman's picture on the cover that summer, along with an in-depth piece about her and her murder. Tim had never seen April before, and had no idea about the story. He wondered why his uncle was showing it to him. Francis held the magazine out.

"I did that," he said to Tim. His nephew looked at him.

"What?" he asked.

"I killed her," his uncle said.

Francis continued. He said he'd walked into her house and shot her twice in the back of her head. "I just walked through the door," Francis told him. Francis only said the woman was pretty and popular, and that he got paid fifty grand to do it. Tim barely looked at the magazine and the photo. It didn't make sense. He never saw his uncle with money; Francis still talked about waiting for his settlement checks from lawsuits he claimed to have filed from his shoulder accident.

Tim was annoyed. His uncle often told whoppers and embellished things, making himself seem much tougher than he was. His family would often discredit his stories as exaggerations or twisted jokes, dismissing them with an eye-roll. That's what Tim did now. Even though Francis had ups and downs with his family, they loved him. He was that quirky relative, maintaining his dirty sense of humor well into adulthood.

Besides, Tim was already preoccupied with how his uncle was behaving—he could see Francis was definitely high.

Tim didn't know of Joseph Mulholland's role in the last month of his uncle's life. In September of 2013, when Joseph left rehab and briefly moved in with Francis, one of the first things he had done was to fill a prescription from Dr. James Kauffman for 120 30-mg. Oxycodone. He would later say he was clean and that the pills weren't for him; he had only filled the prescription to pay back a debt he owed to Fred. The web of connections between Joseph and Francis, would-be cousins, would only become clear later.

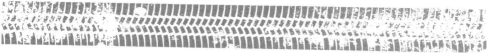

Chapter 9

MOMENTUM

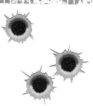

In the summer of 2012, investigators felt they had good momentum in solving the murder of April Kauffman. They were motivated not just to solve a homicide, but to put people at ease. Homicides were uncommon in the city of Linwood and the towns immediately surrounding it. Atlantic City had its share of violence; Pleasantville and portions of Egg Harbor Township did too. But the area where the Kauffman residence sat in Atlantic County was seen as a near-idyllic family community, making April's murder even more shocking.

Linwood lay close enough to Ocean City that a trail actually connected the towns, almost to the bay. The Somers Point Bicycle Path began a few blocks from the Atlantic Ocean, and ran north, parallel to busy Shore Road. Traversing Linwood, Northfield, and Pleasantville, the scenic, tree-lined route brought the different communities together. The trail traveled through neighborhoods, schools, parks, and playing fields, providing a safe route for children to visit or walk to practices. Runners and bikers used it to exercise. Linwood residents called their portion the Linwood bike path. What residents did not know for years was that the same bike path was possibly used as a getaway trail by April's killer.

In the days after April's murder, investigators subpoenaed the two Wawa convenience stores where Jim told officers he had stopped at the morning her body was discovered. They wanted the surveillance video that Jim said would verify his alibi. They also wanted the surveillance video from the Shore Memorial parking garage at Shore Memorial that he said would further document his whereabouts of that morning.

One piece of surveillance video Jim never mentioned was from Mainland High School; the doctor most likely didn't know of its existence. The school stood directly across from the neighborhood of 2 Woodstock Drive, on the other side of Wabash Avenue. The bike path actually ran down the median, splitting Wabash Avenue in two. A smaller street, Oak Avenue, ran closer to the school's entrance, and would fill up in the morning and afternoon with buses and parents' cars for drop-off and pick-up. One of the school's cameras faced The Linwood bike path. Detective Sgt. Hamilton picked up the external hard drive containing video from the School Security Camera System and worked his way through it. The video documented the peacefulness of the dark early morning hours. Puddles formed on the damp blacktop from an overnight rain, and a little mist still hung in the air.

At 5:16 a.m., a Chevy Silverado pickup truck appeared, the only vehicle seen near the bike path on the Wabash Avenue side nearest to 2 Woodstock Drive. The roadway, directly across from the high school, connected several neighborhoods, including the Kauffman's neighborhood on Woodstock Drive. Six minutes into the video a man in a hoodie, sweatpants and white sneakers was seen walking on the Linwood bike path, which ran along the Wabash Avenue median here. He was walking away from the area of the Kauffman house, the opposite direction the Silverado pickup truck was seen driving.

Only one other vehicle was spotted on that same stretch of roadway around that time: a dark-colored SUV, also headed away from Woodstock Drive, in the opposite direction from the pickup. The SUV was seen on the video sometime after 5:16 a.m. Minutes later, the surveillance video from the Wawa on Shore Road would show Dr. James Kauffman stepping out of his dark- colored SUV at 5:23 a.m. These two videos would prove vital to the authorities' case years later, but at this point, the pieces had not come together.

The investigation continued, with search warrants issued for Jim's alarm system, phones, vehicles, and for the couple's home in Tucson, Arizona. In June, detectives traveled to Philadelphia International Airport and boarded a US Airways plane to remove Dr. Kauffman and confiscate his phone, although they did not arrest him. They interviewed family, friends, and coworkers of Jim and April Kauffman, finding a number of people who may have had an issue with either one of the couple.

Neighbors were keeping their eyes on Jim too. After April's murder, all the guns that Jim had kept in his gun room at 2 Woodstock were eventually returned to him. Ballistics tests a few weeks later showed none of the .22s collected from 2 Woodstock and the Arizona home could be the murder weapon. During the course of their interviews, Jim's obsession with firearms became apparent, along with his fabricated stories about his time in Vietnam piled up. These aspects of his personality supported the detectives' sense that he must have known something about the murder and the murder weapon, even given the ballistics test results.

The day after the murder, investigators had done a final sweep and walk-through of 2 Woodstock with a K-9 officer before closing the crime scene and allowing Jim to return. Looking for firearms that may have been hidden in the backyard, the weapons-sniffing dog moved closer and closer to the in-ground pool. The dog signaled his handler to a "hit," somewhere near the pool heater. Authorities searched, but came up with nothing.

The day Jim was allowed back in by investigators, two neighbors told police they saw something peculiar: Jim stood by the pool, wielding the skimmer. They had never seen him cleaning the pool in all the years they had lived there. He swished the skimmer around in the pool, went inside the house with it, then came back out and dropped it on the ground.

Investigators were still trying to pin down exactly when April was murdered. An investigator with the Medical Examiner's Office, Louise Houseman, had documented the condition of the body at 1:15 in the afternoon, one hour and forty-five minutes after April was pronounced dead by medics. She noted that April's body was in full rigor mortis; the temperature taken under her arm, the right axillary, was 85 degrees; and the temperature in the room was at 77 degrees.

Dr. Hydow Park noted those findings in the final autopsy report. On June 15, then-Assistant Prosecutor John Maher sent a letter to Dr. Michael Baden asking him to review the initial autopsy report. Baden is a renowned medical examiner who often reviews autopsies and testifies in court across the country, and appears frequently on documentaries and true crime shows. He responded that after reviewing the autopsy photographs, eye fluid toxicology report, and reports sent from the prosecutor's office, he would put the time of death eleven hours before 1:10 p.m., which would have been at 2:10 a.m. Baden noted that he based his conclusion "...on the time required for the body to develop the extent of rigor and lividity that was present, for the body temperature to drop to 86 degrees and for the eye fluid potassium to rise to 9.4." However, the body temperature provided to Baden was a degree higher than the one Houseman noted at the scene.

In June of 2012, still less than a month after April's murder, Det. Sgt. Mattioli received a call from a frequent confidential informant, who lived next door to Glenn Seeler at the Ramada Inn. This informant had helped detectives in the past with other homicide cases in the county, never asking for anything in exchange. He told Mattioli, "A buddy of mine was running around bragging about the shooting of the lady... the doctor's wife..."

Months later, he agreed to record a statement with Mattioli and Detective Sgt. Hamilton about what he had told police soon after April's murder. The informant went on to say that Seeler was talking about a planned hit on April two weeks before her murder. At the time this individual only knew Seeler as "Slash."

"He's a biker, he's a Pagan... He's the enforcer...," the informant continued, explaining that Seeler had talked about his position of sergeant at arms and what that meant in the club. Mattioli asked him to clarify: "What does that mean from what you know?"

"They do the dirty work," the CI responded. Weeks before the crime, he went on, Glenn "Slasher" Seeler was looking for a hitman and Seeler asked his neighbor for help,

> CI: The first information he says is, do I know anybody that might want a piece of the action?
>
> MATTIOLI: Action of?
>
> CI: Pulling off the hit.
>
> MATTIOLI: When you say pulling off the hit, what exactly do you mean?
>
> CI: To murder the lady, I guess. I guess that's what he meant, to murder the lady?
>
> MATTIOLI: I guess what I'm asking is, was it him that wanted her murdered, or someone else who wanted her murdered from what he told you?
>
> CI: From what I picked up, he didn't even know who the hell she was. He was just doing as he was told.

The CI then went on to say that Seeler, who had a tendency to brag and talk a lot about Pagan business to non-club members, did not admit to being the hitman, but that it sounded as if he knew who was. The day of the crime, he said that Seeler's Harley and his Ford Mustang had remained parked outside his room, and he didn't think Seeler left at all that day.

Police were now confident the Pagans had a connection to Dr. Kauffman, and that they were involved in the murder. It was Glenn Seeler who they started to think was her killer. Another break came to authorities in July. The New Jersey Division of Consumer Affairs sent investigators a list of patients of Kauffman's who were receiving prescriptions every thirty days for 30 mg. Oxycodone Hydrochloride, also known as Roxicodone, from September 2011 through July 21st, 2012. In addition, several were also receiving scripts for Percocet and Xanax. Glenn Seeler, Andrew Glick, Tabitha Chapman, Paul Pagano, Beverly Augello, and Cheryl Pizza were some of the names on that list. Only one person, Tabitha Chapman, was not an associate of the Pagans—but she did have a connection to Fred Augello: her mother dated him. Augello's name was not on the list of patients.

Investigators also learned of the DEA's investigation into the Florida-to-Egg-Harbor pill ring that investigators believed Andrew Glick, fellow pagan Stephen "Little Stevie" Wittenwiler Jr., and a Pagan associate were masterminding. They brought in the Pagan associate to interrogate him in July. That individual told Det. Sgt. Mattioli that his childhood friend, Little Stevie, also known as "Billboard," had brought up the hit job on April a few months before.

"Do you want to make some extra money?" the associate says Little Stevie pitched him. "I know this doctor... from Linwood... that wants to knock his wife off... and was willing to pay about ten thousand dollars." Authorities pressed the associate about who propositioned Wittenwiler to do the job. "Slasher and Chef," he responded, indicating Seeler and Glick. The associate turned CI did not think Wittenwiler had done the job. Mattioli asked the CI if he had noticed whether his friend was suddenly flush with cash, he said no, "He was the typical broke Steve ..."

With this mounting intelligence, investigators were able to get a judge to sign a warrant to tap Glenn Seeler's phone, and two confidential Informants agreed to wear a wire. One of those informants was already working with the DEA. The targets of those CI's: Glenn "Slasher" Seeler and Steve Wittenwiler. Authorities had learned that Little Stevie had been kicked out of the Pagans because of his out-of-control drug habit, and was now receiving outpatient treatment at a methadone clinic. The Feds were hoping his vulnerability, or maybe resentment toward the club, could help them. Seeler was still pushing drugs and had a big mouth; police were counting on him to slip.

The recordings were not as useful as they had hoped. However, they did get Seeler on tape talking about drug sales, which would prove helpful down the road.

* * *

Six months after April's murder, local authorities decided it was time to ask for help from the Federal Bureau of Investigation field office in Northfield. Special Agent Daniel Garrabrant was especially intrigued from the day the murder occurred. The case piqued his interest because it was unlike the average homicide they see in the area. And Garrabrant tended to gravitate toward difficult cases. He offered the FBI's assistance on the case right away—the FBI often lends assistance to local authorities, especially in cases where the FBI's resources could be a major help. It took a while for the Atlantic County Prosecutor's Office to accept the invitation, but when they did Garrabrant was ready with a theory in hand. Garrabrant believed this was a murder-for-hire, and Dr. Jim Kauffman was responsible. He also believed prescription and other records would prove it.

In November of 2013, another investigation into Glenn Seeler's alleged drug trafficking caught up with him. The Ocean City Police Department and the Guns, Gangs and Narcotics Task Force of the Cape May County Prosecutors Office executed a search warrant on November 20 in the 600 block of Wesley Avenue. Glenn Seeler and Cheryl Pizza, both living in the home, were arrested and charged. Police seized four handguns, a stun gun and drug paraphernalia commonly used for the distribution, packaging, and sale of controlled substances. Seeler was charged with four counts of unlawful possession of a handgun, possession of a stun gun, possession of controlled or dangerous substance, distribution of controlled dangerous substance, and possession of drug paraphernalia. Pizza was charged with four counts of unlawful possession of a handgun, possession of a stun gun and possession of drug paraphernalia.

Authorities were still looking for the murder weapon used to kill April Kauffman, a .22 caliber gun, and Glenn Seeler was still in their sights. The ACPO immediately jumped on the discovery of a .22 caliber handgun found in his Ocean City home during the search.

Since the case was in Cape May County's hands, the Atlantic County Prosecutor's Office sent a letter to the New Jersey State Police Laboratory Ballistics Unit asking the lab to test the four "projectiles" found at the April Kauffman homicide scene against the .22 caliber handgun found in Glenn Seeler's home.

"Our agency requests the comparison be given a priority status for completion," Sergeant Ian Finnimore of the Forensic Crime Scene Unit wrote NJSP. But the results came as a let-down for those who had pegged Seeler as "the guy." They were negative: the bullets that killed April Kauffman had not been fired from the gun seized from Seeler's home.

The DEA, FBI and local and county authorities all had their hands in the April Kauffman murder case; but after Seeler's arrest, the momentum in the Atlantic County Prosecutor's Office appeared to come to a standstill.

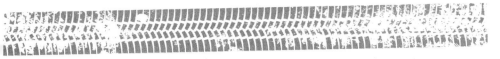

Chapter 10

STANDSTILL

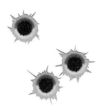

"I feel like she's coming off of a cruise or a vacation...." Kim Pack closed her eyes and described the image she had of her mother in her head: "I'm waiting for her beautiful blonde hair, blowing in the wind... pulling up in that red Corvette as I look out my front door... Somebody took her from me."

It was Friday, May 10th, 2013, exactly a year since her mother's death. Kim Pack nervously tucked her short blonde hair behind her ears and held a microphone in her hand. The past year speaking to groups and the media had revealed a talent she didn't know she had; maybe an undiscovered trait she'd inherited from her mother. If, God forbid, the roles had been reversed, April would have made life hell for police and prosecutors if they hadn't made an arrest by now, and she would have done the same for the person she suspected had committed the crime. Kim had been persistent in her approach to law enforcement handling her mother's case. But she was starting to feel as if no one was communicating with her—that she was off on some island, alone.

The occasion of her talk that night was the dedication of a public bench in her mother's honor. Kim looked at the crowd gathered around the bench, decorated for the occasion in red, white and blue, with photos of her mom set up on the bench's wooden seat. A small plaque with April's name had been attached to the seat back. The bench sat across the street from the 2 Woodstock Drive cul-de-sac where Jim Kauffman still lived, on the Linwood bike path. Today he was out of town on vacation. Media trucks lined the street, and dozens of people, including Legion Riders on their motorcycles, veterans, friends, and some of the many people April helped, among others, had gathered for the occasion. They each took small candles and set them inside paper Chinese lanterns letting them float up into the muggy May night sky.

Kim choked back tears as she thanked the crowd. "This has been the most difficult year of my life... that woman being gone is such a void in my life. She was my sister, my soulmate, my Mom...."

As the anniversary neared, Prosecutor Jim McClain said that he would not declare the murder of April Kauffman a cold case. He told the *Press of Atlantic City*:

> "I consider a case to be cold when all available investigative leads have been explored and exhausted and there is still insufficient evidence to support a criminal charge," the prosecutor said. "The homicide of April Kauffman is an active investigation and is not being regarded as a cold case."

To put April's homicide case into perspective, the Atlantic County Prosecutor's Office reported a solve rate of 62 percent in 2012. There were 29 homicide cases that year; April's was one of 11 homicides from 2012 that remained open. The Prosecutor's office had reached out for help from the public in other cases. Just the month before, they had handed out flyers to generate public interest in another unsolved homicide. But for April's case, they refused most interviews and passed up any chance to put it back out in the news during the anniversary.

McClain told The Press of Atlantic City, "My office has received dozens of phone calls from members of the public offering information. In this particular case, there is no need to release any additional information in order to create public interest or response." King Arthur Gropper, April's former radio co-host, worked to keep April's case alive, mentioning it weekly on his radio broadcast and providing the number for the prosecutor's office. Harry Hurley, a close friend of April's and a fixture on the Jersey Shore radio scene with his popular talk radio show, came to events in April's honor trying to maintain interest in the case. During a vigil on the first anniversary, Hurley urged people to have patience with investigators and suggested trying to raise money for a reward. Near the second anniversary, however, Hurley voiced the frustration that so many others felt about the case. During a vigil for April held then, he suggested that the public get more involved, perhaps by establishing a committee, and criticized Prosecutor Jim McClain. "Prosecutors in high-profile cases; they do updates," Hurley said. "This guy has never said anything."

In the weeks after her mom's murder, Kim would just sit in her home and stare at the walls, still numb. After the abrupt end to the daily phone calls, texts, and visits with her mom, she began to feel the reality of April being gone. Kim would play over and over in her head the things that had upset her mom in the days and weeks before her killing. She gave every piece of information to detectives, as small or inconsequential as it might seem. She offered to record phone conversations with people who reached out to her and claimed to have information, but who were scared to go to police. Her husband did the same. In fact,

Randy was recording conversations with Jim, with the help of authorities. A few days after her mother's murder Jim had worn a short-sleeved polo shirt, and Kim noticed scratches on the inside of his left forearm. She scribbled down what they looked like to show police. The Packs had become investigators themselves.

Kim stopped speaking to Jim completely after an upsetting meeting with him in July 2012. He had asked to meet her for lunch through a mutual friend. They had barely spoken after her mother's funeral, and Jim kept coming up with excuses not to let Kim go through her mother's belongings. Kim was so uncomfortable about meeting Jim this time that she alerted detectives on the case, and suggested they wait near Clancy's By the Bay, a restaurant in Somers Point where she agreed to meet Jim. Jim ordered soup, and Kim sat with a glass of water. She remembers listening to him eating while Tiger Woods played golf on the television. She asked, "What happened to my mother?" Jim paused with the spoon between the bowl and his lips.

"I have no idea," he said. Kim tensed up,

"Why can't you just come with me to the police? Maybe you could shed light or provide a clue or something."

Jim reached across the table and put his hand on her hand. He said, "I have a very expensive powerful attorney, and he doesn't think it's a good idea that I talk to police because the police always frame the husband, and I'm gonna do what he says because he is an expert at this ... we will never know what happened."

"Well, I guess then we are done here," Kim said, starting to leave. "There's nothing else to say...." As she got up from the table, he told her to wait, then said, "Oh, by the way, there's this woman from my past that called me. What do I do? Do I call her back?" Kim was taken aback.

"What are you asking me right now?" Jim fell over his words, saying, "Oh no, no, no; this was a girl that I knew from high school and she called the office to give her condolences. Do I call her back?"

Kim felt disgusted. "I don't know, Jim... I gotta go." Later, she thought he'd been asking for her blessing to get back into the dating pool. There were rumors he had been spotted in her mom's Corvette with a woman.

Kim had never publicly accused her stepfather, but from the moment he had called to tell her of her mother's death, she had been sure he was involved in April's murder. As time passed and 2012 turned to 2013, Kim began to realize that her mother's case was turning into folklore. Once-credible tidbits of information turned into hurtful gossip. People speculated about Jim and April's marriage. There were stories so wild that if they hadn't been about her own mother, she would have rolled her eyes. Instead, they cut Kim deeply. Kim's appearances on the news, where she begged the public for any relevant information, had made her into a public figure in the little town of Linwood. People felt they could approach her and share any thoughts they had regarding her mom's case—in the pharmacy, grocery store, and restaurants, regardless of whether her kids were at her side.

One day, someone approached Kim in a restaurant, saying they had heard that Jim's lawyers had a "little black book" belonging to her mother. This sounded salacious, but it wasn't. It was a small book with a bird on the cover; her mother had told friends she wrote down her life adventures in the book, hoping to hand it to Kim one day. She didn't know where it was—it had vanished from April's night-stand, where a friend would later tell police she had seen it.

In Jewish tradition, one year after someone's death their headstone is "unveiled" at the deceased's gravesite. Jim was not invited to the unveiling. He had promised to order the headstone, but it was not ready for the unveiling. Instead, the small group of friends and family who gathered used a large rock. When the headstone was finally created, it said only

"Beloved Wife"
APRIL KAUFFMAN
OCTOBER 27, 1964 – MAY 10, 2012

This was followed by two lines in Hebrew which read: "In the past," and "Rachel Daughter of Abraham." There was no mention of Mimi, the beloved grandmother to Kim's children, nor of April's being a beloved mother to Kim.

Kim and Jim still had to co-exist in the same small town, and in the same business. Pharmaceutical representatives would pass on to Kim comments made in his office, including a sign that reportedly went up warning people not to ask or talk to the doctor about "current events."

On the outside looking in, however, it seemed Jim Kauffman was living his best life. Nearly a year after her mother's murder, Kim sat at a stoplight and turned her head to see him in his car. They made eye contact; he gave her the middle fin-ger and laughed.

In June 2013, Jim put April's estate up for auction. He hadn't given Kim any advance notice, let alone allowing her to come and take any of the hundreds of collectibles and keepsakes that April had accrued. Kim had begged Jim to let her take her mother's things, but all he gave her was a trash bag filled with some of her mother's clothes, which he left on Kim's doorstep. Some of April's figurines and china dated back to when Kim was a baby. There was also china from her first husband's family, relatives of Kim's father. Jim consigned everything to the South Jersey auction house, even down to her tea collection, hat boxes, a silly witch's hat that she'd worn the previous Halloween with Kim and the boys, and a tea-party hat she'd worn to the baby shower for Kim's oldest son.

Every piece brought back a memory for Kim. The ornate and colorful glass perfume bottles her mother kept on her vanity were also up for auction. Just the thought of them triggered memories of her mother's fragrance.

All of the auction items could be viewed in person at the auction house or online. Lee Darby and Peg O'Boyle, acting as motherly surrogates, went to work for Kim to get as many items as they could. It was a tall task—they would be bidding against people who might have no idea of the emotional weight these items held. Lee and Peg arrived at the auction house for the Friday preview, to identify which items were April's. Several other estate auctions were scheduled for the same sale. They compiled a list of what had belonged to April, and gathered a group of a dozen or so people to bid when the auction opened online on Sunday.

"We hope to be able to procure the most precious treasures that April would say she wanted Kimberly to have, just little simple things. They're critical to maybe a healing process," Lee told ABC-owned affiliate WPVI Action News, who had shown up to cover the story. Jim had no comment through his attorney. In the end, it was a small victory for April's friends who were able to buy April's treasures and preventing them from going into the hands of strangers. It sent a message to Jim that April's army had assembled and they were not stopping.

After the story about the frantic push to get the mementos aired on WPVI-TV, more tips came into police—including one from "beyond." A man emailed who described himself as someone who used a "rare type of dowsing technique that only few knew how to do" emailed Detective Sgt. Hamilton. The man offered thoughts that came to him after reading the story on WPVI-TV'S website. He described his technique saying, "I do testing on energy, or statements." He continued, "All I do is get a picture of the person or name or both for a better connection..." He sent several emails to Det. Sgt. Hamilton. They read like someone jotting down their thought process, with run-on sentences, and in the first email he confused the reporter's name with April's. The emails, strange as they may be, were chilling because of the details he included. He wrote that he believed Jim Kauffman knew April was having an affair.

> ...Dr. Kauffman suspected this and had her followed for about 6 weeks by someone and caught her several times [with] this person involved with sex. At this time... he hired a hitman to shoot his wife for approx. 30K so he would not be the suspect and get revenge....

In another email, the man wrote more about April having an affair and then said, "I tested some kind of life policy for 500K?" And later in another email he wrote "...There were 2 one driver and one shooter... both white males ..."

The writer, who lived on the West Coast, offered his phone number. At the time he wrote the emails, between June 28th and June 31st of 2013, there had been no mentions in the news about a hitman, how much the hitman was offered for the hit or any related details. The man explained himself and his process to the authorities, anticipating their skepticism: "I guess by now you're wondering who answers my questions... I would say the universal gods because they like to help bring lost people home alive or dead and catch bad guys."

There were more messages from beyond. In 2014, a friend of Kim's went to a psychic in nearby Collingswood, Kym Durham, and handed her April's picture. At the time, no details about the Pagans or a hitman were in the news. Durham described the inside of the house with specific details and then described what happened to April. "They walk in and go up the steps, shoot her twice, one of them is standing there watching...," Durham said after seeing April's image. Someone could conceivably have looked up footage of 2 Woodstock from the real estate listing for interior details. But Kim's friend had made the appointment for herself, and showed Durham April's picture towards the end of her session, so chances of the psychic doing research beforehand were low. The description of someone standing and watching April's murder stuck out to Kim's friend, and gave her chills.

Kim wanted to feel her mother's presence. She craved the comfort of knowing that our family is still with us, even beyond the grave, watching over us and keeping us safe. Some nights when Kim would stay up feeding her toddler, she would notice his little hand reach towards the ceiling like he was trying to grab something in the air that Kim could not see. She wondered if it could be her mom reaching her hand out to touch his. Kim knew her mom, Mimi to her grandsons, would break through the walls of heaven to be near them.

One of the first items Kim received from the auction was a Limoges collectible. April had always planned to pass what she collected down to Kim. The small ivory and white porcelain box had a note inside.

To Kimberly from Mom
whenever you look at this you know you're always loved you're so special best wishes for the rest of your life.

Kim put the delicate box next to her bed, feeling a renewed sense of hope after receiving this message from her mother.

Chapter 11

CHUTZPAH

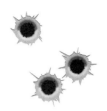

Jim Kauffman avoided the vigil marking the first anniversary of April's murder. He also did nothing to publicly help solve the crime. He did, however, explain to everyone he knew that he *didn't* commit the crime. The only statement he gave to police was the brief one the day of the murder. After that, he was advised by his attorney, Ed Jacobs, not to say anything. But Jacobs would argue that his client was being cooperative. In October of 2012, five months after April's murder, Jacobs wrote a letter on behalf of Kauffman to the Atlantic County Prosecutors Office. Rather than Jim Kauffman sitting down with detectives and speaking with them in person, with his attorney present, investigators had sent written questions they would like Kauffman to answer. The letter from his attorney held his responses.

The letter, addressed to John V. Maher, then Chief Assistant Prosecutor, responded to Maher's request in September for an interview in the Prosecutors' office.

Subject: April Kauffman Homicide Investigation
Major Crimes Case 12044
Our File No. 13,482

Dear Mr. Maher:

A month ago, you asked me if Dr. Kauffman would consent to an interview with your office in the hope that his answers to certain questions would aid you in your investigation into the homicide of his late wife. These questions were as follows:

1. Does he know of any person who would have wanted to harm April?
2. Does he know of any situations that April may have been involved in that could have put her in danger?

3. Does he know of any individuals who would have wanted to harm him?

4. Does he know of any situations that he may have been involved in that could have put his life in danger?

After much discussion, we have decided that as long as you continue to view Dr. Kauffman as a subject or target, it would be imprudent for us to produce him for an interview with your office at this time. Having said that, we have a sincere interest in aiding your investigation in the hope it will lead to the apprehension of the individual(s) responsible for April's death. Below is a summary to the above questions.

The letter went on to offer a story involving an employee who had worked for April at the Cherry Café, and to point the finger at others. The employee had been infatuated with her, and April had fired him over a separate issue. The employee, the letter averred, was believed to have ties to organized crime. Relying on details provided by Jim, the attorney related that April had received uninvited sexual advances from members of the Coast Guard during her visits to the Cape May recruiting base, as well as from veterans connected with the VFW, many of whom suffered from PTSD. A final potential suspect, the letter claimed, was an ex-boy-friend of April's; Jacobs stated that the ex-boyfriend continued to contact April during their marriage.

In response to the question about who might have wanted to harm Jim, the letter suggested two former patients of his with Klinefelter Syndrome, a condition involving an extra X chromosome in males which can result in sexual or personal-ity disorders. Kauffman's attorney wrote that both patients had developed pedo-philic impulses after being treated with testosterone. One of those patients was incarcerated.

The letter ended: "It is important to note that we are not making any accusa-tions against the individuals referenced in the above paragraphs. This letter, which should remain confidential and is not intended to be exhaustive, is simply our best attempt to answer your questions at this time."

There was no mention of Pagans, and no mention of any criminal schemes involving Atlantic Endocrinology Associates, Jim's practice.

Life went on for Jim after May 10, 2012 much as it had before. Besides going into the office every day, he still actively participated in the speaking circuit for pharmaceutical events and conventions. Just a week after April's death, he flew to Chicago to give a speech.

Soon after April's death, Jim started dating again, rekindling a romance from forty years earlier with a woman named Carole Weintraub. Whereas April had been nearly twenty years younger than Jim, Carole and Jim were much closer in age. They had attended Atlantic City High School four years apart, though they didn't meet and begin dating until Carole's senior year of high school, during Jim's hiatus from Franklin and Marshall. Their young romance had ended after about a year and a half.

Weintraub, petite and possessed of big brown eyes and a pretty smile, had founded a successful headhunting business just outside of Philadelphia, growing the business over the thirty-plus years since she had seen Jim. She had also married and divorced and had a daughter.

Even though their breakup had been free of drama, she still had trepidation about reaching out to Jim after a friend broke the news to her about April's death. That trepidation, however, proved brief.

For the past four years, Carole had rented a summer home in Longport, New Jersey. Driving back to her home in the Philadelphia suburb of Bryn Mawr, she often took a route that went by James Kauffman's Egg Harbor Township office, with his name on the sign for his endocrinology practice. Carole remembers wondering aloud once to a friend in the car with her, "Gee, I wonder if that's Jim Kauffman who I dated in high school?"

A friend of Carole's remembered her mentioning her former sweetheart, and called Carole to tell her Jim Kauffman's wife had been murdered after seeing the news of that horrible day on television.

Carole sent a sympathy note with a contribution in April's memory to the couple's synagogue, and then called Jim's office, leaving a message to relay her condolences. Dr. Kauffman saw the message and when he called her back, they spoke for about five minutes. He remembered being curt. Carole thought he was polite and appropriate. Jim called about a week later to apologize for what he thought was his rudeness. They decided to meet for breakfast.

On June 14, 2012, Carole dined with Jim at Steve and Cookie's, a popular Shore mainstay located in Margate by the bay. Reservations are almost impossible to get and require calling or waiting in line on a single designated day a few weeks before Memorial Day, to book reservations for the entire summer into September. The couple enjoyed their dinner on a Thursday night at the busy restaurant, as part of a group dinner hosted by a pharmaceutical company. It was just a month to the day after Jim had buried April.

For Jim and Carole, the courtship even in the early days flourished in spite of the murder investigation even when it looked like Jim was targeted by investigators. On June 22nd, investigators boarded Jim's US Airways flight to Arizona with a search warrant for his phone. They removed him from the flight, and he then boarded another flight to Tucson. When he was able to reach a computer the next day, he blasted an email from his account, hormone69@aol.com, to a group of trusted friends.

Subject: PHONE

HELP! THE POLICE TOOK MY PHONE YESTERDAY SO I HAVE NO
CONTACT LIST. PLEASE E-MAIL ME YOUR CELL NUMBERS AS I
AM GOING TO GET A THROW AWAY PHONE WHILE I AM HERE
SO I CAN CONTACT YOU. ALSO IF YOU CAN THINK OF OTHER
PEOPLE'S NUMBERS I NEED, PLEASE E-MAIL THEM. THE
PHONE I GET MAY HAVE A STRANGE AREA CODE SO PLEASE
ANSWER IT. OTHERWISE, I AM STRANDED. THANK YOU FOR
YOUR FRIENDSHIP.

JMK

Although Jim and Carole had just reconnected a few weeks earlier, Jim
included her among the fifteen or so people he trusted enough to contact at that
moment. The truth was that his circle of trust had been shrinking since April's
murder.

Soon, Carole began working as a consultant for Jim's office, using her skills
as a headhunter. For about nine months, she solicited resumes, searched and interviewed candidates, and helped guide Jim through employment practices and
employment law. There was, in fact, one employee Jim wanted to replace.

In 2012, Kauffman employed about seven people. Barbara Greenling, Jim's
nurse practitioner, had joined the office in 2009. On the day of the murder, like the
rest of the office staff, she had gone over to 2 Woodstock Drive. Barb stayed by
her boss's side and comforted him that day. According to statements given to
police, she noticed that Jim's story of what he had done in the hours following the
murder had changed several times. She also stated Jim told her that if he got
arrested the bail would be set at one million dollars, and that if he were arrested,
he would kill himself; he wouldn't spend time in jail.

Greenling met with detectives days after the murder. She told them about
some strange things she'd observed at the office shortly before April was killed.
She saw a man who looked like a "biker," in his forties or fifties, with tattoos, facial
hair, and a limp. Jim came in to see this man outside of regular office hours. One
of those times, Greenling asked the man his name, and he answered, "Glenn
Seeler." Greenling got the feeling that everything was "not quite kosher in Dodge."
Seeler wasn't on the appointment list; there was no chart for him, and he was
receiving narcotics prescriptions. When Greenling asked her boss about it he
shrugged it off, saying he'd met Seeler at the VFW and was helping him out.

"Don't get us into trouble," she told him. Kauffman was keeping a file in a
manila folder in his office, separate from the other patient files. Seeler would be
one of several people Barb would start to see beginning in 2011 and 2012 who fell
into this new category of patient: "bikers, with no medical files, who come in during off-hours."

Typically, the staff in Kauffman's office made up charts on new patients, and then Jim would see the patients and document them. As a nurse practitioner, Barb was second in responsibility only to the doctor, and she often saw the same patients as Jim.

On the day of April's murder, before the staff got the devastating call, Beverly Augello had called Dr. Kauffman's office to see if they could squeeze her in for a last-minute appointment. When Beverly arrived at the sign shop that morning, Fred had told her to make the appointment. Beverly arrived at the doctor's office around nine a.m., about twenty minutes after she had called. She said it was a routine appointment with Dr. Kauffman. He gave her a prescription for allergies and her usual 120-pill, 30 mg. Oxycodone Hydrochloride prescription, a.k.a. roxies.

But on her way out she did something she had never done before: she picked up an envelope at the front desk. It was a thick white business-size envelope, with the name "Fred" written on it. Beverly left and went to fill her prescriptions at the pharmacy. When she returned to the shop, she handed Fred the envelope and the pills. Fred put the envelope into a drawer he stored money in, and locked it. It wasn't until the next afternoon Beverly claims she heard April had been killed.

The day after the murder, the office staff returned to work, and Barb Greenling gave Jim a ride to the office. Kauffman and his staff did not see any patients that day. At least one employee noticed that the black sneakers which Kauffman wore nearly every day had been replaced by gray Velcro-tab sneakers. That same employee noted to detectives, there were dark stains and chunks of dark material on the floor leading from the entrance of the building into Dr. Kauffman's office. About a month later, Kauffman would begin to wear his black sneakers again, but with fresh, new laces. Over time Kauffman's office began to return to normal, and his office staff appeared to act as his support system.

"Jim was hurting too," a staff member told police. For the most part, they weren't privy to the sordid details of his marriage, including fights and threats of gun violence. The only complaint one employee reported hearing Jim say about April was, "Oh my God, she wants me to cut vegetables this weekend," when April asked for help prepping for a catering order for the Cherry Café. Most of his staff viewed him as a man who had lost his wife to violence, with the killer on the loose.

Kauffman was known to treat his staff really well, even giving some staffers generous bonuses. In 2009 he gave $1,000 at the end of the year, and in 2010 and 2011, it was $2500 quarterly. He gave the bonuses in cash, in an envelope, and didn't document it on the business payroll.

But there was one staff member who kept a close watch on Jim beginning in the summer of 2012. The FBI secured an informant in Kauffman's office, with a mission to investigate more than his wife's murder. That informant's identity was kept secret even years later in search warrants and FBI paperwork.

Kauffman's practice had a lab in the office to draw blood from patients and run routine tests. It was faster and more convenient for both patients and the practice. In 2011 he switched to an outside lab, but asked to have the same two phlebotomists draw the blood. New Jersey law, however, mandated that no money could be exchanged between a physician's office and a lab. This meant that Jim was not allowed by law to rent space to the lab. The outside lab changed its name to Infinity Clinical Laboratories, and the owners of the lab were seen meeting with Kauffman in the office once a month. The meetings, the FBI believed, involved kickbacks Kauffman was receiving after ordering unnecessary blood tests, specifically the Boston Heart test, a wide-ranging cardiovascular assessment. The FBI estimated that the kickbacks amounted to tens of thousands of dollars. The FBI was following one of the lab's owners, Phil Biondello, whom they believed was targeting Medicare patients, many of them disabled or elderly. Lab tests including the Boston Heart test were among the services covered for Medicare Part B beneficiaries.

During this period the FBI worked to build their case against Biondello and his lab scheme. In 2013, one of the phlebotomists who Kauffman had insisted should be kept on by the new lab was fired. Greenling, still working in the office, became more and more suspicious of the bikers who continued to visit. One day she noticed on the copy machine a wage report listing Carole as an employee. Greenling didn't know that one of the reasons Jim had hired Carole was to find a replacement for her. Kauffman had complained to Carole that Greenling spent too much time with patients and that she was "verbose."

Then, in October 2013, Greenling took a strange call from the Cape May County authorities. They had discovered the body of a man whom they thought was a patient of Kauffman's, inside a home in the Villas, New Jersey. The man was dead from a suspected overdose. A bottle with a prescription for 120 30-mg. Oxycodone Hydrochloride tablets had been found next to the decedent on the floor, along with baggies of heroin. The doctor listed on the pill bottle was Dr. James Kauffman. The dead man was Francis Mulholland.

The FBI remained focused on the blood lab kickback scheme, and in the course of a larger investigation, an FBI source in a different doctor's office reported that the doctor was collecting $20,000 a month from Biondello. The source stated that Biondello would go to multiple offices with cash in hand, and the kickbacks were ten percent of what the lab was collecting on referrals. Kauffman had begun working with Biondello starting in November 2011, and the scheme went on for several years.

Patients of Dr. Kauffman's, who thought they were getting routine blood work in the convenience of the doctor's office, started noticing their insurance companies were billing them $1,000 for the test and some would receive a reimbursement check for up to $1,200. When they brought it up to Kauffman's staff, they were told not to worry; they didn't have to pay back the difference.

The Feds caught up to Biondello, and in 2015 he pled guilty to a single count of violating Title 42 US Code Section 1320, a health care violation. Investigators would later find a nasty text exchange between Biondello and Kauffman purportedly printed out by the doctor, just two months prior to Biondello pleading guilty. The text from Biondello to the doctor was testy; it appeared Kauffman may have canceled their arrangement in October of 2015, and that Biondello wasn't happy about it.

Schemes such as this by labs like Infinity appeared to be emerging as a trend. In 2017, the US Attorney's Newark, New Jersey field office found more cases of doctors receiving kickbacks from a blood lab in Parsipanny, New Jersey in a case unrelated to Doctor Kauffman. Biodiagnostic Laboratory Service received more than $100 million in Medicare and insurance payouts from 2010 through 2013. They were giving cash to more than fifty doctors who worked with the lab. It is believed to be the largest number of medical professionals ever prosecuted in a bribery case. In many of the cases, authorities believe the doctors at first didn't realize it was illegal, and then got in over their heads. Others were simply greedy—they risked their already high-income practices for an extra couple of a thousand in cash from the lab per month.

Through all this, Kauffman remained untouched. But investigators were floored when they stumbled upon *another* possible case of pharmaceutical/healthcare fraud operating out of Kauffman's office. Once again, the Feds got involved.

Instead of narcotics or blood tests, this alleged fraud involved unnecessary medications to treat conditions like fungus and erectile dysfunction. The victims in this case were the insurance companies. The scam was a pyramid scheme involving doctors, pharmaceutical companies, and patients with really good medical insurance—the kind that would shell out thousands for a compound cream to be mixed by a pharmacist. In New Jersey, people with state insurance had the best coverage. Municipal workers, firefighters, police, and teachers were all recruited as patients.

The doctors wrote prescriptions for compound drugs including lotions and vitamins or health supplements. The patients did not really need these prescriptions. One of these compounds only cost the pharmacies around ten dollars, a small fraction of the money charged to the insurance company. The insurance company reimbursed the pharmacy anywhere up to $6,000 for that prescription. Boardwalk LLC, which the FBI believed to be a shell company, sat at the top of the pyramid scheme. It took 40% of the $6,000, for example, and Central, the pharmacy, would keep 60%. Maintaining the scam's forward motion required recruiters (most of them pharmaceutical company employees) giving their patient recruits "pre-completed" forms for the compound medications. The doctor would okay the script without giving a reason as to why the patient needed it. Some recipients never even met with the doctor, let alone receiving an exam. The doctors and the recruiters received kickbacks in cash.

The FBI found three doctors at the top of the pyramid; Dr. Kauffman was one of them. Some insurance experts say it looked like the prescription benefit plan provider used by many New Jersey state benefit holders, Express Scripts, did not have a safeguard in place to alert them to what was happening. From January 2015 through June 2016, according to Express Scripts records, Dr. Kauffman prescribed "compound" over 750 times. More than 650 of them were from Central Rexall Drugs, and each charged $5,000 to the insurance company. Sometimes the scripts were for multiple patients in one day.

According to a search warrant, the head of Boardwalk LLC, a former pharmaceutical sales representative named William Hickman, allegedly asked the source in Kauffman's office to become a part of the scam. The source declined.

Dr. Kauffman had the chutzpah to allegedly keep these scams going, on top of the off-the-books income from his prescriptions for his biker "patients."

Jim also had a new partner in life by his side. In December 2012 Jim proposed to Carole at the Four Seasons Hotel in Philadelphia. They took a trip to Puerto Rico, and eight months later they married in a small ceremony at Rodeph Shalom, a historic synagogue on North Broad Street in Philadelphia. In addition to Carole, Jim, and the rabbi, the only guests at the ceremony were Carole's daughter and a friend of Jim's, Tim Mooney.

Tim and his wife had been close friends with Jim and April. Shortly before April's murder, they had vacationed with the Kauffmans in Aruba. On that trip, Tim Mooney had actually saved Jim's life. Jim had nearly drowned after falling off of a water raft, but Mooney, a former Atlantic City lifeguard, had pulled the doctor to safety. Mooney acted as one of April's pallbearers, and had been devastated over her loss. But since he spent most of his time in Florida, he'd missed much of the gossip circling around Linwood about who killed April. When Jim saw his old friend on the beach in Longport, New Jersey shortly before his wedding to Carole, he asked Tim to be his best man. Tim would later say he felt hoodwinked and betrayed by Jim. He ruminated on how April's life would be if he hadn't been with Jim in Aruba to pull him from the water.

After the wedding, Jim and Carole went on a cruise to Europe. When they returned, they decided they wanted to celebrate with a large reception including friends and family. Almost 100 people attended their wedding reception. Most of Jim's office staff were included on the guest list, but Barbara Greenling was not. Some close friends of Jim's thought the quick courtship was odd, happening as it did so soon after April's death. Carole and Jim would eventually settle into a high-end condo in the Symphony House in bustling Center City Philadelphia. The Symphony House on South Broad Street is surrounded by many of the city's flagship arts and entertainment organizations, including the Suzanne Roberts Theatre, the Wilma Theater, the Kimmel Center, and the Academy of Music. Some of the city's wealthiest residents call the building home. Jim could be seen spotted there waving to friends of Carole's as they drove into the underground garage attached to the building in the couple's Mercedes Benz. He was becoming somewhat acclimated to his new life in Center City with Carole by his side, along with their dog Esther, a Brussels Griffon, who Jim affectionately called Shorty.

In Linwood, however, Jim would not let go of 2 Woodstock Drive. Jim spent most of the week down there, seeing patients and keeping up the same schedule at his practice. Carole, however, would never sleep there; she found it too disturbing to be in the house where April was murdered.

Carole shrugged off the stories about Jim having been in the military. When asked if she thought he had ever served, she laughed and replied, "He doesn't seem like that sort of person... that would volunteer to be a Green Beret or even in the military... somebody who doesn't mind getting shot at...." Carole also wasn't fazed by the fact that he frequently used the alias Morgan Shane, when he was online, and sometimes to check into hotels. She claimed he had used that pseudonym back in the 1970s when they were first dating.

As Carole and Jim went through their life as husband and wife, however, those closest to April wondered what Jim might have told her about May 10, 2012.

A few years later, attorneys Patrick and Andy D'Arcy found out what Carole was thinking in a civil deposition as part of a civil case regarding April's life insurance policy.

During the deposition, Patrick D'Arcy asked Carole "Have you ever asked Jim what he thinks happened?" Their exchange went like this:

CK: I asked him if he had any idea who did it.
PD: And what did he tell you?
CK: It could have been any number of instances. It could have been her association with some unsavory people.
PD: And, who's that? The Pagans?
CK: The Pagans.
PD: Is that what Jim told you?
CK: Or vets that were disturbed or police.
PD: He said this is something we think about every day; is that accurate?
CK: Maybe he does, I don't.
PD: Do you think about it often?
CK: No.
PD: Okay, did you ever think maybe Jim did it?
CK: Never.
PD: That never occurred to you?
CK: No.

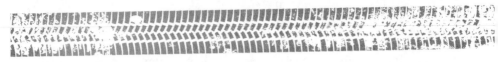

Chapter 12

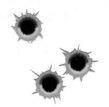

THE D'ARCY BROTHERS

Jim Kauffman's impatience got the best of him in June 2013. He was tired of waiting for the payout from two life insurance policies in April's name, which would total $600,000. As the primary beneficiary, he was entitled to all of the money while he was still alive. So he brought a suit against Transamerica Life Insurance Company to claim it. But Transamerica refused to release the money, after Atlantic County Prosecutor Jim McClain would not provide the life insurance company with a police report to review the case, citing an ongoing investigation. McClain also would not issue a letter to the insurance company that would clear Jim of the crime, even though he was not named as a suspect. The report would have essentially cleared the doctor of April's murder. Transamerica stated in a counterclaim filed in September of 2013 they were "unable to determine whether plaintiff {James Kauffman} may have been responsible for the intentional killing of April Kauffman."

Later, Kim might have viewed this as divine intervention. Transamerica sent her a letter informing her she was the third party beneficiary of her mother's life insurance policies. If she didn't go to court and make a claim, and if he were cleared, or if Jim won the lawsuit he had filed, both policies could go to him. Kim couldn't stomach the idea of Jim gaining anything from her mother's murder. She contacted a high-profile Philadelphia law firm, known for their aggressive approach to cases and flair for media attention. After weeks of no action by the law firm, and unreturned phone calls to Kim, her frustration grew: time was running out for her to respond to Jim's lawsuit. Kim decided to drop the big-city firm, and instead called a local personal injury firm in Egg Harbor Township. Years before, her husband had used them after being hurt on the job. The law firm of D'Arcy, Johnson, Day took her case.

* * *

When Kim pitched her case to her lawyers, brothers Patrick and Andy D'Arcy, they realized the case was more complicated than it seemed. However, both brothers were game to represent Kim, and to Kim they felt like angels sent from heaven. Pat, the older brother by eight years, stocky with light hair and piercing blue eyes, stands a little taller than his brother Andy. Andy looks younger, with thick chestnut hair framing a babyface and dark brown eyes. Their firm focused mainly on cases like medical malpractice, nursing home abuse, and automobile accidents. Together, they had litigated a couple of thousand cases and won impressive settlements.

Kim's situation was different. The D'Arcys were not criminal defense attorneys or former prosecutors. Kim spoke candidly: her stepfather had murdered her mother, and that was why he shouldn't get the settlement. The D'Arcys were prepared to drop that bombshell even without criminal charges against Jim.

They filed a counterclaim to the life insurance lawsuit on Kim's behalf as well as a wrongful death complaint. They argued that Jim Kauffman should not receive the monies because of the slayer rule, part of common law which holds that a murderer cannot retain a property interest in his/her victim's estate.

Jim had not yet been charged by law enforcement. But for the first time, through this lawsuit, Kim could make official and public what she believed. In court documents, the Federal legal filing charged that Jim was responsible for the intentional killing of her mother.

On the day they filed the suit, Kim and her husband crowded into the small lobby of the law firm for a press conference. So many members of the media showed up that they began filling the steps leading upstairs to an adjoining office. Wearing a gray suit with an American flag pin in honor of the work her mother had done for veterans and her patriotism, Kim once again had to take the microphone, but this time it was with confidence that justice might be served.

"I've purposefully tried to avoid talking about what happened," she said, "but now after being brought into this lawsuit, I have no choice [but] to respond and fight for what I know is right. I can no longer sit back and allow what I perceive is an injustice to occur. I know that my mom would not want me to sit back any longer." A poster of April sat nearby on an easel, with a phone number urging anyone with tips to call. In two years, no one had ever done that; the Prosecutor's Office had never urged the public to come forward with information.

Ed Jacobs, Kauffman's attorney, was outraged at the suit. "This is nonsense," he responded in a statement. "Dr. Kauffman has lost his wife in the unsolved homicide. He's cooperated fully with the Atlantic County Prosecutor Office's investigation. Ms. Pack has been interviewed multiple times, multiple times over the course of the investigation and my client has never been charged."

The D'Arcys went to work immediately. Their team had to start from scratch: they received no help from the Prosecutor's Office or their investigators, and were excluded from looking at any files investigators had on the case. The D'Arcys rolled up their sleeves along with the private investigators with their firm, a group that included retired FBI agents and police. They re-interviewed everyone, then found people who had never been contacted—potential witnesses, friends, family, and associates of the Kauffmans—and interviewed them. Along the way, they confirmed the truth that had long been suspected by others about Jim's military service. After filing requests with The National Archives, which holds military records, they found Jim had never served. Then, they delved into Jim's past, going as far back as his college years. Even though this was a civil case, the D'Arcys had subpoena power, and anything they learned about they could ask for, including phone records. It was tedious work.

In April 2014, the brothers subpoenaed the Atlantic County Prosecutor's Office asking for "a complete and accurate copy of the investigatory file" relating to the circumstances surrounding Kauffman's death. Specifically, they were seeking documents that held information including the identities of confidential informants. Prosecutor Jim McClain waited until June to respond. His filing stated, "Disclosure of the identities of the confidential informants, either directly or indirectly, would immediately jeopardize the safety and well-being of those informants." A judge decided the information couldn't be released, but that did not hinder the progress of the D'Arcy's.

One of their significant finds was the "Harry Johnson" phone account. Patrick D'Arcy pored over hundreds of hours of Jim Kauffman's phone records and noticed the familiar phone number. Patrick couldn't believe it. He shared his findings with the Prosecutors Office, telling them, "If you find out whose phone number this is, you will find out the killer." D'Arcy remembers investigators taking notes and writing down the phone number. Although they wouldn't say, their reaction made it seem to him as if they'd never known about that phone number before.

The "Harry Johnson" phone, the "burner" or throwaway phone Beverly Augello later said she had set up for her ex-husband Fred Augello to use, is the same phone that exchanged over three hundred phone calls with Jim Kauffman starting in August 2011, and with the last call made the day before April's murder. The D'Arcys discovered that on the day the "Harry Johnson" phone was activated in August 2011, Jim Kauffman's phone called the number for the first time. That appeared to be a sure sign he already knew the person with the phone, and that they had some preexisting relationship.

The D'Arcys then cross-referenced the contacts in April's phone, and found the Harry Johnson phone number was saved in her contacts as "Motor P." But she never called the number, and "Motor P" never called her; this was something else investigators appeared to have overlooked. After the lawyer's findings over the following year, investigators sought a warrant to re-examine Jim Kauffman's cell phone. According to the details of that search warrant, written by a detective in 2015, "The forensic files obtained from James Kauffman's cellular handset in June 2012 were reviewed to determine if the telephone number... (The Harry Johnson

Phone) was saved in Kauffman's contact list. It was not found within the saved contacts." It seemed to the D'Arcy's even more likely that investigators either hadn't found the Harry Johnson phone or hadn't realized what an important find it was.

The climax of the D'Arcys' case, however, came when they were able to question Jim Kauffman. It was the first and only time he would be questioned under oath. The brothers also deposed Carole Weintraub Kauffman. For Jim, the deposition might seem just an annoyance. But since it would go into the hands of investigators, his story could be checked against his brief statement to police the day of April's murder. If he should ever be charged criminally, this could cause problems for him.

On July 11, 2014, at 10:03 a.m., the deposition of James Kauffman began at Jacobs and Barbone's law firm in Atlantic City, in a modest one-story building on busy Pacific Avenue in Atlantic City, across the street from several casinos. It was two years, two months and a day from the date of April's murder. Edwin "Ed" Jacobs' long-time partner, the seasoned criminal defense attorney Louis Barbone, sat with Kauffman. The deposition lasted nearly five hours. Right out of the gates Patrick D'Arcy fired questions at Jim.

PD: Okay. Doctor, April Kauffman was shot to death in your home; is that fair to say?

JK: Yes.

PD: Do you know what type of gun was used?

JK: No.

PD: Do you know what size gun?

JK: No.

PD: Do you own guns?

JK: Yes.

PD: How many guns do you own?

JK: Approximately 18.

PD: Okay. Have you ever threatened to shoot your wife?

JK: Absolutely not.

PD: Okay. When you left the house that morning, April was asleep. Correct?

PD: Yes, sir.

JK: Have you ever served in any branch of the military?

JK: No.

The D'Arcys already had interviews from multiple sources who said Jim kept bringing up that police told him April had been killed by a .22. They also had the June 2006 police report from Egg Harbor Township Police when Jim allegedly threatened to shoot April, a family friend, and his relative, with whom April had been caught fooling around. Later in the deposition, Jim would deny it:

PD: Are you saying you don't recall if you said that?
JK: I categorically deny ever saying I would kill my wife.

The D'Arcys also had Jim's Philadelphia College of Osteopathic Medicine (PCOM) admissions information, which included his letter about receiving psychiatric care—something that contradicted Jim's answer to one of the first questions Patrick asked.

PD: Have you ever received psychiatric treatment?
JK: No.

D'Arcy unveiled more inconsistencies. Jim said he slept in the master bedroom with April, not the guest room, as he had told police the day of the murder. Instead of the dinner of steaks and wine he had described to police on the night before her death, he stated he had worked on office paperwork before having sex with his wife and going to bed at 11 pm.

Jim had originally told police and several others that when he entered the room after receiving the call from Billy that April was unresponsive, he didn't touch April because he saw she had "lividity." That day Jim had made the macabre comment to Kim and the police, "You've seen one dead body...." But in this deposition to Patrick D'Arcy, Jim claimed he *did* touch his wife as she lay on the floor.

JK: I was feeling for the skin and I felt for a pulse.
PD: What did you feel?
JK: That the skin was cold and I did not find a pulse.
PD: How long were you in that room?
JK: Less than 30 seconds.

The doctor told D'Arcy he didn't try resuscitation attempts because he could tell by April's "pallor" that she was clinically dead.

PD: Do you recall telling anyone that you never touched her?
JK: I don't recall any of that.
PD: Okay. Well, that would be so wrong so—if you wouldn't have said that. Correct?
JK: I don't understand your question.
PD: Sure. You would not have told someone you never touched her, because, as we've just discussed, you did touch her.
JK: I still don't understand your question though.
PD: Okay. You touched her. We've discussed it. Correct?
JK: Correct.

April Kauffman. Photo courtesy of Kim Pack.

April Kauffman and Dr. Jim Kauffman. Photo courtesy of Kim Pack.

April Kauffman and her daughter Kim Pack. Photo courtesy of Kim Pack.

Kim's college graduation. Photo courtesy of Kim Pack.

April and Jim Kauffman's home in Linwood, New Jersey. Photo courtesy of Larry Farnese.

Atlantic County Prosecutor Damon G. Tyner.
Photo courtesy of Atlantic County Prosecutor's Office.

Patrick and Andy D'Arcy, Kim Pack's civil attorneys. Photo courtesy of D'Arcy Johnson Day.

Left to Right: Booking photos of Ferdinand "Freddy" Augello aka Miserable;
Glenn Seeler aka Slasher, Andrew Glick aka Chef,
John "Egyptian" Kachbalian, Beverly Augello, and Joseph Mulholland.

Photos courtesy of Atlantic County Correction Facility.

Andrew Glick takes the stand during Fred Augello's trial. Glick cooperated with authorities and agreed to testify against Augello. His testimony lasted several days and he was considered the "star" witness. Photo courtesy breakingnewsac.com

Fred Augello sits in Atlantic County Court during his trial. Photo courtesy breakingnewsac.com

Kim Pack and Atlantic County Prosecutor Damon Tyner embrace after the jury announced a guilty verdict in Fred Augello's trial.

Photo courtesy of Annie McCormick.

Kim replaced her mother's headstone in October of 2018 shortly after Augello's trial. Kim removed 'Beloved wife' and the last name Kauffman from the original headstone, which was bought by Jim. Photo Courtesy of Kim Pack

PD: Therefore, you would never tell anyone that you didn't touch her?

JK: I still don't understand the question. But if the question is,
        "Did I tell anybody that I didn't touch her?" The answer is "no."
        I did not say that.

During the deposition, Jim readily admitted to Pat D'Arcy that he was not a member of the military, and he confessed to lying about it for years, and misleading others by wearing a green beret and buying marksmanship medals. D'Arcy brought the caricature depicting Jim with a gun and a United States Marine Corps tattoo, that had hung on the wall in 2 Woodstock, and entered it as evidence. Jim admitted he lied to his friends and to April, but maintained that he came clean with Carole when they started dating in 2012. If Jim had lied for financial gain that would be against the law, under the Federal "Stolen Valor" Act. Ed Jacobs stopped that line of questioning. Jim's explanation of his motive for lying about serving came down to his wanting to "help" veterans; that if they thought he was one of them, that would somehow be an advantage. His admissions as to how far he had carried his lies over decades during the proceeding that day were stunning.

PD: Did you ever tell Kim Pack you were in the military?

JK: Yes.

PD: Okay. Did you ever... Did she ever do a project for college and part
        of the project was you being in the military?

JK: Yes.

PD: And you carried bodies?

JK: Yes.

PD: And the torture you had gone through --

JK: Yes.

PD: Especially—hold on, especially on 9/11 and what that made you feel?

JK: Yes.

Jim also said he didn't realize April had been shot when he was at the scene, contrary to what he had said to friends and to police that day.

PD: So none of the police officers at the scene told you she was shot?

JK: That's correct.

D'Arcy questioned Jim about his guns and ammunition. Jim said he had owned eighteen guns in 2012, half of them in Arizona and half in Linwood.

PD: Do you own or have hollow-point ammo?

JK: In Arizona?

PD: Okay. Not here, though, locally?

JK: Umm-hmm.

PD: Why is that?

JK: Because I didn't want any more firearms in New Jersey, because of the laws.

PD: Okay. Do you own any silencers?

JK: Absolutely not.

PD: As of May 10, 2012, did you have hollow point ammunition in New Jersey?

JK: Yes.

PD: Did you have a revolver in New Jersey?

JK: Yes.

D'Arcy also tried to get answers about the blood lab run out of Jim Kauffman's Endocrinology office that currently was under federal investigation.

PD: Did you have any financial incentive for people to the lab company?

JK: Absolutely not.

PD: And you've never received any cash from anyone associated with the lab?

JK: Absolutely not.

Then D'Arcy brought up the blow-out fight on Christmas Eve of 2011, the one that caused April to stay with her friend Lee Darby for nearly a week:

PD: Did you ever threaten to take April, Kim and Kim's children out if she pursued a divorce?

JK: Absolutely not.

PD: She never threatened to expose you about not being in the military. Correct?

JK: No.

PD: Did you ever threaten to go nuclear on April, her daughter and her grandchildren?

JK: Well, I've never used the term nuclear so the answer is no.

D'Arcy started grilling Kauffman about the temperature of the room to determine how cold April's body must have felt, then he caught Jim tripping over his words.

JK: Me or my ex—my divorce, my divorce... my murdered wife.

PD: Yes, your murdered wife.

D'Arcy took this up a little later:

PD: Did April ever tell you she wanted a divorce?
JK: No.
PD: Did you ever tell her you wanted a divorce?
JK: No.

And further on:

PD: Would you describe your marriage as a happy marriage prior to
      her murder?
JK: As happy as every other marriage.
PD: That I don't know. I don't know how every other marriage is.
      I'm asking you, you—
JK: Everybody has ups and downs.
PD: Okay...

D'Arcy returned to the theme again later:

PD: Would you consider the marriage you had with April as a happy
      marriage?
JK: Yes. And we had planned to do things, that's why she was redoing
      the kitchen, and her long-term goal was to sell the big house, get a
      condominium here, till I stop working here.

Pat D'Arcy asked who Jim thought had committed the crime. Jim shared a lot
more ideas than he had listed in that October 2012 letter to the Prosecutor's Office.

PD: Who do you think did it?
JK: I thought it could be somebody in the police departments.
PD: Is that Linwood?
JK: Linwood or other. I thought it could be someone who was one of
      the veterans who had PTSD and something happened obviously.
      I thought that some of the people April, on her radio show, went after,
      correctly went after but went after, obviously could have done this.
PD: Like who?
JK: There were people who were either anti-veteran or, there was one
      gentleman, I don't remember his name, who owned some building
      in Somers Point who was almost like a slumlord to the veterans.
      She was very, very good at this. And, but she raised some hackles
      I'm sure. And I also, the last choice was that it was someone in a
      motorcycle gang.

PD: What motorcycle gang?

JK: The Pagans.

PD: Why would you think that?

JK: She had some bizarre relationship with somebody in the Pagans who
        I've met a couple of times. And it just didn't seem appropriate.

PD: Do you know his name?

JK: No, I do not.

PD: Have you met him?

JK: I met him twice.

PD: When?

JK: It has to be a year or so before her passing. We were in Smithville.
        She said there was a meeting with the Pagans and there was some
        music or something, so I went along with her. And there was a whole
        group of Pagans sitting there which is not my normal circle of
        motorcycle riders.

D'Arcy picked this up later:

PD: The Pagans is a motorcycle gang?

JK: According to what I see on TV and in the paper, they are more than
        just a motorcycle gang.

PD: Right. Do you have any contact with them?

JK: None whatsoever.

PD: You don't have any patients that are Pagans or anything like that?

JK: If I do I don't, I don't know who they are.

Jim went into detail about April's run-ins with a Linwood police officer, then
about veterans with PTSD who could have turned on her in the course of her
charity work. He brought up others, including exes of hers. But he circled back to
the Pagans, bringing up that April had told him about a Pagan who came into the
Cherry Café.

JK: She mentioned on only one occasion that one showed up at her
        restaurant, unannounced, and whether it was flirting or doing
        something like that, asking her out or something and of course she
        turned him down and he wasn't very happy.

In the deposition Jim did not put a name to that Pagan; the names he would share
with authorities would come later.

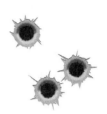

Chapter 13

NEVER TRUST A PAGAN

"Never trust a Pagan."

Andrew Glick said this all the time. But for going on six years, Dr. James Kauffman appeared to trust the Pagans wholeheartedly, to the extent of abetting the expansion of their illegal prescription drug ring. Kauffman, known as "Doc" to his new friends, was ballsy enough to raise the price on the group of bikers, their friends and family coming in monthly for narcotics: between 2011 and 2016, he jacked the cost of a 120-pill Oxycodone prescription from $100 to $500. There was an ease now to the process, a deceptively regular routine. Kauffman now gave out his own nicknames. He didn't call Freddy Augello by his club nickname, "Miserable"; Kauffman called him "Hollywood."

At the beginning, Kauffman only wanted seven people in the ring, nine tops. He also kicked some people out of the arrangement at his own discretion. One of those people was Joseph Mulholland, who had returned from rehab and was reportedly on methadone. Mulholland did not share this information with the doctor when he came in for his narcotics prescription. However, methadone prescriptions are monitored, and as a result, Kauffman's office received a call. The doctor could see serious reprimands from the state board on the horizon—his medical license could be in jeopardy. Kauffman sorted out the situation by explaining that his patient had not informed him about the methadone. He then kicked Mulholland out.

The doctor was having other issues with the Pagans. Francis Mulholland, the alleged hitman, who was not even a patient, reportedly came barging into the office months after April's murder. "This fucking nut came into my office," the doctor complained to Glick, and it sounded to Glick as if "the nut" had leverage. Months after his unexpected visit to Kauffman's office, in October 2013, Francis Mulholland would be discovered dead in his Villas home.

By late 2016, Kauffman had started to lose his cool. The doctor did lose it with Beverly Augello during an appointment in March 2017. He yelled at her, enough to worry Fred when Beverly told him about the encounter after the appointment. Fred called on Andrew Glick to handle the situation, telling him Beverly couldn't deal with another encounter like this one. Andrew didn't have an appointment with Kauffman for at least ten days, but he called in for a visit.

"What's going on, what's the problem?" Glick asked Kauffman. The doctor revealed the issue: his lawyer had heard through a contact, someone who worked in the county jail, that a Pagan in county lockup was talking about the murder, and who did it. Kauffman told Glick, "You better take care of it." But he gave Glick no further information to go on.

"You got a name? Is he in Atlantic County? Any county? Can you give me something? I need a little more than just a Pagan," Glick demanded. Kauffman said he would ask his lawyer. Meanwhile, Glick started digging. He checked to see if any Pagans were in jail, but everyone was accounted for. The doctor's tantrum threatened what had become a smooth pipeline of pills and rattled the symbiotic relationship between the doctor and recruits. Fred was so fed up, he demanded a meeting with "the Doc." Glick had just picked up his new prescription, so he had to make up a reason to go to see the doctor to give him Fred's message; this time he decided an infected toe would be a good excuse.

"We're not taking no for an answer," Glick told Kauffman in the exam room. "You need to meet with [Fred]. I'll call you by the end of the week." But Kauffman "sweated them out," as Glick put it, and didn't call either Glick or Fred for eight days.

At this point, the operation was still working as it had back in 2011. They would recruit people to be patients. A patient would see Kauffman for a prescription; then, either Fred would get half the pills, or the patient would sell him the whole bottle for cash. Andrew was now trying to recruit more people, but when they heard who the doctor was, with the cloud of an unsolved murder over his head, many wanted no part of it. Andrew had two steady patients; Fred had six. On average, they were splitting $1,700 to $1,900 a bottle three ways.

The agreement with Kauffman wasn't anything complex. Even though the arrangement involved the Pagans, it wasn't a club-run operation. Fred had no current connection to the club, and Glick never told the mother club about the operation. There was no Sopranos-like hierarchy of boss, lieutenants, soldiers, and earners. It was more like Amway, but they were recruiting addicts or drug dealers instead of sales people. They looked for someone they knew and could either trust or intimidate to make sure they followed the plan.

Andrew brought in two other Pagans for a few months here and there. Fred had his ex-girlfriend's daughter, Tabitha Chapman; his ex-wife and business partner, Beverly Augello; an old bandmate; and Pagan Glenn Seeler and his wife Cheryl. Joseph Mulholland had three or four people. The number of recruits working for each person had varied over time, and sometimes Kauffman would cut someone off.

The idea of running a pill mill through a local doctor was not a new thing to the Pagans. Back in 2011, the DEA and FBI had intercepted the note from Glick to a Florida Pagan proposing an arrangement with a Florida doctor, setting up a pill pipeline by using several Pagans as patients. In Levittown, PA, Dr. William O'Brien III ran a similar system out of his office starting in March 2012—around the same time as Kauffman's operation was starting up. Federal prosecutors say O'Brien also worked with the Pagans, recruiting "pseudo-patients" to buy fraudulent prescriptions. They were charged $250 cash for the first appointment, and $200 cash for every subsequent visit. He sold 30 mg. Oxycodone, and the Pagans resold the pills on the street. Investigators claim 700,000 pills containing Oxycodone and other Schedule II controlled substances were distributed by those involved in the conspiracy. The doctor was sentenced to thirty years in federal prison. At least two Pagans were sentenced to nine years and twenty years for their role in the case.

In late 2016 and early 2017, the national chapter of the Pagans was on the cusp of a transition into new management. Many of the old-school guys who had retired, had "patched over" into other clubs—they swapped one motorcycle gang patch for another, even joining rivals like the Hells Angels. But now they were making their way back in.

The release of Keith "Conan the Barbarian" Richter from prison in 2017 promised to shake up the organization. Law enforcement sources say Richter formulated a plan while he was in prison, aimed at taking over the Pagans upon his release. Richter had been sentenced to sixteen years in federal prison on conspiracy to commit murder and racketeering charges. In the late 1990s, Federal authorities said Richter had ordered the hit on the manager of a topless dance club in Long Island after he refused to pay the Pagans for protection. The gang had been extorting thousands annually from multiple topless dance clubs, according to prosecutors.

Once "Conan" got out, the then-national Pagan president got a severe beating, sources say. Immediately, law enforcement began to track Conan's push to regain control of North Jersey territory from the Hells Angels, with similar activity involving chapters all the way up to Rhode Island. The FBI would eventually send out a memo throughout New Jersey warning of violence in response to Richter's mandate.

When Fred went off the grid on May 10, 2012, the day of April's murder, Seeler and Glick worried that the Mother Club would get word immediately. After a few days of silence from Fred, Seeler finally caught up to him. Fred told him to remain calm, act as though nothing had happened, and just go on with his life. "Nothing is going to come back to us; it's golden," Glenn later related what Fred confidently told him to Andrew. Andrew knew that he could have and should have confessed to the Mother Club about the pills and what knowledge they had about the murder, but he clammed up. He knew this was bad—as he put it, "It was like shitting myself bad."

At that point though, Andrew didn't really know all the details about April's murder, and he didn't want to know. Andrew wasn't with Fred in a sidekick role, as Joe Mullholland was. Glick was more buddy-buddy with Seeler. Glick thought Glenn Seeler and Joseph Mulholland were working as liaisons between the doctor and Fred. Fred himself never set foot in the office, and never had a prescription in his name. "Freddy's Crime World," as his associates referred to it, had other jobs going on, but they all agreed it was Fred who gave the orders. Glick reminisced about the old times when they'd have fun together, when Fred was always looking for work. They would operate as muscle, or protection, for a variety of people, and get cash or gift cards for stores like Harley Davidson.

During 2011-2012, associates describe Fred as being obsessed with finding a shooter for the doctor to kill April. Joseph Drinhouser had acted as Fred's sergeant at arms at one time, and together with Seeler, worked for Fred collecting debts, or roughing up people for one reason or another. Drinhouser says Fred took him for a drive one day sometime in that period, and pulled up to a house with orange garage doors, just like the ones at the Kauffman home at 2 Woodstock Drive.

"That's the house where the doctor wants his wife killed," Drinhouser says Fred told him. Drinhouser recounted that Fred said he'd give him ten grand for the job. Drinhouser turned down the job. Joseph Mulholland says Fred also drove him by the house and offered him the same amount to do the job. Mulholland claims he said no. Mulholland also claimed the doctor grew so impatient that, unbeknownst to Fred, he asked Joseph to take care of the job, offering him $100,000. Mulholland reported the doctor telling him that he looked like a guy who could get it done.

During Fred's search for a gunman over this time, Glenn Seeler's wife Cheryl Pizza started to hear more. She was an addict, and happy to have a steady supply of pills coming her way. She didn't really pay much attention when she began hearing about Fred floating a sinister assignment like murder for hire. She said to her husband, "I'm not scared of Fred; he's like a billy goat." Seeler looked at his wife and replied, "Don't underestimate him. He's a cold-blooded killer." Pizza thought half the stuff her husband said was a lie anyway, so she didn't make much of it, slipping easily back into her daily pill and drug-induced haze.

In 2013, however, things started to change. "Irish" now had a 200-pill-a-month habit, and went into rehab. Seeler was arrested in 2013 on an unrelated drug charge, but continued to get prescriptions from the doctor until 2015, when he moved with Cheryl to North Carolina. Their marital troubles would later blow up, so to speak, when she shot him through a door. Their accounts differed about what the fight was over, but after the shooting, dual restraining orders against each other would keep the lovebirds apart. Fred and Andrew became closer, and with Joseph "Irish" Mulholland in rehab, Andrew became the conduit between the Doctor and Augello.

Still, the mother club had said nothing—they hadn't approached Glick even as rumors of Pagan involvement in April's murder and the pill mill began hitting local Facebook group pages. As a chef, Glick was used to having a demanding job with pushy clients and bosses. He had learned how to stay calm under pressure from the round-the-clock demands of working in the kitchens of Atlantic City casinos. In the nineties, Atlantic City was still drawing celebrities and high-rolling guests. As the chef for Caesars in charge of room service, Glick created meals for the higher-end clientele, and knew how to handle difficult, entitled people.

With or without Dr. Kauffman, Andrew Glick was an established drug dealer. Andrew's drug-related side business had slowed down after the 2011 FBI-DEA investigation into the pill-running operation between Florida and New Jersey, but then started to pick up again. His main supplier of meth and coke was a fellow Pagan named Jazz who rode with the Cumberland County, NJ chapter. Andrew only knew him by his nickname—a common situation among members, which could protect identities when trouble developed with the law. Andrew described Jazz as Puerto Rican, bilingual, and connected to the Sinaloa cartel through his ties in Vineland, NJ. Sinaloa is the organization led by notorious drug lord El Chapo. It is an internationally powerful, vast and ruthless syndicate. Vineland, in the midst of South Jersey farmland, has drawn a large Hispanic population through migrant work, and law enforcement reports connections to the Mexican cartels.

Once a week, Glick would get a half-ounce and an ounce of meth, and a half ounce of coke from Jazz. The arrangement between Andrew and Jazz ended somewhere around 2014 when Jazz got nabbed on drug charges, but Andrew wasn't ready to dial back on the dealing. He started networking, and during an East Coast event with the club, he met another Pagan, "Valdez," who told Glick he had a good supply and could give him a better deal. As a fellow Pagan, Glick trusted him. During the annual Roar to the Shore in September of 2015, Glick made his first buy off Valdez. He bought 4 ounces of meth for $4,000; Glick sold an ounce for $1,500.

Glick found another source for cocaine through a customer, and bought 4 ounces of coke for $3,500. The more he bought, the bigger the discount he got. Glick changed chapters after he lost his diamond with the Cape May County chapter. He remained a rank-and-file member for about eight months before he was voted in as vice president of the Atlantic County chapter.

At first, Glick just dealt to other Pagans; then he branched out to their friends. Since it wasn't his main source of income, and carried the high potential downside of prison time, Glick promised himself he would stop dealing after he reached a specific financial goal.

After the deal with Valdez, Glick was able to expand his side business by offering better prices. He now sold to about six people who came in about once every week to ten days. Glick quickly rose to the position of a supplier, meaning he sold to other dealers. Some of his friends, like Joe Drinhouser, still bought from him for personal use.

Just as the drugs flowed from one Pagan to another and then outward to civilians, so did the gossip, especially club gossip. A year after April's murder, while Andrew was still president of the Cape May County chapter, the higher-ups in the Pagan organization heard rumors that some Pagans were involved in the murder-for-hire of a doctor's wife. James "Jersey Jim" Coles, then the president of the mother club, called Glick and told him to get his officers together—Coles was coming down to "talk" with him.

"Is something wrong?" Andrew hesitantly asked. "Nah, I'll tell you when I get down there," Glick remembers him replying. Coles arrived accompanied by a group of associates whom Glick described as his "gooney squad." Coles was pissed. Even though Andrew was tight with Jersey Jim, he said Coles did a "maniac in the basement routine," trying to threaten Glick into explaining the story that Pagans were responsible for a murder-for-hire plot. Coles had heard rumors and gossip, not just within the biker world, but also on the Internet.

Just as any CEO would be upset with staff who had done something completely unsanctioned, the Mother Club was worried: they might be implicated in something that was really the work of lone wolves. Andrew responded with one of the biggest lies of his life, denying any involvement in the job. Andrew admitted later that if Coles had taken things further and started kicking the shit out of him, he would've spilled. He would have dialed Fred's number himself. But Coles stopped short of hurting him, and left having no idea what had really gone down.

The gossip did not end there. One of Glick's major buyers, another Pagan who sold meth, started running his mouth to a buyer. What he allegedly said made its way to police years later, in 2017. Another informer would come to police in 2018, reporting something they'd heard about a Pagan associate claiming to have a role in the job, who said he'd been hired by Fred to kill April, and then to kill the hitman.

By the spring of 2017, Glick and Augello were getting fed up with Kauffman. Glick had resented Kauffman acting like he was in charge from the beginning. He had shared his issues with Fred early on when the doctor began to express impatience about not finding someone to kill his wife.

"I was like, first of all [Kauffman] asked you to do this," Glick said of his conversations with Fred. "We're going to tell him what he can do. We'll kill his wife when we want to, and we're going to string him along, and we're going to get ten more dudes going [with the pill operation], and if he does anything, we're going to tell [him] flat out, 'Yeah, go see your fucking wife....'" Glick complained to Glen Seeler that Fred was pushing to have April killed. Besides the moral implications of killing someone, Glick saw no financial advantage in the job—they were already making good money. Fred responded, telling him the Doctor was going to sell a Corvette to pay Fred to find someone to do the hit.

"...He's trying to sell his car or something and he's going to give me the cash from that. I'm like, is it a fucking Rolls Royce? Because the money I'm talking is... I'm doing the math in my head and I'm like, we got him. I'll even do this; I'll go to him and say we ain't killing your wife. I'll tell [him] a little piece of information for the future: never trust a Pagan. Never. You're fucked. You will go along with our agenda. We have you. We own you..." Glick tried his best to convince Fred not to jeopardize the good thing they had going with the doctor, telling him, "Fred, this is the golden goose.'" Once the job had been done, though, it was too late.

Now, the doctor was again trying to call the shots. After Kauffman revealed his concerns about the loose-lipped Pagan in the county jail, Glick told the doctor that Augello wanted to meet with him. After nearly two weeks, Kauffman responded: "Tell Hollywood, tomorrow. Shoprite at noon." According to Glick, Augello and Kauffman met in the parking lot of the Somers Point ShopRite and smoothed things over. There were reassurances that no one in county was ratting.

Then the doctor made a new request of Fred. He wanted a nine caliber gun, untraceable. In payment, he would knock off two scripts for it. He wanted something that couldn't be traced, because the guns he already owned were all legal. He didn't say what he needed the gun for. When Glick heard about the request, he figured it could have been intended to harm Kim, Kauffman's stepdaughter, or one of April's best friends, whom Fred described as "a persistent bitch." Every spring as the anniversary of April's murder would approach, Glick remembers Fred saying, "They're never going to let this go...." Andrew would answer, "There's no statute of limitations on murder."

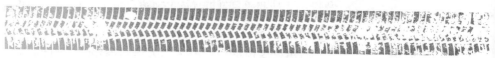

Chapter 14

NEW SHERIFF IN TOWN

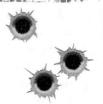

Superior Court Judge Bernard DeLury stood in front of a happy family of five in the midst of a proud moment, in an Atlantic County courtroom on March 15, 2017. The Tyners had gathered together at the front of a packed courtroom. Folks watching from the audience, including many family and friends, could see Damon Tyner's three children, between Tyner and his wife Nicole—his high school sweetheart—who was tasked with holding the Bible. The kids' eyes went back and forth between the Bible and their dad. Everyone was smiling, their faces shining with pride.

As DeLury asked Damon G. Tyner to raise his right hand and repeat the oath of office, history was being made: Tyner became the first African American to be sworn in to the position of Atlantic County Prosecutor, the top law enforcement officer in the county. Heavyset and bald, the caramel-skinned Tyner always looked sharp with a perfectly trimmed goatee, designer suits, square-rimmed glasses, and a quiet confidence. Since 2014, the 46-year-old had been serving as a judge on the Superior Court of New Jersey. Prior to that, he had served as an administrative law judge. Tyner had been interested in the Atlantic County Prosecutor position when he was in his mid-thirties; he had also run, unsuccessfully, as a Democrat for the New Jersey State Assembly in 2005 and 2011.

Tyner followed in the honorable footsteps of his father, Henry Edward "Hank" Tyner, who had served Atlantic County first in the Atlantic City Fire Department, and then over a thirty-year career as a police officer. He had taken a break from the police force to serve as the first president of City Council under Atlantic City's newly established Mayor-Council form of government.

Not many choose to leave a judgeship to run for the prosecutor's office, but Tyner did. The position of top prosecutor in the Atlantic County office had been fluid since Ted Housel retired from the post. Housel had been appointed by then-Governor Corzine in 2007 and had planned to retire and return to his lucrative private practice in 2012. His last day happened to fall just weeks after April

Kauffman was found murdered. Jim McClain, who had a thirty-year career in that office, took over as acting prosecutor; Governor Chris Christie appointed him two years later. In July of 2014, he was sworn in. Shortly after that, Christie nominated McClain to a Superior Court judgeship. In the summer of 2016, McClain took his seat on the bench in civil court and Diane Ruberton, a longtime prosecutor in the office, became acting prosecutor until Damon was appointed.

Tyner began assembling his team right away. He picked Cary Shill as first assistant prosecutor to lead the office's team of prosecutors. Shill started in the office in 1989; a career prosecutor, by 2006 he had worked his way up to chief assistant prosecutor, supervising the trial unit, gangs, the drugs and narcotics unit, and violent crime. He was the last prosecutor in New Jersey to obtain a death penalty verdict before the state abolished capital punishment. In one of his first orders of business, Tyner met with Shill to reorganize assignments for chief assistant prosecutors in the areas of major crimes and homicides.

Tyner hired his brother, Michael Graham, to the position of Agent to the Prosecutor. That decision ruffled some feathers, but Tyner was confident in his choice. He trusted his older brother, who came with experience. Graham had retired in 2016 after twenty-five years as an Atlantic City police officer. Thirteen of those years he was assigned to the Atlantic County Prosecutor's Office Major Crimes Squad, handling homicides. Graham might have been the lead investigator on April's case, but on the day April was killed he was assigned another case in Atlantic City.

Graham, like Tyner, had public service in his blood, specifically blue blood with deep ties to law enforcement. Graham and Tyner have the same mother, Beatrice, who married Damon's father after Michael's father's death left her a widow with five children. Michael's father, Clayton Graham, was the first Atlantic City Police Officer killed in the line of duty, in April of 1962, when Michael was 18 months old. Beatrice and Hank would go on to have one son together, Damon.

Tyner, Shill, and Graham sat down with the office's lead investigators: Lieutenant Thomas Finan, Lieutenant Kevin Ruga, and Captain Kevin Hincks. The new Prosecutor asked for copies of all open homicides dating back to 1970. Tyner had been a news junkie, even as a kid. He remembered some of the open cases, including ones his father had been involved with. Among the cold cases was the 1984 murder of seven-year-old Gary Grant, the son of a police officer who was found bludgeoned to death. Tyner had been thirteen at the time. The boy's father coached Damon Tyner's basketball team, and he remembered the agonizing search that followed his disappearance. Another cold case from over a decade before involved the slaying of four prostitutes whose bodies were found in 2006 behind a motel in the West Atlantic City section of Egg Harbor Township.

Damon asked his colleagues which of the open cases was potentially solvable. The consensus was the April Kauffman case. Tyner learned that April's case was not cold—that there were many leads that might prove fruitful given the right amount of attention. The case had been neglected. Damon found that a lot of work on the case had never been done. For example, James Kauffman's DNA had never been obtained. A motion had been filled out requesting a sample from Kauffman, but no one ever followed through; a Post-it note in the file said to hold off, but it wasn't clear why.

Within weeks of his new appointment, Tyner welcomed the D'Arcy brothers, Kim Pack's civil attorneys, into his office. Over a three-hour meeting, they laid out all of their information including interviews, leads and theories, just as they had when Jim McClain was prosecutor. Tyner met with the management of the local FBI office to underscore his desire for a strong working relationship. The new prosecutor already knew there was a gem in the FBI: Special Agent Dan Garrabrant. Through all of the investigators on the Kauffman case over the years, it was Garrabrant who had kept the April Kauffman case on life support.

Tyner then promoted assistant prosecutor Seth Levy to be lead prosecutor on the Kauffman case. As a judge, Tyner had observed Levy arguing many cases in his courtroom, and he liked what he saw. Levy was meticulous, paid attention to the small details and was quick in the courtroom when the defense threw a curveball. When he spoke to the jury, he took complex cases and boiled them down to make them easy to understand. Levy had grown up right in Linwood. The thirty-nine-year-old graduated from Rutgers Camden law school in 2004. Tall and well built, Levy was an intellectual who had been seen filling the waiting periods in court thumbing through the Iliad rather than scrolling through a smartphone.

Levy had several homicide cases under his belt. The Kauffman case might be a career changer, but it wouldn't be his first interesting, dramatic case. He had obtained the conviction of a husband who had set up his wife's death as a gun-cleaning accident, and who would have benefitted from a large inheritance. Levy also successfully prosecuted the case of the State vs. Loretta Burroughs, whose second husband died under suspicious circumstance, and third husband disappeared; his frozen body parts were discovered by police years later, stored in numerous Tupperware bins in Burroughs' home. The grandmother told police she sometimes took his head out to speak to him because she missed him. Burroughs is now serving a life sentence.

Tyner, Shill, and Levy met with Linwood Police Chief Doug Carman and John Hamilton, who was now a captain. In their meeting, they discussed the challenges moving forward and what they had from the original investigation. They also met with Kim Pack. They did not make any promises, but Tyner told her they would investigate the case like it had never been investigated before.

From the county's major crimes unit, Tyner assigned Det. Sgt. James Scoppa to lead the investigation. Scoppa, a veteran of the office since 2001, had been with Major Crimes since 2014, and previously had been with the gangs, guns and narcotics unit around the time when the Kauffman investigation was just heating up. Scoppa was assigned to the case full-time.

In the Spring of 2017, FBI Special Agent Dan Garrabrant was working with the New Jersey Child Exploitation Task Force spearheaded by the Atlantic City office. Prostitution in and around Atlantic City kept the force busy, with agents estimating that they freed twenty-five to fifty girls and boys from forced prostitution each year. Garrabrant had long experience, both as a street cop and as a seasoned federal investigator. He had a no-bullshit approach to the criminals he worked with and was easy to talk to.

All this time, Garrabrant had continued to work the case. He and his family happened to go to the same community pool that Kim and her family went to. As much as it bugged him, he couldn't approach her and tell her he knew details about the case that he felt sure would lead to solving it. Tyner's appearance as the new Atlantic County Prosecutor was welcome, as he made clear that he was willing to put more resources into the investigation. Garrabrant knew that was what they needed in order to connect the dots of data they had gathered over the years. Garrabrant felt confident enough to tell Kim during the meeting with Damon, "I've been working on this case a long time, we're going to solve this."

Assigning an agent to the Prosecutor's office, as in this case, is fairly common. Garrabrant was happy to help; in addition, he'd made a promise to Kim early on to keep track of her mother's case.

Two weeks before the fifth anniversary of April's murder, the Prosecutor's Office filed a Motion to Compel, ordering Kauffman to give a sample of his DNA. If Kauffman refused, Tyner and his team would argue the matter in court, leaving it to a judge to decide. In an interview with ABC-owned affiliate WPVI Action News, Tyner chose his words carefully in revealing this development.

"We are asking for a sample of his DNA so that we can use that as part of our investigation," Tyner said. The reporter asked him about the current status of James Kauffman and whether he was now viewed as a suspect. Tyner responded, "He is not, and we are not naming him as a suspect at this time." The end of the sentence "at this time" lingered in the air. In five years, no one had ever given this much information to the media before, or even spoken the word "suspect," let alone Doctor Kauffman. Kim felt cautiously optimistic. Perhaps the wheels of justice had come alive and slowly start to turn.

The Friday before Memorial Day weekend, Ed Jacobs appeared at the Atlantic County Court in Mays Landing, hoping to convince Judge DeLury that James Kauffman should not be forced to give his DNA. Jacobs was accompanied by his associate, defense attorney Patrick Joyce. Since Kauffman did not have to appear, his lawyers came to court without him.

The prosecutors' motion to be argued in court that day stated:

> On May 10, 2012 multiple blood stains were identified in the second floor master bedroom where April Kauffman's body was located. In addition to the blood recovered from the area of the victim's final resting place, biological stains were located on a blanket in a second bedroom located only feet from the primary crime scene.
>
> On June 7, 2012 a swab from the aforementioned blanket was submitted to the New Jersey State Police Central Regional Laboratory. The NJSPCRL determined the sample to be that of a male contributor however the lab cannot come to any additional ... or definitive conclusions without a known DNA sample by which to compare the forensic sample.
>
> In his recorded deposition, Dr. Kauffman acknowledged that he was the last person to see the victim alive. Dr. Kauffman asserts that as of 5:30 a.m., May 10th, 2012 as he left for work, the victim was alive. There is no evidence to support such a claim. Furthermore, soon after the passing of the victim, Dr. Kauffman put in a claim for $600,000 life insurance that had been taken out on the victim's name. Such opportunity and motive lead this affiant to believe there is a reasonable and well- grounded basis that Dr. Kauffman may have committed the crime of murder, and it is necessary to obtain his buccal swab. Only by obtaining a DNA sample from Dr. Kauffman can the lab compare his DNA to that of the blood recovered only feet from where Dr. Kauffman later discovered the body. A result showing that the DNA sample taken from Dr. Kauffman does not match that taken from the guest bedroom would further the investigation by suggesting the possible presence of another party near the scene of the murder.

Levy said they wanted the doctor to provide a cheek swab with his DNA. If the DNA was not a match to the doctor, then this could rule him out as a murder suspect.

In court, Jacobs argued that a warrant is needed to take blood, and to get a warrant, probable cause must be established. "Five years is enough. It's time, in our view, for the prosecutors to turn their attention to other directions," Jacobs said in defense of his client. Jacobs also asserted that his client had been fully cooperative: "We have provided at least seven investigatory leads to the Prosecutor's Office in writing over these five years."

Jacobs started referred to help his client had provided following his 25-minute conversation with authorities on the day of the murder. Jacobs even boasted his client never once pled the Fifth in the course of the 232-page deposition he gave in 2014—the long deposition conducted by the D'Arcys.

Judge DeLury said he would take the holiday weekend to mull over his decision and would notify both sides on Tuesday. On Tuesday, the judge gave his decision: Dr. James Kauffman had to provide a buccal swab of his DNA. However, the Judge did agree with one of Ed Jacob's arguments; the decision would remain sealed so the media would not know the results. On June 5, 2017, James Kauffman's swab was taken. The New Jersey State Police Laboratory tasked with testing the DNA wrote the results in a report filed on July 12, 2007. The results stated that the DNA profile from Jim Kauffman matched the "major DNA profile" from the blanket found in the guest room. That was the "specimen" the prosecutors had specified in their plea to Judge DeLury. But the lab also tested Jim Kauffman's DNA against several swabs taken from the crime scene, including from under April's fingernails. Under the fingernails of April's left hand, the lab found a mixture of DNA profiles; April was the source of the "major DNA profile" and Jim was the source of the "minor" DNA profile." Tyner and his team's filing the motion had set the wheels of justice turning in the downfall of Dr. James Kauffman.

* * *

There was something else that made The April Kauffman case seem solvable to Damon Tyner. Just five days after Damon Tyner's swearing-in at Prosecutor, on March 20, 2017, a letter arrived at the Atlantic County Prosecutors' Office with little fanfare. In fact, Jim Scoppa, the ACPO's lead investigator, didn't even notice it for weeks after it was put into a file. The sender—the Jacobs and Barbone Law Firm—was the firm representing Dr. James Kauffman. The letter named the subject in the heading: the investigation of the death of April Kauffman. The letter was addressed to Erik M. Bergman, the Chief Assistant Prosecutor of the Atlantic County Prosecutors Office at the time. It was a supplement to a letter sent to the ACPO by Ed Jacobs back on October 4, 2012, six months after April's murder. It said:

Dear Mr. Bergman:

This letter is a supplement to my October 4, 2012 correspondence addressed to John V. Maher Jr., former Chief Assistant Prosecutor, attached. Regarding Paragraph 1, the names Francis Mulholland and Ferdinand C. Augello have been brought to my attention. As to the latter, he may be a resident of Absecon or Ocean View, New Jersey. Either or both may have an association with The Pagan Motorcycle Club. We know nothing of the accuracy or reliability of this information.

The letter was signed by Kauffman's defense attorney, Ed Jacobs. Dr. James Kauffman was carbon-copied on the letter.

The information in that letter was the first time anyone told authorities that Ferdinand "Freddy" Augello and Francis Mulholland had anything to do with April Kauffman's murder. The letter, at first sitting unnoticed in a folder inside the prosecutor's office, would not go ignored for much longer. Investigators could never have guessed how much of an impact the letter would have on their case.

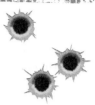

Chapter 15

THE BEGINNING OF THE END

"No! No! I'm killing myself!"

Dr. Jim Kauffman yelled at Detective Jim Scoppa. Scoppa had just entered Kauffman's office with a search warrant in hand. Seconds later, Kauffman pulled a 9 mm. Ruger handgun from his waistband. It was just after 6:41 on the morning of June 13, 2017, exactly two weeks after Judge DeLury's decision that the doctor must give the court a sample of his DNA. Teams of local, county and federal authorities executing the search warrant stood on the lawn fronting Kauffman's office, waiting for him to appear at the door. They had watched through the windows as he unlocked a door leading to the hallway, then unlocked the main door. He had stepped outside, a look of surprise on his face.

Kauffman, wearing light-colored medical scrubs, pulled out the legally registered weapon and pointed it at his chest while slowly backing into his office. Scoppa quickly retreated to the front lawn as Officer Charles Champion of the Linwood police covered the detective. Champion, pointing his gun, screamed, "Don't!" Kauffman had already run back inside.

From the lawn, police officers yelled for Kauffman to surrender: "Sir, drop the gun; let's talk." Another officer joined in, "We only have a search warrant." Facing the exterior of the beige medical office, investigators with the Atlantic County Prosecutors Office (ACPO), Linwood and Egg Harbor Township Police Departments and the FBI stood with weapons drawn.

"You are not under arrest!" one of the men yelled. Kauffman reappeared by the main door. He was visibly nervous, still holding the gun in his hand.

"I don't believe it!" He yelled back, "I'm not going to jail for this. I'm going in the back room and I'm going to kill myself."

It was the statement, "...I'm not going to jail for this" that had some wondering if "this" meant the murder of April Kauffman. Scoppa already thought he knew what Kauffman meant, but those charges would not come today. Authorities were trying to tell Jim they were not there to arrest him, just to search his office. The search warrant had been scheduled for a week, and they had held a tactical meeting the day before. They had no idea it would go down like this, but they were prepared.

Officers stayed back, tossing the search warrants into the mulch by the manicured shrubs in an effort to coax Kauffman to pick up the documents. They wanted him to understand that they were there to search his lab and medical records as part of a medical fraud investigation.

Finally Jim emerged, grabbing the paperwork off of the ground, then ran quickly back inside.

Five years earlier, following his wife's murder, authorities had searched Kauffman's Linwood home and seized a cache of weapons from his gun room. Those guns were later returned to him, but today at least, one of the officers remembered. He warned the others, "He does a lot of shooting, a lot of target practice." After several minutes, you could hear the tension rising in the officers' voices. They needed better cover, more weapons. "Get another car up here," one officer shouted. "More assault rifles are coming."

The entire ordeal was all captured on the police body camera video, a mandate from the FBI for this type of search. Officer Champion was tasked with the recording. The body camera, affixed to his chest, showed a tribal tattoo on Champion's left forearm and a tiger tattoo on his right forearm. On the recording, the detailed body art dwarfs the tiny image of Kauffman standing scared in the doorway. Champion was steady and calm for the nearly hour-long standoff.

Finally, word came. Investigators had managed to get Kauffman on the phone. An officer yelled directions to the others: "He's cooperating. He said he doesn't want to hurt any cops but he doesn't want to be handcuffed." Still cautious, the orders continued.

"Call him out to the BearCat." This referred to the Ballistic Engineered Armored Response Counter Attack Truck, a tactical truck used by many SWAT teams. The officer continued, "...Open his shirt, spin him around and duck. We're going to grab him. If shit goes bad, be aware of a crossfire."

Forty minutes later, after multiple conversations with Kauffman over the phone, the standoff ended. During those calls, investigators promised to meet his requests, including handling him delicately while restraining him, due to a shoulder injury. Kauffman surrendered with his hands up. He turned around and got on his knees following a command amplified through a bullhorn. He gave a yelp of pain as authorities used double handcuffs. Whether he was in real pain, they didn't know, but they kept their promise.

The video of Kauffman's arrest was released in full months later. It showed more detail than the version prosecutors played for Judge Bernard DeLury at Kauffman's detention hearing a few weeks after the incident. In the longer video, Kauffman scoffed at the authorities' insistence on handcuffing him, even though he had pulled a weapon when police arrived. "You guys are killing me," he lamented. But later on, the doctor had apparently changed his attitude. He shared the codes to his garage and his phone, telling detectives where to find keys, locks, and the gun, which he'd in the office upon surrendering.

Authorities then walked him away from the building as they executed the search warrants on his office and SUV. They would also be searching his residences in both Linwood and Philadelphia.

"Do I get my car back?" Jim asked, annoyed, when FBI Special Agent Daniel Garrabrant explained what they were doing. Another lawman answered, "Yes." Jim clarified, "I mean today?"

Since Kauffman had threatened suicide, protocol required that he be taken to the hospital for evaluation. "I'm fine," he kept saying to the EMT. "Why am I going to the hospital?" he asked. The EMTs called over Detective Scoppa, who climbed into the back of the ambulance to try and calm the doctor down.

Walking into his office that June day just after 6 a.m. was the last time Jim Kauffman would ever walk free. If he hadn't pulled a weapon that day, he might have stayed out of jail; he might have gotten away with murder.

While Kauffman was being evaluated at the hospital and later booked, investigators served search warrants on his car; his Linwood home on 2 Woodstock Drive; his condo at the Symphony House in Philadelphia, including the storage facility there; his home in Arizona; his medical office; and his childhood home, which his mother still owned in Margate. In total, that day seven search warrants were served. Authorities listed the numerous crimes they were investigating: Insurance Fraud; Health Care Claims Fraud; Destruction, Alteration, Falsification of Records; Falsifying or Tampering with Records; and Homicide.

Specifically, they were looking for any and all files, documents, and/or any electronic data, like computer desktops, laptops, tablets, portable drives, cell phones, anything containing patient records concerning the issuance of narcotic medication, fraudulent prescriptions, and/or blood testing. The warrant continued that they were searching for any and all evidence of fraudulent medical practices, including cash and gifts. The Feds also wanted pre-completed forms that pertained to fraudulent medical practices, including "straw patients."

The warrants specified any and all evidence related to contacts with Boston Heart, or any other blood lab involved in kickbacks related to unnecessary blood testing, Infinity Labs or its affiliates and evidence related to contacts with Boardwalk Medical LLC and/or Central Rexall Drug, Inc., and/or any other organization, corporation or individual similarly involved in kickbacks for fraudulent medical practices. Also included were any and all evidence, electronic, documentary or otherwise, related to Dr. Kauffman's military service records, as well as anything related to divorce proceedings between April Kauffman and Dr. James Kauffman. Investigators confiscated $100,000 in cash from the office. In Kauffman's SUV, they found a loaded gun.

Nine members of the ACPO and two members of the FBI descended on 2 Woodstock shortly before 10:30 a.m. Inside they found wads of cash: $20,000 on Jim's desk, $1,150 behind his downstairs television set, $6,000 in a wooden box in his first-floor office, and $2,000 more behind the box. They took stacks of paperwork and medical and patient files. Then they took a photo and removed a portion of the dining room floor where, even after six years, a bullet remained lodged in the floor from a fight April and Jim, during which she had reported to friends and a neighbor that he'd fired his gun and missed her. A separate search warrant had been drafted specifically for that "bullet defect" in the wood floor. Investigators also found bins full of prescription meds, some in other people's names.

In Philadelphia, investigators knew what they were looking for before the warrant was signed. A confidential source had told ACPO detectives that Carole and Jim Kauffman had hired someone to install shelving in a storage unit they kept in the Symphony House. The shelving in the 4' by 6' storage room needed specific measurements in order to store "totes" containing Jim's files. The source said Carole described the totes as 33" long by 21" wide by 17" high. The shelving was installed in the summer of 2016. Investigators believed the files were Kauffman's medical files, and they knew from Kauffman's staff that he kept patient files for seven years.

Inside the beautiful condo on the 22nd floor, agents laid out what they had confiscated to be photographed. The front door opened to a foyer with an Oriental rug, wooden armoire, and shelving. A chandelier hung from a trey ceiling. The hallway opened into a large living room, with the kitchen off to the side. In the dining area next to the kitchen, there was a table seating six. The table sat alongside floor-to-ceiling windows with a city view; a telescope on a tripod pointed outside. A light fixture that could double as a piece of modern art hung over the table.

The condo was organized and neat, and the FBI left it that way. In a home office, agents photographed computers, laptops, and financial information. A desk plaque engraved with "Nasty Woman" sat close to a mouse pad with a picture of Esther, the couple's dog. Two guns were discovered, and a shopping bag full of cash with at least six thick envelopes, some labeled "1,000" in ballpoint pen. Agents seized at least fifteen military medals, including a Purple Heart.

* * *

On the morning of June 13, Andrew Glick was driving to work in Ocean Heights around a quarter after nine. Passing Kauffman's office, he thought there must be a fire. "Oh no, Action News, oh crap," he said to himself. He couldn't get his mind off what might have been going down at Kauffman's office. Glick was so nervous he practically sleep-walked through the morning. He heard on the news that federal and local investigators were serving search warrants on Kauffman's home.

Glick couldn't take it. Fearing the police would come to his house next, he left work, arrived home and cleaned out his house, top to bottom. Dripping with sweat on the hot June day, he packed up everything including drugs and guns, drove to a storage facility, and rented a storage unit that day. Meanwhile, Fred was peppering his phone with calls, totaling seven to eight times throughout the day.

"I know. I'm busy. I'll call you asap," Glick texted Fred. The next day Glick met up with Fred at The Cheese Board, a restaurant in Linwood. "Do you think it's about us?" Fred asked him. Fred, Glick explained later, was getting all of his information from radio host Harry Hurley's Facebook page. Glick knew this was bad. "Prepare for the worst, and hope for the best," he told his friend.

* * *

On June 21, 2017, the day after Judge DeLury ruled Kauffman had to remain in jail until his trial, a recorded conversation between Jim Kauffman and Carole Kauffman took place.

Jim:	I love you. I'm so upset for you. I should've just shot myself and been done with it.
Carole:	First of all, let me just remind you you're on a recorded line....
Jim:	I know, but I should've done something to myself. I wouldn't have put you through all of this.
Carole:	Jimmy, Jimmy, you're on a recorded line. Don't say anything.

Carole Kauffman had been talking with Jim this way for a while. She was getting used to having to wait twenty seconds from the time her phone rang until she could hear her husband's voice. "You have a collect call from Jim." "Jim at the Atlantic County Jail." This call may be monitored or recorded..." the prompt said every time before she accepted the call.

"You there, Jimmy?" she would ask. On the other end, she could hear Jim's voice: "Yeah, how ya doing?" Jim's attorney was appealing the decision to keep Jim in jail, after unsuccessfully asking the court to allow his client to remain on home confinement. Kauffman's medical license was also in the process of getting revoked. Their conversation continued:

Carole:	How are you?
Jim:	Terrible, beyond depressed...
Carole:	Everyone is asking for you.
Jim:	I know. I just can't believe the guy didn't let me out."
Carole:	Well, neither can anybody else. Ed filed an appeal....

In New Jersey, lawmakers had recently voted to eliminate cash bail. The court appoints someone to assess the chance that the individual could pose a danger to themselves or others if released while awaiting trial. A nine-factor algorithm was instituted to assess whether a defendant is dangerous or likely to flee. Based on this, defendants are now either detained or released with electronic monitoring. The court appoints someone to assess if the individual could pose a danger to themselves or others if released while awaiting trial. The judge hears arguments during a detention hearing set within a certain amount of days from a defendant's arrest. Kauffman had no prior arrests, but he did pull a weapon with more than a dozen police at his door. Jacobs argued that Kauffman did not point the gun at the officers, but at himself, and he threatened suicide. The body camera video played in court did not help Kauffman's argument to be released, even though he had rated number 1 on the point system, for the lowest risk. Levy argued that if law enforcement had not been so calm during the standoff, and in turn kept Kauffman calm, Kauffman could have been justifiably shot. Judge DeLury ruled he must remain in jail.

At that point, Kauffman had been behind bars for seven days. In court, his tanned face showed an overlay of white stubble. He looked tired, and his hair, dyed dark brown, was now fading from back to white.

Carole had been frantically trying to keep their bank accounts, car leases, mortgages, attorneys' fees, and payroll in order while caring for Jim's mother, Ruth, who was moving between a nursing home and rehab. Jim's office was shutting down. His office manager, Terry Warner, scrambled to keep things in order before the office officially shut its doors in August. Carole functioned through the crisis like a machine: showing up for court dates, making arrangements, moving money from Jim's 401K. She also began to prepare to sell 2 Woodstock and the Arizona home. Over the next several weeks, she also began working to sell the Lincoln Navigator and the Corvette in Arizona and to get rid of her Mercedes lease. She rarely broke down, but when she did, it was either because of people who showed her compassion or who were incredibly difficult. Jim complained about the food and the conditions, as well as the medical care.

From their conversation on June 28, 2017:

> Jim: There were incredible fistfights over shoes... Now when we are outside the area, [the guards] are going to toss everybody [search prisoners' cells]. I have everything neatly labeled in my box so when I come back, they said everything will be on the floor.... These assholes, they do stupid shit, then whatever....I'm losing my mind. I can't think straight. The breakfast today was a half cup of cereal, two slices of white bread, and a tablespoon of peanut butter; it's just inhumane here... this is not fun. I'm not comfortable here; it's insanity... they put the AC on so everyone is freezing... We were all joking we were going to write a Broadway play about this, about the Atlantic County Jail... It would be a hit; there's some comedies, music, and then grave cold facts of how inhumane people can be.

From June 29, 2017:

> Carole: How do you feel right now Jimmy?
>
> Jim: Physically terrible, mentally terrible. I hope I make it the next three weeks, and yesterday, I thought I was going to die. I have to tell you I really didn't care....
>
> Carole: Here's the thing: you do care because you want to get out....
>
> Jim: Physically, I got sick...

Jim's emotional roller-coaster careened between thoughts of suicide and hopes of starting over. He complained daily about the food options: oatmeal, stale bread, sliced bologna, then change the subject to ask about their dog, Esther, and if she missed her "Pop." He talked about what he would do when he was released, which he expected would be soon, and of his hope to change the quality of life inside the Atlantic County Jail. He also talked about getting back to work.

From June 7, 2017:

> Jim: I have patients all lined up. You have no idea, the guards all want to come back. I have a guy next to me whose aunt, grandmother want to come out. I'm sure I'll have half a practice when I come out. Terry tells me the patients come out in tears....I'm going to get my license back and start over, a smaller practice. Stay in Philadelphia or Florida with the money to be collected... I'm optimistic... I just need to get out of here....
>
> Carole: We'll make some money on the book you're going to write... I have a feeling you won't do it. I'm going to do it....

Jim never admitted to doing anything wrong. He had no comprehension as to why the Feds had accused him of Medicare fraud. Instead, he thought of himself as a political prisoner, the target of a personal vendetta by Tyner and DeLury. Even Carole, his lifeline, began to get frustrated with Jim's inability to grasp the gravity of his having pulled a gun with a wall of police facing him outside of his office.

> Jim: Why are you angry with me?
>
> Carole: You're kidding me, right?
>
> Jim: You were angry at me?
>
> Carole: Yeah, a lot of what's going on here is self-inflicted ....
>
> Jim: Whaa? Well I'm sorry you know, I'm human. I screwed up. Don't be angry with me; you're the only person I got....
>
> Carole: You better be nice to me then.
>
> Jim: I didn't want anything to happen. I didn't want anything to happen five years ago. I didn't do anything.

Carole: Well, actually that's not true. You did... I'm talking about recently... your behavior.

Jim: I was stressed to the max—what can I tell you....

Carole: Well, if you didn't have those [guns] at your disposal....

Jim: Whaa?

Carole: They shouldn't have been there; this wouldn't have happened...

Jim: Please don't be mad at me.

Carole: It's stupid, just stupid. They're not my words; they're your lawyer's words.

Jim: I understand....

Carole: You made a not so bad situation really bad.

Jim: I understand... I'm sorry I called.

By September, Jim realized that he could be inside the entire time up to the trial, while he sat anxiously awaiting information from his attorneys. He began sharing a new narrative with a close circle of friends: Somehow, his dead wife should take the blame, not only for her murder, but all his troubles.

From September 7, 2017:

Jim: I made the paper. I don't understand.

Carole: Jimmy...

Jim: I'm just a regular guy who's been a physician for thirty-five years, helping people.

Carole made some disparaging remarks about April, and brought up the idea that Jim's marrying April had been what led to all his trouble.

Jim: Just because I had a marriage with that person doesn't mean I'm not a regular guy.

As summer turned to fall, Jim became more comfortable in his role as inmate. He had plenty of money in his commissary account, and he would make calls for other prisoners who lacked privileges, or ask Carole or other friends to send a message for them. The corrections officers had a rapport with him. Jim asked friends to help him figure out crime-themed trivia questions that the guards posed to him, such as the type of gun Jack Ruby had used to kill Lee Harvey Oswald, and the name of Ruby's nightclub. (The answer: a Colt Cobra 38 caliber revolver, and the Vegas club. The other inmates also came to him with their medical problems, and called him Doc. He told friends that he was diagnosing inmates with diabetes left and right, and blamed the poor food options inside.

But when Jim started to see the discovery materials his lawyers had obtained about his case, he again turned to his small circle, asking them for favors that could be interpreted as intimidation of a witness. He called a close friend who also worked in the medical world, and told him that his nurse practitioner had turned on him, and he wanted everyone to know.

Friend:	Hey, Big man...
Jim:	Yo, my man... So listen to this one... I get this thing from the prosecutor that they're trying to confiscate the money because they have a confidential informant that says I'm a Pagan... Who do you think the CI is?
Friend:	You're a Pagan? What, do you do that in your spare time?
Jim:	Barbara Greenling.
Friend:	No.
Jim:	Honest to God, I've got the paperwork in front of me... Can you believe this shit?
Friend:	I... that one I can't believe...
Jim:	I got it in writing... and it says this has to be confidential because, you know she may be injured because the Pagans or whatever... I'm sitting there going you've got to be kidding me...
Friend:	How would she know you're a Pagan? Even if you are a Pagan, how would she know that?
Jim:	I'm not arguing with you. I would say I'm not not affiliated with them or nothing....Isn't it amazing? But... they're going to use that to confiscate the money....
Friend:	Confiscate the money ? Because you're a member of quote a gang? I guess the woman who I know pretty well, as you know, is willing to testify to that? She has to have proof of that?
Jim:	I guess so, I don't know how...
Friend:	Well, that's a Jacobs thing; he needs to move on that.
Jim:	I know, but I also need you to spread the word in the town....
Friend:	Spread the word of what?
Jim:	She's a confidential informant, OK? I need that on the streets so people know what the hell they are dealing with. This is insane. I'm getting railroaded by every possible person. I need some defense on the outside.
Friend:	That's just fucking insane. I hear ya.
JK:	Gotta rock 'n' roll....

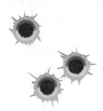

Chapter 16

ALL I WANT
FOR CHRISTMAS

"We should've whacked this dude a couple of years ago."

All Fred Augello wanted for Christmas was James Kauffman dead. It was five days before Christmas 2017, and Augello, the former president of the Cape May County Pagans chapter, stood in his kitchen venting to his former vice president, Andrew Glick. Together the two Pagans discussed a plan to kill Kauffman while he waited for his trial on weapons charges in the Atlantic County Correctional Institution. It had now been six months since Kauffman's dramatic arrest. That morning, Glick had called Augello in a panic and rushed over to his house.

"My boy called and said his guys from 'in there' called, and saw US Marshals take the Doc out last night. He said the reason they knew they were Feds was because they had the US Marshals jackets." The guys from "in there" Glick referred to were current inmates and associates of a drug dealer Glick knew through his connections with the Sinaloa Cartel.

In recent weeks, Glick had kept Augello up to date about his ongoing conversations with his Sinaloa contact. He had taken the lead in arranging a hit against Kauffman in jail, acting on Augello's insistence in the matter.

"You don't think that they found them out, that they wanted to whack him, do you?" Augello asked. Glick's update from that morning had Augello concerned. If Glick's information was correct and Kauffman was in the custody of US Marshals, that could mean big problems for Augello and Glick. Among the Marshals' responsibilities is the transporting of federal prisoners. Up to this point, Kauffman had been held in a county jail on state charges, for weapons violations from pulling the gun on police. Now, both men wondered aloud in the kitchen why the Feds had removed Kauffman from the county lock-up. Maybe he was finally going to face a grand jury on federal indictments for one of the alleged scams Kauffman was running out of his office—either the kickback scheme involving the compound creams or for the blood lab operation. Neither of those had involved the Pagans. But it could still pose a problem for them; more charges against the doctor could mean more leverage for investigators to get information from Kauffman about who killed April.

Augello had been paranoid about Kauffman since the previous March, when Kauffman had revealed his fear over a jailhouse Pagan snitch to Glick. That had proved to be a false rumor. But something else had put Augello on edge back in March. A letter sent to the prosecutor's office had suggested that investigators look into Fred Augello and Francis Mulholland for the murder of April Kauffman. What really riled Augello was who wrote it and who had been copied on it. This was the letter written by Jim Kauffman's attorney Ed Jacobs and sent to the Atlantic County Prosecutors' Office back in March 2017. And Kauffman himself had been cc'd on the letter.

Glick's attorney, John Zarych, had learned about the letter and was able to get a copy of it which he gave to Glick. Glick had told Augello about the letter in November 2017 and brought him a copy once he got his hands on it. They sat together in Augello's van, parked outside a Wendy's fast-food restaurant that November night. Augello was stunned.

"This, to me, without getting into a big conversation, is amazing, like I can't figure out for the life of me, why these people would do this?" Augello said to Glick.

"Well, they're bringing this up because of the new prosecutor, Damon whatever...," Glick speculated. Fred responded to the mention of Tyner with a racial slur. This letter created a massive problem for Fred Augello, one that he would obsess over for the coming months.

Inside the van, Fred held the letter in his hand, thinking out loud. He said he had never been a patient of Kauffman's, had never met the doctor. A group of people going for pain meds couldn't be easily connected to murder.

"I didn't murder this woman," Fred defiantly repeated to Glick, and, "I don't know this person," referring to the other individual named in the letter, Francis Mulholland. As his frustration grew, his thoughts turned back to Dr. Kauffman. "The guy was trying to throw me under the bus, throw us under the bus," Fred said, and Glick wholeheartedly agreed, echoing Fred's words. Glick reflected back Fred's thoughts as he continued to stew: "From the beginning," Fred muttered, and, "He's a fucking asshole," referring to the doctor.

As he continued to ruminate, Fred seemed to grow paranoid, asking Glick to turn off his cell phone.

"If you can't shut your phone off that's one of the signs... that they're tapping your phone," Fred said, looking at Andrew. Fred would then claim he heard "through a source" that police were listening to Andrew's calls, and he feared the same for himself.

"I'm convinced that my phone is tapped, that's why I told you I've done nothing wrong... So that's where we are at, that's why I talk to you about this like this, and I am totally convinced that they are, that every time I talk to you on the phone they are listening..."

In this case, Fred's paranoia was well grounded: his entire conversation with Glick was being recorded and listened to by authorities in real time.

Even with those worries, Fred did not stop talking to Glick over the next several weeks about the letter or about the doctor. On December 20th, as the two spoke in the kitchen of Augello's home about a jailhouse hit on Dr. Kauffman, the conversation grew more intense. Augello's raspy voice got softer, as if someone was listening in.

"Here's my deal with the doctor. I think there's going to be a point in his life where he says fuck it...," he said. Glick interrupted in agreement, "He's gonna give everybody up for spite..."

At 61, Ferdinand "Freddie" a.k.a. "Miserable" Augello had a good life. He was living with his schoolteacher girlfriend in the southern New Jersey suburbs, in a beautiful four-bedroom home with a pool, in a wooded neighborhood of Woodbine, New Jersey. He owned and ran both the sign shop and Freddymade Guitars, a business making and repairing guitars. Besides motorcycles, music was his passion. He fronted a band, Who Dat, a staple year-round at events and bars throughout the shore. The band's name was a hat tip to New Orleans and the blues-rock type music they liked to perform, but they also played covers of songs from Michael Jackson to Jimi Hendrix. Augello had started Who Dat with his cousin Dan Haines to play a Hurricane Katrina benefit, and decided to keep the band together. As a retired Pagan, Augello could still wear the Pagans colors and jacket, and come and go freely to the clubhouses and events, although he no longer had to pay dues.

His once long black hair, now gray, was usually pulled back into a long ponytail. Reading glasses were now a permanent fixture atop his head. He had settled into the role of family man, carpooling his girlfriend's children and hosting Christmas Eve dinner. But investigators were beginning to think Augello, who had never been arrested, had a murderous edge—that he had something to do with April's murder.

Independent of Augello's conversations with Glick, investigators suspected that Augello had already begun looking for options to get rid of Kauffman and that he'd been testing the waters with a Mafia connection. But Glick offered up an alternative plan, even offering to spot Augello the ten grand it would take to get the job done.

Outside the kitchen, the grandfather clock chimed twelve times signaling noon. Augello stepped out of the house, leaving Glick alone inside the well-kept, nearly half-million-dollar home. As Glick waited for Augello to return, he admired the Christmas decorations set up around the house, the train set Augello had set up for the holidays, and the large Christmas tree. When Augello came back Glick offered a comment about the tree, but Augello quickly shifted the conversation to the topic that obsessed him: the letter Kauffman's attorney, Ed Jacobs, had sent to the Atlantic County Prosecutor's Office. He wondered aloud whether Ed Jacobs' having sent the letter might not sit well with another criminal client of his: Philadelphia wise guy Joey Merlino, and possibly other members of the Philadelphia "family". Merlino himself was about to head to trial in federal court.

"These mafia guys I know," Augello started, "…The one guy is the direct underboss of the guy that is running Philly, and they told me… [Ed Jacobs is] doing Merlino's case now, and they wouldn't be happy with this lawyer knowing he put my name on there," Augello said. Francis Mulholland, the other name in the letter, was dead and couldn't share what he knew.

Glick had to leave. Before he did, he assured Augello they would get the job done; they would kill Kauffman in jail. Augello walked Glick out to his truck

"Me and you are always good," the long-haired tattooed biker assured Glick. Augello continued, "You're no rat… come over Sunday after five." Glick agreed to come Sunday, which was Christmas Eve, and promised to bring a bottle of Jack Daniels. He then got into his pickup truck, drove a short distance away and met Detective James Scoppa from the Atlantic County Prosecutors Office. Just as Glick had been doing since early November, he handed over the recording device and microphone he'd worn into Augello's home, and briefed the detective on everything they had talked about.

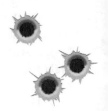

Chapter 17

FLIPPING ON FREDDY

The road to Glick's betrayal of Augello had begun months earlier, when Glick walked into defense attorney John Zarych's office in July 2017.

"I could possibly have all the information to solve the biggest case in Atlantic County in the past twenty years," Glick said to Zarych, boasting of his inside information about April's murder.

In spite of his size and impressive tattoos, Glick managed to come across as friendly rather than intimidating. He cracked jokes and peppered most of his sentences with "Yo," the popular Philly greeting. Glick often sounded more like Sean Penn's Jeff Spicoli from Fast Times at Ridgemont High than a fifty-two-year-old professional chef and biker. He was also smart and good with finances, always looking for a way to make a buck and save one too; he worried about savings and 401ks, and made sure to use discounts. Glick and his wife Vicki were going through a contentious divorce after she caught him cheating, and since he was the breadwinner it was proving costly for him.

Glick walked into Zarych's office just three days after he realized he was under the authorities' microscope. Glick had sought out Zarych on the recommendation of a Pagan brother. Glick told the attorney what he knew about April's murder; he also told him what he didn't know, such as where the gun used to kill her could be found. Fearing his arrest was imminent, he paid Zarych a $7,500 retainer.

Glick retained legal counsel after he realized he might have drawn suspicion on himself a week earlier, when he voluntarily went into the Atlantic County Prosecutor's Office on Unami Boulevard to claim his medical records. During the raid on Dr. Kauffman's office, all patient files had been confiscated. The ACPO had put out a message on local media alerting all Dr. Kauffman's patients to retrieve their records. With Kauffman now in jail, Glick needed to go to a new endocrinologist to treat his diabetes, and he needed his records. Glick called the office several times, finally hearing back from Sgt. Jim Scoppa. Scoppa told him to come in on July 22nd at 12:30 p.m.

Glick, who had never been to the prosecutor's office before, followed Scoppa down a long hallway and into an interview room. Scoppa offered him a seat and returned ten minutes later with Lieut. Kevin Ruga.

Ruga and Scoppa immediately started asking questions about Glick's relationship with the doctor. Glick thought he could skate by. He truly did have a patient-doctor relationship with Kauffman; the doctor saw Glick regularly for his Type 2 diabetes, ordered labs on him three times a year, and prescribed Glick medications to control his diabetes that Glick received through the mail. Glick had insurance and paid a $50 co-pay each visit.

The investigators asked whether Glick saw Kauffman after hours. Glick's initial visit with Kauffman in 2012 had been on a Saturday, a day the office was normally closed, but after that it was always on a Friday, since Glick worked some weekends at the retirement home.

When Scoppa and Ruga asked about pain prescriptions, he offered a cover story. He received pain meds for shoulder and back pain from a motorcycle accident, he said. The accident was real, but the pain was not.

Scoppa told Glick he believed that he and other Pagan members and associates had been receiving illegal narcotics prescriptions from Kauffman, and that Glick had been approached by Kauffman to kill April.

Specifically, Scoppa wanted to know about a prescription the doctor had written for Glick dated May 11, 2012, the day after April's murder. Had Glick gone into the office that day? Glick didn't tell the investigators, but he knew about that prescription. Kauffman had written it ahead of time, a month prior. He dated them every thirty days, and Glick had not gone to the practice that day. It was a coincidence.

Glick wasn't talking. He was the former president of a Pagans chapter, and they had a code: no snitching. He could be killed for violating it. Glick also knew from this line of questioning that he was in trouble; he needed a lawyer.

Glick called Fred after the meeting and told him that things were bad; the investigators knew details. Glick immediately stopped selling drugs, fearing the authorities were watching him. Since 2015, business had really picked up with his cocaine and methamphetamine distribution. Even though it was a side business, he had generated nearly $40,000 in cash so far. But as weeks passed, and then months, Glick began to think he was off the hook. Always looking for money, he wanted his side-hustle back up and running. On October 22, 2017, he held an open house at his home to let his customers know "Andrew's Crime World," as he called it, was back. Most of the clients were friends; that day he spotted many of them to a half- or quarter-ounce of meth and coke, just to get his customer base back. A couple of days later, he replenished his stash with eight ounces of meth and four ounces of coke.

The authorities had not forgotten about Andrew, however. Andrew's Crime World gave them the opportunity for which they were waiting. On November 1, 2017, Glick had gone inside a shed on his property on Ridge Road in Egg Harbor Township, and was unloading cash and drugs he had just transported from an apartment he rented on the Ocean City Boardwalk. He was using the temporary winter rental as a place to stash drugs and cash. That night he thought he would take everything home, to count how much cash he had and check his drug inventory.

Glick heard what sounded like a diesel truck pull up outside the shed. Then a loud amplified voice screamed, "Andrew Glick, we have a search warrant!" It was already dark out. Glick, walking with a flashlight, approached his white perimeter fence. The fence was as tall as he was, with tight slats, so he couldn't see through it to the driveway. A vehicle pushed the fence in.

"Drop your weapon!" he heard. Glick dropped the flashlight, felt a gun touching the side of his head and instinctively dropped to the ground. While Andrew lay there for about a half-hour, with his face in the dirt and his hands zip-tied behind his back, authorities scattered through his house and around the property, confiscating $37,000 in cash stored in a briefcase in his Chevy Silverado pick-up, over a pound of crystal meth, five ounces of cocaine in a blue Igloo cooler, and seven legally registered weapons. They also took loads of gear with Pagans colors and symbols.

They transported Glick to Northfield Police, where Sgt. Scoppa and Special Agent Garrabrant met with him in an interview room. Glick called his lawyer, John Zarych, who arrived there within the hour and began working on a deal with authorities. It was at that moment Garrabrant knew: this was it. He was confident Glick was going to be the line to connect the dots and explain the bigger picture, to answer the questions about April's murder after all this time. The trio of Scoppa, Garrabrant, and Glick would form a team, with Garrabrant playing the straight man to Scoppa and Glick, and Glick as the funny one with his wicked sense of humor that kept both lawmen on their toes.

Glick spent the night in the interview room with his hands cuffed in front of him. Facing a possible forty-year sentence, Glick eventually agreed to wear a wire. The voices Scoppa and Garrabrant wanted to hear on that wire were Augello and Seeler.

Glick told the ACPO and FBI that their perception of how the prescription drug ring worked was correct. He went on to confirm that Augello had told him that Dr. Kauffman wanted his wife dead. Augello had asked Glick if he knew anyone who would do the job. Glick revealed more details to authorities while he sat handcuffed. He mentioned how Augello had said that Dr. Kauffman planned on selling a Corvette to obtain the cash to pay for her murder. And that as part of the agreement, Dr. Kauffman would continue writing fraudulent scripts to individuals sent to him by Augello.

Glick did not hold back. He said he told Stevie Wittenwiler about the job to kill April Kauffman. Wittenwiler, Glick said, was not only aware of it but said that Dr. Kauffman had already approached him. And that when Wittenwiler told Augello he'd started contacting Dr. Kauffman directly, Augello had cut Wittenwiler out of the deal.

That night, as he waited for food in the holding room, Glick explained to his questioners that after being approached by Kauffman, he heard nothing about the murder for five months, until he saw on the news that it happened. About a year and a half after the murder, Glick said Augello told him that the male individual he had hired to kill Dr. Kauffman's wife had the last name of Mulholland. Mr. Glick stated that he and Augello had a mutual friend at that time named Joseph Mulholland a.k.a. Irish, but Augello said that it wasn't Joe—it was someone else with the same last name. Augello also told him that the individual had recently died from an overdose in the area of Rio Grande, New Jersey, and that they didn't have to worry about him any longer.

Special Agent Garrabrant told the agents with Glick to get him food from McDonald's before he headed to the county lock-up. He had to go to jail to make his arrest look legitimate. They gave him no guarantees that they would reduce his charges, even after he had answered their questions and agreed to wear a wire.

Glick spent six days inside the Atlantic County Correctional Facility in the medical pod. Although he and Kauffman were inside the same facility, they did not cross paths. When he was released, Scoppa and Detective Jason Dorn picked Glick up from jail and drove him home. Back home, he savored the feel of a hot shower and the taste of real food after days of over-processed turkey and bologna sandwiches, food he claimed he wouldn't even serve his dogs. Glick couldn't go back to jail, let alone prison. He didn't want to cooperate, but feared it was his only option. He had twenty-four hours alone in his house before his new handlers would be back to get to work. One of Glick's friends had been taking care of his dogs in his absence. The friend drove Glick to his house in Ocean City, lent him his Dodge Challenger, and told him to keep it as long as he needed.

Scoppa and Dorn picked Glick up at 2 p.m. Their first stop was a cell phone store. The detectives handed him some cash to pay for the new phone. Glick thought it was his cash, from the briefcase they'd confiscated—he had a certain way of folding his cash that looked familiar.

Then the authorities went right to work. They went over how Glick should set up meetings with Augello, Glenn Seeler, and other people they had discussed in his interrogation. They took over his drug shed and set up a camera system in seven areas of Glick's property. The property was very private, sitting about 200 feet off the road from Ridge Avenue, with the closest neighbor about 250 feet away. The ACPO also rented Glick a truck, since his had been seized in the raid on his home.

November 10 was showtime, when Glick officially became "Newark Source CI FBI." He drove his borrowed Challenger to meet with Scoppa and Garrabrant behind the Northfield FBI Office around seven p.m. As Glick and Special Agent Daniel Garrabrant began getting the wire ready, Fred called.

"Yo," Glick greeted him, "I'm just walking out of my house... so... getting in the car and I'll be there in less than ten..."

Garrabrant stood next to Glick listening to his call, meanwhile making sure the wire and transmitter were all set to work. It was a pocket-sized transmitter about the size of a credit card. Glick also had digital audio recorders, and Scoppa and Garrabrant had receiving devices so they could listen in on the conversations.

"You good?" Garrabrant asked Glick. "Where's the card?" Glick wondered. All this equipment was new to him, and he didn't know where to put it.

"Put it in my pocket?" he asked. Garrabrant responded, "Leave it there, it's very touchy." Garrabrant didn't want anything to go south, technically.

"What is it though?" Glick asked. He didn't know what to say about the recording device was in case it was spotted. "It's a storage facility key," he was instructed. You could hear the nerves in Glick's voice as he repeated it to himself, "Ok, just say storage facility key, just say storage facility key."

Garrabrant gave his new source instructions: "After you're done, head this way and we'll make sure he's still not following you. I'll get in front of you somewhere, just head towards your house." Glick tried to lighten the moment.

"Yeeahh, just stage a briefing area in my driveway, haha,"

"Probably go to the park," Garrabrant responded, all business. Then he repeated, "Make sure he's not following you."

Glick got behind the driver's wheel of the Challenger. The Red Hot Chili Peppers blared as he drove to the meeting spot. When he pulled up, he shut the door to walk towards Fred, his best friend and Pagan brother. "Yo," Glick's voice sounded normal. The detectives had coached him for this moment: not to panic, to take shallow breaths, and make eye contact. There was no instruction sheet, and this didn't come naturally to Glick. He was flying by the seat of his pants.

Chapter 18

THE WIRE

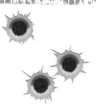

"Shut that off! You don't have it turned on, do you?"

Those were the first words out of Fred's mouth recorded on Andrew Glick's wire in early November 2017. From now on, authorities would listen in on any conversations Glick had with Augello, up to and including their conversation around Christmastime about killing Doctor Kauffman.

Clearly, Fred feared that Andrew's phone was bugged. This conversation carried a lot of weight for Andrew—it was Andrew's only chance to prove to Fred that he hadn't flipped while he was in jail.

Fred wasted no time letting Andrew know he was concerned and skeptical about talking to Andrew. He knew the authorities were watching Andrew's house, he said. He questioned why Andrew was driving the borrowed Dodge Challenger, instead of a truck Augello had seen in Andrew's driveway.

"Yeah, the whole thing's... here, I'm going to tell you right now. It's like really creepy," Fred said to Andrew.

"Right," Glick replied. Fred went on: "What I want to do is hear what happened to you and hear what these people had to say." By "these people," he meant the authorities who had arrested Glick. Fred knew about the arrest and was spooked by the thought that authorities might have flipped him. Andrew had to not only allay Fred's fears in that regard; he also had to get Fred to say something incriminating about April's murder on the wire. He hoped to convince Fred that his legal problems could be a good thing for them in a way: his defense attorney was working to find out what authorities knew about The Pagans.

Glick took Fred through the arrest, his conversations with authorities, and his stint in county, mixing truth and fiction as he went. He even added an embarrassing tidbit, saying he'd pissed his pants when he had a gun to his head. "I spent five days in bologna-land, man. It's fucking..." Glick started laughing, painting his description of the jail and its inhabitants with obscenities and racial slurs.

Fred listened, then opened up to Glick. "I'll be honest with you," he said. "It made you look like you were bad... Cops all around... Andrew is in the place overnight until the morning. What the fuck is he doing in there? And then John, John should have called me... and I've been wondering for two or three days, and I went over there..." John was John "Egyptian" Kachbalian, an old-school Pagan who had served time. He lived by the code, that you never flip or talk to authorities. Kachbalian was somewhat of a barometer for bullshit and rats; he had let Fred know that his antennae were up about Glick cooperating with authorities. As Fred continued to rattle through the chaos of his thoughts over Andrew's arrest, Glick began to empathize. The poor guy seemed to be going crazy.

In addition to Fred, Kachbalian was another person whom Andrew had to convince of his motives. After Glick got released from jail, he had to check in with his Mother Chapter. Kachbalian acted somewhat like a legal department for the Pagans. Augello wanted Kachbalian to review Glick's charging documents, and judge whether it was safe, or not, for club members both retired and current to talk to him. Glick informed Scoppa of the pending meeting with Egyptian, and explained he had to sit down with him in order to look legit.

Glick needed to get two sets of paperwork about his case from the prosecutor's office. But the only set that mattered to him to stay alive were the dummy versions concocted by ACPO to make his arrest seem kosher. The dummy versions would also serve as his official paperwork in the New Jersey Court system. That way, under the new bail reform program, his actual offenses would be significantly lowered. The plan was that this would allow his release when his case was argued in court so that the ACPO could continue to use him as an informant. The hearing actually turned into a close call, with a prosecutor fighting to keep him in jail, unaware of the sting operation her colleagues had cooked up with Glick acting as an informant and as a decoy to catch others.

As he conducted the "legal review" for the Pagans, Kachbalian was checked for the amount of drugs and illegal weapons seized from Glick during the raid. This would affect the likelihood of Glick's being released by police. For example, if the paperwork spelled out the actual amount Glick had been caught with, there was no way state or federal authorities would let him out on his own recognizance, or by the state's new point-based release system.

After their meeting in Wendy's, Augello called Glick and said that he believed him; he knew Glick was "straight up." Augello assured Glick he wouldn't talk to Kachbalian anymore. "John wants to control things," Augello told Glick on the phone that night. Kachbalian had shared information about Glick that made him think "funny things." Basically, Kachbalian had shared his hunch that something was funky about Glick's arrest. But Augello decided to trust in his best friend Andrew's perceived sincerity instead.

The meeting at Wendy's was the first time Andrew had worn a wire with the intention of recording his friend. But soon Andrew Glick, former Pagan President, began acting as an agent. "Glick had become a pro, it was almost like he was an investigator himself," Scoppa said about him.

Scoppa was successful in laying the bait through Andrew using the letter naming Augello and Francis Mulholland as possible suspects in April's killing. "You think this is a legit letter?" Fred asked Glick. Glick didn't waiver: "I think it's... legit... Fuck yeah."

The Feds had also offered a possible motive for Fred to have killed April, Andrew told Fred. They had told him April had hired Fred to make a sign for her restaurant, but she'd never paid him for the job.

"So that's kooky, so that usually means they need some bizarro scapegoat fantasy and then... that's their proof?" Fred responded.

Fred seemed convinced this was all a ruse by detectives. He said nothing during that conversation that could prove he had contracted with someone to kill April Kauffman under the direction of Jim Kauffman. However, at one point in the transcript, he did something that would take their investigation to another level.

FA: Well, here's the deal dude, um... What's this... I'll get rid of this.
       I'll write it here. Don't say it.
AG: All right.

[Sounds as if someone is writing]

FA: Can you read that?
AG: Mm-hm.
FA: That's what's gonna happen.

Portions of the recording suddenly went quiet except for the sound of whispers and a light scratching noise. Glick would tell authorities that scratching noise was indeed the sound of someone writing: Augello used a brown Sharpie marker to write on the back of a business card, "Kauffman will be dead in two days."

AG: That, that, that would, you know, be a game-changer.

The sound of paper ripping filled the next gap of silence in the recording.

FA: Cause of that person's of, deal there...
AG: Right.
FA: The person that um we're saying...
AG: Right, that...
FA: Remember the Mafia?

AG: Right, uh-huh, got it.
FA: They're...
AG: Yup.
FA: That's bullshit.
AG: That is bullshit.
FA: That guy couldn't write that letter without him doing it.
AG: Fucking A! I saw it, I was like he's a fucking asshole!

Glick spilled more information to Augello about what authorities had asked him, all of it true. He told Augello the investigators had brought up Glenn Seeler, Joseph Mulholland, and Steve Wittenwiler Jr.; they were confident that a roundup—multiple arrests—would happen by the end of the year; and that someone or several people would be charged with April's murder. At this point, the pill operation seemed like background noise to them, but April's murder investigation was moving ahead quickly. Fred and Glick talked about giving each other a heads-up call if the police were planning to arrest one of them first, a kind of "code blue."

Fred wondered if the investigators had been trying to communicate to him through Glick:

FA: Did he give you like a message to give to us or something ?
AG: Who?
FA: The cop?
AG: I think the Thanksgiving was the message. I mean I'm just reading into it. He said enjoy your Thanksgiving.
FA: Did he say anything about your friends? Tell your friends?
AG: He just said... tell your family, you and your family, enjoy your Thanksgiving.
FA: Did he mean us as your family, Pagans?
AG: We're brothers, I don't know. [Pagans] did say... you never get out of the club... the only people who get out of the club are beaten out of the club.

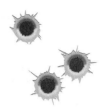

Chapter 19

NOVEMBER

After Glick claimed to his handlers that Augello had written the message "Kauffman will be dead in two days" on the back of a business card, the investigators became concerned that Jim Kauffman's life could be in danger. No one had heard Augello say it on the wire, and Glick didn't have the written message to show anyone. But his word was strong enough for investigators. Acting on this, Scoppa requested a warrant to tap Augello's phone, and Judge Bernard DeLury signed it.

With the wiretap on his phone, authorities could see who Augello was calling and texting. Around the same time, he was calling and texting Glick about getting his hands on the letter naming him as a suspect, Augello also received a call from Joseph Mulholland. Augello had just told Glick he hadn't talked to his friend Joe in years. Their conversation on the phone centered around a paint job Joseph was going to do for Augello. Joseph was a painter by trade, but investigators thought the two men were speaking in code. They might have been thinking of the old Mafia code, as when Jimmy Hoffa famously said, "I heard you paint houses," on meeting the infamous mob hitman Frank "the Irishman" Sheeran. In this case, investigators wondered if the paint chips mentioned in their conversation were code for the letter Ed Jacobs had written wrote to the prosecutor's office, or whether it meant something else altogether.

From the recorded conversation on November 11, 2017:

FA: ...We're going to stop at the store around three, around you know 3:30 and pick up them, uh, swatches, them paint swatches at that, uh, Benjamin Moore joint.
JM: Yeah.
FA: You'll know I have them.
JM: All right, cool.
FA: And then I'm going to head on back to my place. What are you doing?

JM: Nothing, just doing shit around the house right now. Well, give me
       a call I might be able to shoot up there.

In between these seemingly casual business calls with Mulholland, Augello
kept texting and calling Glick nonstop about the letter. Glick and Augello agreed
to meet at 3:45 that afternoon, at the same Wendy's where they'd met the night
before.

One of the detectives on the surveillance team called Scoppa.

"Yo, we don't know who this is, he's been talking to him for a little while now."
Although they had a warrant to monitor Augello's calls, the surveillance team had
to stop listening in on a conversation if it wasn't pertinent to the investigation,

"What's he saying?" one member asked.

"He was talking about some other shit like picking up a ladder, then talking
about this other girl that was at a bar the other day, and how she likes black guys,
and started being racist ....do you think you should minimize it?" One of the
detectives responded, "They're obviously talking about Pagans. If they're talking
about the Pagans then keep it up..." Then he mentioned the satellite tower they
were receiving the call from: "It's hitting off tower off Shore Road, Route 9." The
tower locations gave them an idea of the radius within which Fred might be
calling.

Today's meeting was the second between Glick and Augello. Dan Garrabrant
had just returned to the country from an overseas assignment. The Special Agent
and Scoppa had to hash out the kinks of the recording devices, but they thought
the meet, and the tapped calls earlier that day, were a success. They didn't realize
yet that when Fred and Joseph Mulholland discussed paint chips, they actually
meant paint chips. However, they did have a different problem: Augello was again
writing notes during the meeting with Glick.

After the meeting ended, Augello went back inside the Wendy's to hit the
men's room. Glick started up his truck again, sighing heavily. The sigh sounded
like a weary man with the weight of the world on his shoulders. He cranked up the
radio and listened to The Red Hot Chili Peppers. As he started to leave the parking lot, his phone buzzed. It was Scoppa.

"Yesss....," Glick answered. Scoppa, who had been listening in, wasted no
time.

"What did he write down?" Scoppa asked, then added without waiting, "...
and did he bring them papers inside with him?" Andrew didn't have the notes Fred
had written. He told Scoppa, "The one paper... the envelope with the letter is on
his floor, and he got the paper towels in his pocket."

"He wrote on paper towels?" Scoppa asked. Andrew replied, "Yeah..." Scoppa
rushed on: "What did he write on them ?" Andrew and Scoppa set up a meet
point, and while Andrew was driving on Ocean Heights to Route 9 toward the

FBI office, detectives ran into the men's room of the Wendy's and searched the trash cans, but they found no paper towels that had been written on. Glick parked at the PNC Bank in Linwood and waited for the investigators. When they arrived he filled them in: "The other note says basically no one witnessed where and when Augello met with the doctor, and... the arrangement to kill April was made." Scoppa asked, "He writes that down?"

"He writes that down," Glick continued, "that no one but the Doc have that information." Glick also informed Scoppa that it didn't look like the plan for Kauffman to be dead within two days was happening. Glick said Fred made a gesture, swiping or slashing his hand away, insinuating that the timing had been pushed back. Again, without video or material evidence, the investigators had to take Glick's word for all this. Just after the meeting ended, the surveillance team saw a call coming in to Augello from Joseph Mulholland. This time investigators knew for certain Fred was talking about the letter.

FA: I'm, we're good, but um, I got that paperwork.
JM: Yeah is it good, or...?
FA: It's, It's just, um, well I don't know, it mentions...
JM: Yeah.
FA: People, like I said, it does, and uh, it shows...
JM: Oh, okay.
FA: It shows that um, that um, and it's dated from a long time ago, so...
      So it shows that you know, uh, it, it, there's a supplement to it that
      has some big fucking insane... something just, retardedness...
      But it just introduces these people to, um, these names... I don't know
      this other guy on the thing, I don't.
JM: Yeah.
FA: I don't know this doctor, it's fucking ridiculous.
JM: Yeah.

The next morning, Sunday, November 12, ACPO and FBI surveillance was in place outside Fred's Woodbine house when Joe Mulholland arrived around 11 am. They watched as Joe pulled up in his 1993 black GMC Sierra pickup truck, and stayed through his hour-long visit. Investigators believed Joe was there to see the letter. The investigators continued their surveillance on Fred that day. First, he called Beverly to find out whether they had actually done any sign work for April Kauffman. Although Beverly was no longer working for Fred, he knew she could look up past records, and she told him there was no record of it.

Augello then began calling and texting Glick about getting hold of the original letter Jacobs had written to The Prosecutor's Office in 2012, for which the second letter was the supplement. Augello wanted to see if the first letter had mentioned any other names.

Glick was under major stress. Not only did he have to keep up with Augello's texts and calls while still juggling his full-time job as a chef; he was also dealing with his divorce from Vicki, and he had recently learned that his new girlfriend, who already had two children from a previous relationship, was pregnant. Sometimes Augello called and texted so much that Glick would miss a call or a text. Then someone from the Prosecutor's Office who had been monitoring both their phones had to go to Glick's house to remind him—sometimes waking him up—that he had to answer every time Augello called, and every time investigators called. That was the deal.

As Fred began to sound less evasive on the phone, Glick took the opportunity to try and see if Augello would talk about how he knew Francis Mulholland.

AG: I never [knew] Irish's last name was Mulholland, I don't know his first name.

FA: Right, I don't know, I don't know that other person who's on there, I have no idea who they are... The dude that I know, Joe... is a friend of mine, that's not his first name, I don't know who this guy is. He [Joe] is a painter, he's doing, he's doing paint work for me, painting... my house. That's a different guy, there's a million people with, that's a really common Irish last name.

More texts and calls from Fred to Andrew followed, all with Fred wanting the original letter Ed Jacobs had sent to the prosecutors in 2012. Augello shouldn't have been so worried about that letter. It was far longer than the supplement, but in no way pointed toward Fred or any other Pagans. In other conversations Fred would rehash reasons he couldn't have done the crime, and then they would switch to talking about football, or about Glick's divorce. Fred was also anxious about an upcoming meeting Glick told him he would be having with the FBI as well as his attorney the following Tuesday. There actually was no such meeting—Glick hoped it would be a catalyst for Fred to tell him other details, which he suggested would help him navigate the meeting. Glick assured Fred that he had his back; he wouldn't say anything incriminating to the Feds.

By the next morning, Monday, November 13, Fred called Glick again. That night, after Glick was done work, they met in the little town of Marmora, in a CVS parking lot.

They sat in Fred's van again, this time with the radio volume turned up high to the Rush Limbaugh Show. Fred remained adamant that no one could link him to April's murder.

FA: My DNA is not in the house.

AG: We had the talk, you know, that it's impossible...

FA: We are not part, part of that.

AG: Right.

FA: Because you didn't do it and I didn't do it. I'm not going to jail for murdering some woman I didn't murder.

AG: I, I understand that, but they're gonna, they're just gonna, as you said, they are going to make life hell for us, and make life hell for some people…

FA: That's my point. They can beat people and chain them down, but nobody can give them what they want, what they want, because none of them people did that.

FA: (after a moment) You didn't do it.

AG: I didn't do it, nope. Fuck that

FA: I didn't. I didn't do that.

AG: No.

FA: You know this thing doesn't exist.

AG: Right.

Glick explained to investigators that when Augello said "This thing doesn't exist," he cocked his fingers into a gun shape, to indicate the murder weapon.

Augello asked Glick to meet him on Wednesday, November 15, at the Wawa in Somers Point, before Glick headed to work. Augello again cranked the radio up really loud, and the listening device Scoppa had was cutting in and out. In the debrief with Scoppa, Glick said Augello wrote certain things down again. This time Augello had written that only three people knew everything that happened with regard to April Kauffman's murder: Augello, Joe Mulholland, and Glick.

That afternoon, working undercover, ACPO investigators Scoppa and Det. Jason Dorn followed Augello as he picked up a friend and then drove to the Borgata in Atlantic City. The friend was a member of The Pine Robbers, a Pagans support club. Inside The Borgata, the two met a man that the FBI had listed as a known member of La Cosa Nostra. The three met in the food court underneath the race and sports bar area of the casino.

The ACPO investigators, working with Borgata's security team, tapped the surveillance system and were able to zoom in on a piece of paper Augello held up and showed the two men. Though they couldn't read it, in this close-up view the paper looked strikingly similar to the letter from Ed Jacobs: the placement of the header, the length, the size of the blocks of text. Detectives believed Augello was trying to set up a hit on Kauffman. But the man he was meeting with from Philadelphia was not a made member of the Mafia. They speculated that Augello showed him the letter to back up his story, so it would be reported back to Philly Mafia members. Joey Merlino had formerly headed the Philadelphia mob and was currently on trial for a Medicare fraud scheme. His attorney was Ed Jacobs.

Augello thought the letter made Jacobs look like a rat, and he thought Merlino and his associates would agree.

Later that night Fred talked to his friend, who had set up the meeting at the Borgata. They talked about houses and construction, which sounded to the investigators listening in like a legitimate meeting.

"I felt that went well." Fred said, his friend replied, "Yeah it went *very* well." The authorities did flag one part of the conversation, which they thought might be related to developing plans around the letter:

> FA: ...I was like, uh, just talking about his interest in that situation, you know, don't help me out with anything if it's going to you know put you in a weird... you know what I'm saying...
>
> FRIEND: Yeah and, uh, he mentioned that he liked that, uh, that you did that ...
>
> FA: Cool.
>
> FRIEND: He goes, I like that. He is old school, you know, he goes, uh he goes, if he was you know, a younger guy, the way these guys are nowadays, he goes, they are all, you know, they don't know how to fucking do things...

It had been eighteen days now since Glick had flipped on his friend, but it seemed that Augello still had no idea. As they walked towards the Cheese Board in Linwood on Saturday, November 18 to have breakfast, the two of them shot the breeze. Augello spotted a couple, and commented that the woman was way out of the guy's league.

"What the fuck is that guy doing, right? See that girl with that dork?" Augello pointed to the couple.

"I see," Glick laughed. For a moment it sounded like the two were buddies again, not someone spying on a brother. Special Agent Garrabrant would be dining with the two men, or rather near them, at a separate table. He equipped Andrew with audio and video recorders and told him to bring a notebook—they needed to see what Fred was writing.

"Can we get eggs here?" Augello asked Glick. Glick realized the restaurant they'd picked might not be where Fred wanted to eat today. He had to figure something out so as not to divert from the plan.

"Yeah, I'm pretty sure they sell breakfast," Glick said. Fred asked what Glick was getting. Glick responded, "I don't know, let's see what they got."

"Is there a diner around here?" The two went back to the van and drove across the street, to Romanelli's. Special Agent Garrabrant and the team scrambled to follow the two over to the new location without Fred noticing. Garrabrant slid into a booth sitting parallel to Glick and Augello, but not close enough to hear them. Garrabrant had wanted Glick to focus this meeting on figuring out the money trail for the payment Augello had allegedly received for April's murder. Fred and Glick sat down.

Over a breakfast sandwich for Glick and an omelet with light American cheese and a tomato juice for Fred, Glick tried to prompt Fred to talk about how he knew Francis Mulholland, using the ruse of mentioning questions he said his lawyer was asking him.

AG: He asked me these four things and he said how confident... why did they come up with that guy? I said, we don't know this cat....He said, how did the Doc and Ed get these names together...

FA: Fantasy ...

Glick told Fred he knew Francis Mulholland was dead, because Zarych, his attorney, had googled his name and the police report was posted in the local newspaper down in The Villas area. Fred insisted he didn't know him.

Andrew would tell his handlers that during that morning's breakfast, they wrote on six different pieces of paper. Glick asked if "Irish"—Joe Mulholland—was a rat, and Fred wrote zero, meaning zero chance. Augello also used gestures as he had before, saying without "this" and "this"—amplified by the cocked-hand gesture for a gun, and a slashing motion across his neck—"the police have nothing." When the check came, Andrew picked up the papers they'd been writing on and said he would throw them away. But Augello took them out of Glick's hand and crumpled them up, then looked at the bill.

FA: Fantasy story. How much is it?

AG: I got it.

FA: You sure?

AG: Twenty bucks.

FA: I'll leave a tip.

Fred went to the bathroom while Andrew waited in the lobby, surrounded by people making orders for Thanksgiving pies. The investigators again went to try and retrieve Fred's notes in the trash, but they found nothing.

The next day, Sunday, November 19, Andrew Glick started a shitstorm that almost blew the entire surveillance operation, with a text message. At this point he still didn't have Augello on tape admitting he did the crime. Scoppa told Glick it was time to get Glenn Seeler to talk. Glick had already told investigators during his interrogation that Seeler had been approached by Fred to kill April. Andrew fired off a text.

AG: Yo, it's Andrew, this is my new number. Need to talk. Give me a call tonight after 6. Very important.

GS: Not going to lie should I even call?

Glick's text sparked a domino effect of escalating paranoia. Seeler texted Fred, and Fred called Seeler back. Andrew sent another text to Seeler, while Seeler was in mid-conversation about the drama with Fred.

AG: Why wouldn't you call me? Is someone telling you not to? Wouldn't call if it wasn't important and didn't have... impact [on] you.

Augello was pissed that Glick had reached out to Seeler; it seemed shady to him. In a fit of anger, he drove his gray van over to Glick's house and stormed up onto Glick's front lawn, where he was raking leaves. Augello demanded to know why Glick was calling Seeler. Glick explained: he had just wanted to update Seeler about all of the police questions over the pill operation and April Kauffman's murder. Augello looked at Glick.

"I trust you," he said, and got into his van and drove away. Again, he had chosen to believe Glick.

Glick talked to Seeler that night for an hour and forty-five minutes. But no one knows exactly what they talked about. Glick had failed to use an app investigators were relying on to record the calls. He blamed it on not being tech-savvy. Scoppa made him recap the conversation as well as he could. The ACPO needed Glick to do better: they informed him he would have to take a road trip to North Carolina, where Seeler had moved, and wear a wire in Seeler's house.

Chapter 20

KILLING KAUFFMAN

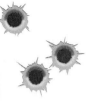

"How you doing, Chef man?" Most of Andrew Glick's co-workers had no idea what the executive chef was juggling as they greeted him at work on December 6, 2017.

"Hey, how ya doing?" he responded with a smile. It had now been a full month since Andrew agreed to be an informant and wear a wire. It was busy in the kitchen, the phone was ringing with orders, and there was a situation with the fruit assortment.

"We don't have any more of the cantaloupe," one of the servers said to Glick. He looked around.

"What do we have? Honeydew? Extra grapes? For fruit cups?"

"Yeah," the employee responded.

"Just put extra honeydew or pineapple," Andrew instructed. Since this was a retirement community, the dinner rush was more of an early bird hour, running between 3 and 5.

Glick still had to go over the budget for the kitchen, and orders for dinner were still coming in. He kept answering the phone, "Dietary, how can I help you?..." One of the residents with signs of dementia kept calling for the same order. Glick saw his room number pop up again.

"This guy is going to drive me crazy," he said to himself... but on the phone, he only showed patience. "Dietary how can I help you? Kitchen..." He listened to the same order for the third time, and just repeated it back: "...You got it, hot meal, ice cream, two large drinks..."

Playing double agent was starting to wear on Glick, mentally and physically. Glick had pink eye and a cold. Plus, his divorce was proving brutal, and his girlfriend had moved into his house with her two kids. Glick wasn't ready for that—he felt like she was moving too fast and too soon for him. Luckily for him, his arrest for drugs had taken care of that problem. His girlfriend's ex had called the New Jersey Department of Child Protection, and she had to move with her kids out of Glick's house after living there for just a few weeks. Glick was also carrying the torch for another ex-girlfriend, his "Russian." He reached out to her in the midst of his new life as an informant, but stopped short of telling her how his world was falling apart because of his own choices. On top of everything, Glick's beloved dog Bob was gravely ill.

Glick let out a big yawn as the phone calls slowed down. One of Glick's co-workers had become a confidant. She knew everything that Chef was dealing with, and it was good because tonight, Glick needed someone to listen. She asked him when he was leaving for North Carolina to see Seeler.

"So, are you going to leave tomorrow or tonight?" she asked. As usual, Glick tried to inject some humor.

"That's what they [FBI] want to do... at first I was driving down [by myself] and they were following me. Now the guy today tells me today, 'Oh, I'll be driving with you,' and I go, 'Oh... my dream come true, eight hours in the car with an FBI agent.' I said, 'I can cross it off on my bucket list.' He... just looked at me. I go, 'Yeah, that wasn't on your bucket list, to ride with a Pagan?' I was like, 'Imagine that, yo. I put it on the who woulda thunk it list.'"

Glick told his co-worker the plan. He would sleep on the way down, and they would head to the North Carolina FBI field office to pick up a car, about twenty minutes away from Glenn Seeler's house.

"Then," Andrew continued, "I'm going to go where the cat [Seeler] lives. I mean, he was a really good friend of mine."

Glick's confidant interjected, "...At one time." Glick started to think about back in 2011 and what Seeler had told him at that time.

"He kinda put the bug in my ear when it first happened and I was like, 'The guys gonna do what?' ...And I was like, 'What is "Slasher" [Seeler] telling me?' I was like, 'Sounds like a terrible idea.'" Glick recounted to his work friend how Seeler had first told him about the search for a hitman to kill April.

"I never thought at all it would ever be done... " Glick said, and then went quiet. His friend softly consoled him.

"...What can you do?" Glick said, almost reassuring himself. "...Yeah, yo yo... Geez ..."

The dinging text-message alert was going off on Glick's phone—Fred was waiting for him in the parking lot.

Glick walked to Augello's van and got inside. The radio was blaring.

FA: They are really screwing him. All this Trump shit is bullshit. The Feds are like doing all kinds of weird, weird shit.

AG: Well they called, they're interested...

Glick got right to business, shutting down Fred's tangent about what was going on with politics in Washington DC. Glick was talking about a fictitious middleman who was purportedly arranging the murder of Jim Kauffman in jail. Augello had met Glick at work to discuss it; Glick lied and said he would be meeting the middleman in person today.

A couple of hours later, Glick met Augello again, this time outside Augello's house. He reported that, following their meeting in the parking lot, he had met the middleman—in person, not on the phone—to arrange the details of killing Kauffman in jail.

> AG: They want the, uh, he said if it's easy with the food, he said five, but if they gotta do it the other way, then we gotta take care of it for five, and he gets his five. So it's either five if they can do it with the food...

In other words, his middleman was saying the fee would be $5,000 if they could put poison in Kauffman's food. If they had to do it any other way, say by stabbing or beating him to death, the fee would be $10,000.

Fred said he had no money. Glick responded, arguing that if Kauffman died it was good for his case too—good for both of them. And as far as paying for the hit, not to worry. Glick would take care of it.

By a week before Christmas, Glick was still meeting with Augello and talking about the fictitious hit. In the weeks since he began wearing the wire, Glick had also recorded conversations with several other people. They included Seeler and Joe Drinhouser, a former Pagan, talking on camera about how Fred had approached them to kill April Kauffman. Glick was singlehandedly building a case for The FBI and ACPO.

Each time Glick spoke with Augello, there was the potential for more information to spill. As time passed, investigators hoped Fred's guard would go down.

The morning of December 22, Augello and Glick walked outside Fred's house. Glick told him that Kauffman had been returned to The Atlantic County Jail, and that the doctor would be killed on Christmas. With that arrangement seemingly finalized, Glick pushed forward to talk to Augello about evidence that could tie them to Kauffman. He claimed that the middleman had asked him if there was anything he was concerned about from the meetings he had in Kauffman's office, and notes that Glick said he had passed from Augello to the doctor.

> FA: He has details from every meeting...
>
> AG: I thought I took every note, but I don't know, maybe he copied them when he took that fucking shit in the other room.
>
> FA: Here's my biggest concern, that he was wired or something, but he turned the radio up when I was in the car with him, and said my name in conversation, he said my name.

AG: Fuck. He's got something... he has some recordings... he's got some
       insurance policy, he does, fucking, I bet you he wired fucking up in
       the office too...
FA: In the office.

Then Fred brought up another matter: that Kauffman had paid Augello with
money he made from selling his Corvette.

FA: [My attorney] is worried about the car, if he ever tells him about the
       car, buying the car and they get the two people, you gotta sell the car,
       you know what I mean?
AG: Yup. Okay, well, I'm going to work. He said he's gonna be by like
       around one in the morning. So that's all I know, but he did say once
       you get that money, it's over. There's no contacting, there's no...
       ya know it's going down.

While the two men were talking, Glick speculated about their suspicions that
Kauffman could flip, maybe even go into witness protection. He compared
Kauffman's case to another notorious murder-for-hire in New Jersey. Rabbi Fred
Neulander was convicted of hiring a hitman to kill his wife, Carol Neulander. In
1994, she was bludgeoned to death in their Cherry Hill, NJ home. Paul Daniels
and Len Jenoff were paid $18,000 to carry it out. Daniels served fourteen years
and Jenoff served ten years. Neulander is in prison for thirty years to life. Glick
figured that law enforcement would be equally punitive toward Kauffman:

AG: You remember the Rabbi that hired the dude that killed his freaking
       wife, he was bragging, the dude that killed her....He gets busted, but
       then he wears a wire, goes to the Rabbi asking for more cash, and this
       is the guy that killed the lady and everything, ya know, he got five
       years, and the Rabbi got life, like forty, but the dude that got the
       money, and did the stuff... the Rabbi was a high-profile thing, that's
       why when you said maybe witness protection, that's just, no fucking
       way, that would be just fucking out of control.

Augello was worried about Andrew, and did not want him to be alone on
Christmas Eve. An animal lover himself, Augello knew Andrew was taking his
dog's final days hard, and he didn't want Andrew sitting in his big house by himself. Glick had already volunteered to work at the retirement home on Christmas
Day, figuring to give one of his colleagues the holiday off with their family, while
he could use the distraction.

On Christmas Eve, Andrew walked into a warm holiday welcome at Fred's house, bringing a bottle of Jack Daniels and wearing a vintage Eagles jacket. The jacket had belonged to Fred's father, and Fred had given it to him as a gift.

"Wow, holy cow, that's a lot of cookies!" Andrew proclaimed to Fred's girlfriend and their family as he walked into their house, looking at their decorated Christmas cookies and homemade gingerbread house.

Christmas movies were playing, and there was a huge food spread, including Fred's meatballs, along with fresh rolls he'd picked up from Atlantic City. Andrew made a plate and sat down with the family. Fred and Andrew started talking about football—star Eagles quarterback Carson Wentz had just gotten hurt, and Nick Foles, the backup, was going to play on Christmas Day when the Eagles were taking on the Oakland Raiders.

Christmas music filled the house, along with the sound of the kids playing and Fred's family laughing. Then Andrew and Fred's conversation turned back to killing Kauffman. Glick told Augello he'd given the middleman five grand for the job, he explained how he would be killed, "I gave him the [$5,000] already....They have a full syringe of fentanyl ready for him... they're going to shoot him up and OD, they're hoping that... I don't know whoever is getting in... a guard, nurse or whatever." Glick assured Fred the job was close to being done.

"I'd do it myself if I could, " Augello said to Glick. Glick responded, "I'd like to choke him to fucking death."

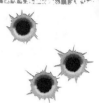

Chapter 21

WHO DAT

Fred Augello woke up to the sound of screams. His girlfriend jumped out of bed, and Fred tried to put on his jeans while running, tripping as he darted towards the sounds of his girlfriend's daughters' cries. It felt like the house was shaking. The Native American dreamcatcher hanging on the wall rattled over the couple's bed.

"What is that, who is that?" his girlfriend yelled.

"Wait!" Fred screamed to her, but she wouldn't listen, and followed her instinct to run towards her children.

The SWAT team smashed in the door. The family dog ran in circles barking as the officers threatened to shoot the dog. Fred raced down the stairs and saw green laser beams coming from the top of semi-automatic weapons, the lights bouncing off the walls. It looked like members of the military, armed and wearing camouflage, were filling the house. He could see the front door was hanging half off its hinges; the halogen lights they had set up outside streamed into the foyer.

Fred could hear the team yelling his name, saying that he was under arrest. It was around 5:30 am on January 9, 2018. Fred had never received a heads-up call from Glick, as they had discussed. Maybe they hit Fred's house first, he wondered.

The arrests he'd expected around Thanksgiving had finally come—it was happening now. It all went down in about a minute and a half. The whole family—Fred and his girlfriend, her teenage daughter, an older daughter, and her boyfriend—were handcuffed and brought outside into the ice and snow, barefoot and without winter coats. Fred's bare feet stuck to the ice on the back porch. The oldest daughter's boyfriend curled his toes trying to keep his bare feet warm.

Dozens of agents in plainclothes entered the house, then let the family back inside. They led Fred into the foyer, his hands behind his back. His usual ponytail was loose, his hair a mess, having been jolted out of bed. Fred had on a black Rock the Boat Music Festival T-shirt and jeans.

By this time it was 5:44 a.m. Garrabrant, neatly dressed as always, wore a shirt and tie and tan pants underneath a parka labeled "POLICE" on the back, and "Police" and "FBI" on the front. Scoppa stood next to him, wearing a black wool overcoat over his suit and tie. Neither man seemed to be dressed for a raid. It looked like they were dressed for court, or maybe a press conference.

Fred was disheveled and outnumbered. "So I got a lot of stuff in here, you guys going to steal all my shit?" he asked. "What's going on in here?" he continued. Garrabrant held a green hoodie that belonged to Fred in his hands. He was silent while Fred complained to him, his hands handcuffed in front. Garrabrant threw the hoodie over Fred's head, and with the help of another FBI agent, tugged it over Fred's shoulders and zipped it up, covering Fred's arms and cuffed hands.

"Well, the FBI is the government," Garrabrant replied calmly. "The budget is bad, but not so bad we have to take your stuff. Anything taken out of here, it will be documented before and after." Fred was scanning the room with his instruments, his most prized possessions,

"What, are you taking out a guitar amp?" Fred asked. Garrabrant answered, "We're not sure..."

A room next to the foyer held a lot of music equipment: amps, guitars, a sound system. A confederate flag hung on the wall, a kind of tribute to Lynyrd Skynyrd, the Southern Rock band that Freddy covered, among others, when playing his gigs. Another room was full of workout equipment. Fred acted bewildered, frustrated, and increasingly antsy as the FBI and ACPO took total control of the home he shared with his girlfriend's family.

"Don't you want to know where my legal guns are?" Fred said to Garrabrant. "Sure, you can tell us that," Garrabrant replied, walking into the other room. Fred shouted to Garrabrant, "Get me a drink of water."

The FBI agent came back with a coffee cup full of water. Fred looked at him incredulously.

"It's all I can do, bro, unless you have a straw someplace." Garrabrant held out the cup. Fred leaned his head into the cup and you could hear him trying to suck up the water but it wasn't working. Garrabrant said, "Why don't you lean your head back....Put your head up. I got kids, I've done this before....Once we get back to the office, I'll give you a bottle of water."

Fred said nothing. When he was done, he just gave a fatalistic nod. Whether Garrabrant was being compassionate or pulling a power move, he'd succeeded in making Fred feel smaller than he must have already felt.

Garrabrant took Fred up on his offer to show them his legal guns. Fred, still handcuffed, took the agent and several others upstairs into his bedroom, where he kept the keys to his gun safe stored in a bag decorated with a Native American dreamcatcher, leaning against the wall.

"That's my black powder gun," Fred said, pointing out the difference between his real guns and the ones he used for his reenactments. Fred frequently took part in Civil War reenactments as well as Native American reenactments, and he was still worried about the G-men, as he called them, taking his stuff.

Garrabrant laid the situation out to Fred: "We're the FBI. We have a forensic team of fifteen people coming in here. They will photograph the entire house, they will document every single item we remove from the house. You will get a copy of that as well as the affidavit....No one is going to take anything you don't know about. Anything we take of any value, a piece of paper or a weapon, you'll have an itemized list of everything..."

Fred overheard a female agent say, "We're going to bring in the dog."

"There's not any drugs in here," Fred replied, exasperated.

"That's my question," the agent said to him, "Are there any drugs in here?" Fred was adamant.

"Nooo—why? What are you looking for?" Fred yelled. "There's nothing in here illegal."

Garrabrant explained to Fred that the narcotics dog was a precaution. "We run a dog because that way, when people are searching and they come across a suspicious item, and the dog hits on it, we know it's not drugs. With the Fentanyl and everything else today, we are concerned about people searching that could come across [drugs]."

Fred was shocked, "Fentanyl!?". He and Garrabrant went back and forth. "Fentanyl, methamphetamine, anything," the agent explained.

"I don't have any drugs," Fred protested. The agent answered, "I'm not saying you do."

Before they headed back downstairs to leave for The FBI office, Fred needed his dentures. After some awkward back-and-forth between Fred, Scoppa, and the other agents, Fred managed to pop his dentures in, even with his hands in cuffs. He gave Scoppa a smirk.

Back downstairs, Fred started to get upset. Concerned about his girlfriend and her daughters, he confronted Garrabrant.

"Come on, why are you doing this to these women for? And you bring these *mulignan* in my house..."

Garrabrant quickly replied, "Don't be disrespectful."

"What do you mean disrespectful?" Fred asked. *Mulignan*, Sicilian dialect for eggplant, is used by some Italian-Americans as a racist reference to a black person.

Garrabrant switched the focus back to Fred's concern for his family.

"They are uncuffed, with the dog, and we're not taking anything apart."

Fred's shock at what had happened started giving way to anger.

"You could've called me and said, Come on down to the FBI," he said. "This is a shock value thing....My lawyer is on his way here. Why don't we sit and wait for him?"

Garrabrant wasn't fazed. "Tell [the lawyer] to come to [the Northfield FBI office]. It'll be faster for him."

"Who contacted him?" Scoppa snapped. Fred answered, "Me. I called him when you guys were bashing the door down....Why wouldn't I do that?"

* * *

Augello's arrest was only one of several arrests orchestrated simultaneously by the FBI on the morning of January 9, 2018. The first arrest that morning was carried out at 5:40 a.m. in Summerland Key, Florida, where authorities apprehended Beverly Augello. In North Carolina they picked up Glenn Seeler, and they arrested Seeler's wife Cheryl Pizza in South Carolina. In New Jersey, they hit Upper Township, for Fred Augello; Villas for Joseph Mulholland; Absecon for Tabitha Chapman; and Egg Harbor Township for Paul Pagano.

The FBI and ACPO fanned out across the area—today was their Super Bowl. Three hundred members of law enforcement took part in the arrests that day. Garrabrant and the prosecutor's office had begun preparing for the arrests several weeks before, quietly getting search and arrest warrants signed by Judge DeLury. Each FBI agent and ACPO investigator was hand-picked to match each suspect's personality. Garrabrant and Scoppa knew they were the ones who needed to be with Augello. Garrabrant's skill set as a behavioral analyst with the bureau prepared him for Fred, who he deemed narcissistic and manipulative. In fact, Garrabrant looked at Jim Kauffman and Fred Augello has two men whose personalities were strikingly similar; they fed constant lines of bullshit and did not take responsibility for anything. But there was still a lot of work to be done; the next step began in interview rooms at various locations.

Fred Augello, sitting inside the Northfield FBI Office, was the one authorities wanted to talk to most of all. His attorney, Shaun Byrne, arrived. Fred wasn't talking.

In the other room, Joseph Mulholland was at least talking with Garrabrant and Scoppa, but his statement was all over the place, starting with claims of innocence.

"I don't... murder? Come on, man. I have fucking sisters. I have a mother. No way."

Then he began to admit he knew something, but quickly clammed up, "You can lock me up for a hundred years, but I'm not talking... nope, nope."

And then he moved on to denial: "I'm being charged with something that, that I didn't do, and I ain't involved in... I don't really give a fuck."

Garrabrant did not roll over. "Well, Joe, let me explain to you why you should give a fuck, okay?" He brought up Mulholland's Achilles heel—his history of addiction to pills and booze. Mulholland was sober now, but back in 2011-2012 he'd been struggling to stay sober and trying to help Francis stay sober too.

DG: It is what it is. Just real quick, and I just want to come down in here before anything else happens. I want you to assume, and I believe that you're telling the whole truth, but I want you to assume that Fred's gonna talk to us and try to help himself out. So I just want to make sure that if you withheld anything of the story that you tell us now, in case Fred tells us something different, okay? So I believe what you're saying."

JM: Uh-huh.

DG: But I just want to tell you that, uh, I'll tell you Fred's here... and his attorney's here as well. So they're talking if they decide to talk. I just want to make sure that your story is gonna jive with his.

JM: Uh-huh.

DG: This is your opportunity. When we walk out...

Garrabrant's statement hung in the air with an unspoken threat. This was Mulholland's last chance, and he seemed to have taken in what Garrabrant had said. When they brought him out into the hallway, handcuffed, preparing to check him into the Atlantic County Jail, Mulholland had a change of heart. He returned to the interrogation room; this time, in addition to Garrabrant and Scoppa, ACPO's Detective Joseph Rauch joined them.

Rauch, like Mulholland, had grown up in South Philadelphia, he turned this connection into a crucial point of trust. Joseph Mulholland had come up in the Grays Ferry section of Southwest Philadelphia, and hung out on "Two Street"— the locals' nickname for South Second Street. It's also where the Mummer's clubhouses are. On New Year's Day, the day of the Mummers Parade, Two Street fills with informal Mummer revelries. Mulholland had been a mummer, marching with the Second Street Shooters and The South Philly String Band.

Unlike Garrabrant, who grew up in North Jersey, and Scoppa, who is a native of Atlantic County, Rauch had grown up at Second and Jackson in South Philadelphia. As soon as he mentioned that, Mulholland felt at ease. In fact, he reached across the table and shook Rauch's hand.

That morning, Mulholland told Rauch that Fred had first approached him, proposing that he kill April Kauffman for $10,000. But soon after that, Dr. Kauffman had spoken with Mulholland himself, right in the doctor's office. The doctor, Mulholland said, offered him $100,000 for the same job.

JR: Tell me the first time that the doctor asked you to kill his wife.

JM: He said to me, you can make a lot more money than what I'm gonna pay him.

JR: Talking about what?

JM: About Fred.

JR: And what does he say about that.

JM: If you find somebody to do it, or you do it, I'll pay you... I'll pay you a hundred thousand dollars.

JR: He told you he would pay you a hundred thousand dollars.

JM: Yup, yup.

JR: And what does he say—to kill my wife, or what does he say?

JM: To kill my wife.

JR: What does he tell you [about] how you guys could do it—explain to you how it could be done?

JM: He said, The door's open all the time in my home. Just walk in and do it. Walk in and walk out.

Mulholland told Rauch he had turned down both Fred and the doctor. But when Fred asked again, he introduced Fred to Francis Mulholland. Francis, Joseph explained to the detectives, was his friend, but because of their last names they jokingly called each other "Cuz," or cousins. The doctor wanted the job done, Fred told Joseph Mulholland, because April was spending the doctor's money on purpose, to bankrupt him; and in addition, she was cheating on him. Fred also told Mulholland that April was planning to tell investigators what she suspected of the pill operation the doctor had going with the Pagans. Not only would this bring that lucrative arrangement to an end; they could get arrested and locked up.

JM: He explained it to me what she did, what she was doing to the doctor, and this, that, and the other. I told him, Listen, I don't do that. I'll fucking steal, I'll do whatever, I said, but I ain't...

JR: Okay. Did [Augello] ever say, like... did he ever say that, Hey listen, this how we were gonna do it, or how it should be done, and how the Doc wants it done? Was there a time frame set [on] any of that information?

JM: Well, the Doc—the doctor was actually pushing this, really pushing this.

JR: Uh-huh.

JM: And [Fred] said, Yo, you got to find me somebody then. Can you find me somebody, blah blah blah blah blah, and I introduced him to Fran.

JR: How did you come to decide on Fran?

JM: Well, he said to me, the one day he said, Man, I'm really fucking
     hurting for money, dah dah dah dah dah, and I said, Well, I could
     hook you up with this guy, maybe you can sell some pills for him.

JR: Okay.

JM: And then I introduced them two, and then I hear that he's gonna
     do this fucking hit.

JR: How do you hear that?

JM: He told me.

JR: Francis told you.

JM: Fran told me, yeah. He goes, Yo, I'm gonna make a ton of money
     doing this. I'm like, Don't get involved with them guys, I'm telling
     you.

JR: What exactly, what exactly did Francis tell you about that?

JM: He said that [he] was gonna shoot the doctor's wife.

Mulholland told the investigators that he'd received a phone call from Francis
to pick him up after the hit. But he didn't see the gun, didn't know where Francis
had gotten it, and he didn't know who had driven Francis to the Kauffmans'
house. Joseph also admitted to being part of the pill scheme and giving half of
every prescription to Fred. However, Joseph Mulholland wasn't telling the whole
truth. He lied when he told investigators he had only picked up Francis that morning because his friend said he needed a lift from the Courthouse Diner, and that
he had no idea Francis had just pulled off the hit until Francis told Joseph when
he got to the diner. Joseph also denied knowing anything about the gun, or how
much Francis got paid. Joseph did report that later, Fred had tried to give him five
grand, but he didn't take it.

Scoppa emphasized that they needed the whole truth.

"It's not making you any more guilty of anything," Scoppa urged. Mulholland
lied, "I'm telling you everything. Why would I fucking hold that back?"

Joseph said that after the hit he distanced himself from Fred, especially after
he had entered rehab. They weren't completely out of touch, and would talk every
few months. Joe would even stop by Fred's shop. But recently, in the past two
months, Fred had been calling him several times a week. Fred would ask him to
help find someone to "take care of" the doctor in jail, which Joseph took to mean
beating the doctor up. He'd blown it off. The investigators asked about the ax
handle found in Francis's house, with "Mulholland" and "ICEMAN" written on
either side. Joseph claimed he'd never seen it, but that Francis's brother's nickname was Iceman.

Joseph's role in April's murder was in fact much bigger than he admitted to
that day. Having protected himself as much as possible, he did his best to leave the
investigators with the worst possible impression of Fred Augello.

"He's evil," Mulholland said. "He's an evil motherfucker..."

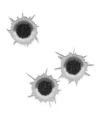

Chapter 22

ROUND-UP

In North Carolina, ACPO Detective Jason Dorn and Special Agent Dean DiPietro from Atlantic City's FBI field office worked on getting Glenn Seeler to talk. Seeler walked in cautious, but friendly, throwing out a defensive screen of dumb jokes and chumminess. He told a sob story about his bike accident and how the hospital hadn't done an MRI, which would most likely have saved his leg, and how he'd been paralyzed for a period of time. Going on about how his medical problems had snowballed, he pulled up his pant leg to show how the leg had shrunk due to muscle atrophy.

As detectives tried to get him to admit to buying and selling pills, Seeler became evasive and difficult. But the biker wasn't as smart as he thought.

JD: Do you know anyone else in the club that was going to see the Doc?

GS: I think there was like a couple...

JD: I don't want to make this like...

GS: A cat and mouse game?

JD: Extracting a tooth here...

GS: Sometimes you have to with me.

JD: I'll ask you specifically, can you just expand on your answers a little bit...

GS: Relevance?

JD: The charge against the Doc.

GS: I know you guys obviously want this scumbag bad... (throaty laugh)

JD: Well, it's a distribution conspiracy [in] addition to some other things, and we're just trying to establish... Well, we've already established, we're just trying to corroborate... the fact that, yes, these other individuals did know this person. That yes, they were being prescribed pills, it's not known from other sources. So, I just ask for honesty from you, and then in return you get the same.

GS: Honesty and favors! Those cigarettes were great, bro!

JD: You would go to his office to get the scripts and stuff like that?

GS: ...I mean, the doctor did save my life, guys....

JD: I understand... He also took one.

Seeler's chummy act was wearing thin on Dorn. He pulled out Fred's picture, put it on the table before Seeler.

JD: So, tell us about Mr. Miserable [Fred Augello]. Other than from the picture, it looks like an appropriate nickname.

GS: Yeah, he was a miserable fuck. I'll give him that. Ya know, when he was in charge he ruled with an iron fist. Nobody, ya know... when Chef [Andrew Glick] was in charge he did things right; talked to us, listened...

JD: Keep in mind...

Seeler put down his pen and cradled his head in his left hand.

JD: ...We know the answers to these questions.

Seeler still didn't look up, seeming deep in thought, as if weighing what he was about to say.

DD: Here's where it's time to step up.

GS: Here's where [blowing out air] ...like I said, I want to be honest with you guys... I don't want to do any time for not doing anything ... I mean it's not right...

Dorn and DiPietro went back and forth with Seeler, telling him they could not make any promises about what prosecutors would do, but urging him to tell the truth. They asked questions about what role Fred had in the pill scheme, and how Seeler got involved. The investigators told Seeler they felt he was not the "main guy," and they indicated that other people were talking. Seeler seemed to loosen up.

JD: When did he approach you? and I'm not talking about the pills. You know damn well what I'm talking about, when did he come to you? Because we know... when was the first time you were approached? Because that's why you're sitting here....

DiPietro had left to get Seeler some water, and came back into the room just as the tension was spiking. Seeler twisted his face nervously, moved uncomfortably in his chair, pulled up the sleeves of his sweatshirt. He made a wide swipe across the table with one hand, then looked up and stared at both investigators.

GS: You must be talking about the shooting?

JD: Yes, I am. When were you first approached?

Dorn, done with Seeler's evasiveness and long pauses, shifted his posture, leaning back in his chair. Seeler sighed heavily and looked down.

GS: There's gotta be some kind of deal made... (nervous laugh)

JD: I... I will tell you this, that is going to be what pretty much locks it in for you as far as whatever consideration is being given to you... I don't have the authority to do that right now.

GS: Who does?

JD: The Prosecutor. You want me to get him on the phone? I'll get him on right now.

The three left for a cigarette. When they returned, Seeler opened up:

JD: What did [Fred] say about the scheme? Tell me as much as you can remember...

GS: Swear to God, you guys better help me.

JD: You're helping yourself.

GS: That was the scheme. It was easy. It was, I'll pay you this, he leaves the door unlocked, he leaves at 6 a.m. every day. All you have to do is walk in, go up the steps, do it, and walk out...

JD: Was there an exit plan, a strategy? How do you get out of there?

GS: Beats the hell out of me... maybe you just go through the back door?

JD: Is there somebody to be a driver, a getaway driver or... was he going to supply you with a gun? Did he get into any of that?

GS: (raising his hands, shaking his head) "Who knows? Like I said, I know certain info, but as far as getting a [gun], this or that, and everything else..."

Seeler ended up getting extradited to New Jersey. Dorn wouldn't answer Seeler's questions about his best friend, Glick. In the interview, Seeler had sung Glick's praises. "He was my president for a while, good man, great man—absolutely great man, I couldn't think any higher of anybody, seriously." When Dorn asked if Seeler considered him a friend, Seeler went a step further. "I consider him family. He's just an amazing man, he'll help you out, he's so smart and he's such a great guy... he really is. I can't speak highly enough about him, he is a true brother."

That "true brother" was far away from Atlantic County on January 9, the day Seeler and the others were arrested. The night before, Glick had bolted to Maryland and stayed at a La Quinta Inn, eating his meals at Cracker Barrel and holing up in his motel room. Still cautious with his money even though the ACPO was paying for Glick to stay in a motel for his safety, he made sure to use his AAA discount, paying $79 a night. Glick could only stand the isolation for two weeks.

The ACPO wanted him to get even farther away. Instead, he went to his sister's house in Delaware. Glick lost his job at the nursing home and began collecting unemployment. He paid $20,000 to buy back the Chevy Silverado seized during his drug arrest, but then found himself in a real financial pinch. Over the next several months, the FBI and ACPO would pay Glick a total of $7,000 to help cover his living expenses including the mortgages and homeowner association fees for his New Gretna, New Jersey rental property and the Egg Harbor Township house, both of which he'd purchased with the proceeds from his drug dealing.

In the days before January 9, Glick distanced himself from Fred.

"You still among the living?" Fred asked when Andrew called him back on January 8, after Fred had left several voicemails. The last time they'd talked at length was on New Year's Day. Fred had consoled Glick over the death of Bob, Glick's beloved Samoyed. Fred expressed concerned not only for Glick, but for how his old friend's other dog, Rocky. was holding up.

FA: All right, well, you're doing good, I just called to see how you were making out.

AG: I appreciate it. I was hoping he would pull through or something, but he just got sicker and sicker.

FA: Rocky, Rocky, yeah. How's he doing?

AG: He's alright, he's wandering around looking, like where he at?

FA: Yeah, my dog did that for a long time, it was just him, it was like a year, he'd go out and sit waiting for the other dog.

AG: Right. He like, walked around the yard sniffing for his scent and stuff, ya know? Rocky is 9 months older, so you know, Bob was with him the whole time.

FA: Right, just like when we had Delia, she was here first and then he came, so he never knew anything without her.

AG: Exactly. Yup, yeah, it sucks, but…

FA: You did the right thing.

AG: I know.

FA: You can't have the animal in pain.

With Andrew on the lam under police supervision, Fred, Joseph Mulholland, and Paul Pagano were locked up in Atlantic County Jail. Seeler was on his way, awaiting extradition from North Carolina. Beverly Augello and Cheryl Pizza were also waiting to be extradited, from Florida and South Carolina respectively. All faced racketeering charges. Fred's racketeering charges were more serious, and he also faced murder charges for April's murder, and attempted murder charges, for allegedly attempting to kill Jim Kauffman in Atlantic County Jail. Like Fred, Jim Kauffman faced murder and racketeering charges too, although he was no longer at The Atlantic County Jail.

Fred didn't know what Joseph Mulholland had told police. But Joseph told authorities that he feared for his life, now that he was in the same jail with Fred. Fred, Joseph said, had made a slitting-throat gesture when the two men saw each other in jail in the days after January 9th. Investigators had already made their arrests, but they were still building their case; Joe Mulholland's latest statement strengthened it.

On January 9, investigators had also gone to Stephen "Little Stevie" "Billboard" Wittenwiler's house. But they made clear they were not arresting him. Investigators instead asked him if he would voluntarily come to headquarters; they even said he could drive himself.

"Has anyone ever talked to you or brought up the murder of Dr. Kauffman's wife?" Garrabrant asked after putting Wittenwiler in an interview room.

"NO!" the 37-year-old, overweight former Pagan yelled. Wittenwiler shouted back. Garrabrant kept going: "Has anyone ever discussed it with you?"

"ABSOLUTELY NOT, ABSOLUTELY NOT!" Wittenwiler shot back even louder, his goateed face reddening. Garrabrant asked again, "So if you were on tape, if you were on tape talking about it... would that be a problem?"

"Yeah, that would be a major problem," Wittenwiler answered. Glick had actually gone to Wittenwiler's house wearing the wire, but Wittenwiler had wanted little to do with him and spoke evasively. However, several other people had mentioned Wittenwiler's name to authorities as someone who was floated the job to kill April. The investigators laid out a group of pictures, as they did with everyone else that morning, including the images of the seven people charged. Wittenwiler looked at them and didn't say much at first, except that he hated Glenn Seeler's guts, and Fred had been the best man in his wedding.

"I'm not a rat," he said. "I'm not just going to give up a name, I really honestly don't know what happened to that man's wife..." Later he added, "I'm not testifying against anyone."

"I'm not asking you to testify," Garrabrant explained. "...I have no intention of arresting you today, I have the intention of you being a witness. I honestly mean what I say, I'm not lying to you. I'm telling you right now if you continue to go down this path, then I may decide that you're part of the problem."

"I'm not part of the problem," Wittenwiler told the agent. "I didn't even do anything..."

"But Steven, I didn't say you—you're not the shooter," Garrabrant responded. "We know that, we understand that... What I want is what you know and when you knew. We know you knew about the job. We also know you didn't do it. That's why we're talking to you as a witness. "

The two men went around and around:

SW: I was never asked to do it.
DG: How did you know about it, then?
SW: Huh?
DG: How did you know about it then?
SW: What do you mean?
DG: How did you know about the doctor wanting this to happen?
SW: Stab who?
DG: No, I didn't say stab, I said, how did you know about the doctor wanting this to happen?
SW: You're confusing me with these questions.
DG: Okay, so this doctor.
SW: Okay, Dr. Kauffman.
DG: Wanted to have something done with his wife. How did you know about that?
SW: People talking, you walk by and hear people saying stuff...
DG: Yeah but this isn't like Wawa conversation...

Wittenwiler eventually let some things slip. Since he had been kicked out of the club years before due to his addiction to heroin, which had been banned by the club, he hadn't been let in on this prescription ring.

"I knew this was eventually going to happen," Wittenwiler said to Garrabrant, referring to the drug ring imploding. The Special Agent asked, "Was it crossing a line?" Wittenwiler got colorful in his response: "No, it's fucking stupid, you don't think it's fucking stupid? ...I mean, don't you think... this whole scheme was retarded, and the bubble wasn't going to eventually pop?"

Wittenwiler wasn't arrested that day, although he didn't give investigators everything they wanted. When they parted ways, Garrabrant said, "I think you have been 75% honest, and I think you know more than you want to tell us, because that will make you more than a witness, um, and I understand."

"I think you're right," Wittenwiler responded on his way out the door.

Two days after the arrests police found Joe Drinhouser, already locked up for another crime, and sat him down to talk to him about what he'd said to Andrew Glick while Glick was wearing a wire. On November 24, Drinhouser happened to stop by Glick's property as authorities were outfitting his shed with recording equipment. Glick took the opportunity to try and get Drinhouser to talk about how Fred had approached him. Glick and Drinhouser had talked, but had also traded a notebook back and forth; the notes were never found by authorities. They wanted Drinhouser to tell them what he said to Andrew that day.

When investigators sat Drinhouser down he was already in orange, head to toe. He was locked up on eight felony charges in completely separate cases, for possession of a weapon, two aggravated assaults, and not being permitted to have a weapon. His detention hearing, set for that Friday, would determine if he could be released until his trial. Special Agent Garrabrant wanted to get Drinhouser to spill on his claim to Glick that Fred had approached him about the hit.

JD: You got to take care of my family.
DG: Yes, absolutely.
JD: You gonna take care of my family.
DG: Absolutely, Joe, look at me. There's a very good chance that you're gonna be home within a week.

Garrabrant and Scoppa wanted to know about other "jobs" Fred had approached Drinhouser about, some on behalf of a successful local contractor. Drinhouser admitted that Fred had ordered him and Glenn Seeler to rough up a guy in Ventnor. He didn't know why, he just followed orders. They had driven to Ventnor in Seeler's Mustang to punch a guy in the face. Then Garrabrant and Scoppa began asking about more crimes.

DG: How about the fire off the parkway?
JS: Up in Ocean County.
JD: My God (unintelligible), I want my lawyer!
JS: That's fine Joe, and then we'll—
JD: I, I wanna help!!

Scared and worked up now, Drinhouser lost it. Scoppa and Garrabrant kept him talking and got him to come to their side. To date, authorities have never expanded on the matter of the fire on the turnpike, but it was apparently serious enough to make Drinhouser fold.

DG: You're not a big fish in this Joe. You're not the big ringleader, you're not the guy we, we want. But you're a piece of the puzzle, Joe, you understand? We understand things happen and crimes were committed, and although I can't make any promises to you, and I make no promises to you now, um, you're essentially uh—Would you rather be in here under arrest, and we never want to talk to you about this case because we don't care, or do you, would you rather be on the side with the Prosecutor's Office and...

JD: I, you know what I want to be? Umm, I want to be in a position where my wife and my children are going to be safe.

Drinhouser opened up at that point. A year before April's murder, he told them, Fred had driven him to the Kauffman house and said he had a job for him—to kill the doctor's wife. Fred didn't tell him a name, but Drinhouser said Fred had offered to pay him $10,000 for the job. The door would be open, and he would just go in and take care of the wife. It was a big house with orange garage doors. After Drinhouser offered all this, Garrabrant and Scoppa warned him not to talk to anyone, especially any other Pagans. With so many Pagans in jail with him, it would put his safety in jeopardy.

DG: Okay, so, so Joe, here's the thing. What's the most important thing? You are not going to talk about this thing to other people, only your attorney, right?

JD: I'm not gonna talk to anyone. Come on, guys.

DG: I'm just saying.

JS: Don't talk to Fred about this, don't talk to Glenn. Glenn's gonna be in county jail soon, as he's getting shipped up from North Carolina.

DG: Fred's over there, okay?

DG: And if any prison guards come to you and start passing messages, you just keep that to yourself and pretend like you are on Team Pagan, and don't say a word to anybody, okay? You understand me?

JD: You guys actually care about people like me?

DG: Absolutely, why wouldn't we care about you, Joe?

JS: Because you're not, you're not, the ringleader?

DG: [You've been] a gentleman to us. If you were in here telling me fuck you, I'll kick your ass, then I'd be like, Go fuck you too. But you've been a gentleman, there's no reason not to care about you, Joe.

JD: Because I think Hillary belongs in jail

DG: Well that's fine, that's your opinion.

JS: Who likes Hillary?

They all laughed.

The arrests on January 9 spurred more people to come forward, some with credible information, others not. One interesting call came to the ACPO from a confidential source. It concerned a man they had investigated in 2017, whose name had been included in the warrant on the Harry Johnson phone number. The warrant stated Jim Kauffman had called this individual the day *before* the Harry Johnson phone number got set up. The informant told investigators that the man in question was a Pagan associate; he had bragged that he and Augello were responsible for the murders of April Kauffman; he also claimed that he and Francis Mulholland (then still alive) had the murder weapon.

Detective Jim Scoppa asked the informant if they would wear a wire, or whether they could urge a mutual friend to wear one. In 2017, Scoppa interviewed the Pagan associate. The individual then had a pending criminal case and was facing a prison sentence. He denied any involvement with the murder, and any affiliation with the Pagans, and investigators had not pursued it any further.

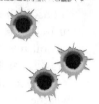

Chapter 23

BONFIRE OF THE VANITIES

"You might as well take me out to the lawn and shoot me, this is just ridiculous."

Dr. James Kauffman sat with his hands handcuffed together and attached to a wide brown belt around his waist. A group of mugshots were spread out on a table in front of him next to charging papers. He sat inside one of the interview rooms under the gaze of a camera, inside the Northfield FBI Office, a nondescript space with bare walls and fresh wall-to-wall carpet. Special Agent Daniel Garrabrant sat next to him. The ACPO's First Assistant Prosecutor Seth Levy also sat at the table.

Kauffman was another person hauled in for questioning on January 9, 2018, although he'd come from a prison cell. It was 1:34 p.m. Levy began reading the list of new charges the doctor faced, as Kauffman listened with a look of shock.

"The first thing I want to tell you," Levy began. "You are being charged with a racketeering..."

"What!" Kauffman exclaimed. His head shot back as if he'd been hit.

"With you as a member," Levy corrected himself, "not as a member but with members of the Pagan motorcycle gang..."

"Jesus," Kauffman said under his breath, rolling his eyes. Levy continued, "...including a number of people: Fred Augello..."

"Who?" the doctor asked, his face quizzical.

Kauffman had lost weight in jail and his orange jumpsuit was so large, it hung on his small frame. His red hair was now white and closely cropped, his ever-present tan had faded. Two sets of reading glasses hung from the V-neck collar of his prison-issued uniform. He denied knowing any of the people in the pictures displayed in front of him.

Kauffman was unaware that just six hours before, Fred Augello had sat in the very same chair after federal and local authorities raided his home and hauled him out in handcuffs. Investigators officially charged 68-year-old Kauffman and

61-year-old Fred Augello with murder in connection with the death of April Kauffman. Additionally, they charged them with racketeering related to the illegal distribution of narcotics through Kauffman's medical practice. Augello was also charged with conspiracy to commit the murder of James Kauffman. The names and faces on the table in front of Kauffman included Joseph Mulholland, 52; Beverly Augello, 47; and Glenn Seeler, 37, all charged with first- degree racketeering. Additionally, Paul Pagano, 61; Tabitha Chapman, 35; Cheryl Pizza, 36, were charged with second-degree racketeering. The racketeering charges rose out of the oxycontin drug distribution ring. The suspected hired hitman, Francis Mulholland, was not charged because he had died of a drug overdose a short time after the murder, but he was named by authorities as the actual killer.

"...We don't want you to say anything, without..." Levy tried to remind Kauffman not to say anything without the presence of his lawyer, but Kauffman couldn't help himself.

"I'm just... my wife gets killed, and they blame me six years later, and I don't get it, man... and I... just whoever this Fred Aug—" Kauffman leaned over the table, waving his head dramatically left and right, scanning the mugshots.

"Who's that?" he continued. "He's not on here..." Garrabrant moved a bottle of water obscuring Augello's printed-out mugshot. Kauffman looked down at the photo.

"Oh. Okay," he said.

Kauffman knew Garrabrant from his arrest in June, and he knew Levy from having watched him spar with his attorneys in the courtroom over the past few months.

Even in the interview room, Levy looked ready for court, in a perfectly tailored blue double-breasted suit. His dark tie had a tight precise knot; a handkerchief peeked out of his front pocket. Garrabrant wore the same outfit he'd had on during that morning's raid: dark slacks and a light sports coat; a lanyard with his ID hung around his neck. After notifying Kauffman of his charges, they had one more thing to tell him. He had to be moved from Atlantic County to Hudson County, New Jersey because there was a threat against his life. Levy broke the news to him.

"We find it to be credible, um, and we have knowledge that some of the people that you are charged with racketeering...," Levy's words drifted off as if he was waiting for a response from Kauffman. "...You are charged as part of the Pagan outlaw motorcycle criminal organization. They have ties to South Jersey, and we're moving you to North Jersey because they don't have a strong presence up there."

Kauffman deadpanned, "It's funny, because I have all my teeth and no tattoos."

"We are not saying you are a Pagan," Garrabrant said. "We're saying your connection to them puts you in danger down here." Levy once again brought up the man Kauffman claimed he didn't know.

"Augello was specifically the one who made the threat." Kauffman let out a heavy sigh. In total, it took about twenty minutes to explain the charges and what would happen next. Before he was transferred, Kauffman lamented to both men, comparing his situation to a 1987 Tom Wolfe novel about ambition, racism, social class, politics, and greed in the 1980s.

"This is surreal; I mean I feel like this is the Bonfire of the Vanities." In response to the Doctor's strange analogy, Levy blurted, "In that case, the guy was guilty... Don't answer that."

That morning when police had come to private cell 2F to pick up Jim at the Atlantic County Correctional Facility, he didn't understand why the guards told him to take his belongings, which all fit into one large white trash bag.

"No one tells me anything, " he had complained to the Police officer. The officer who began shackling Jim up for transport didn't have to ask him to face away from and hold his arms away from his hips—by now Jim knew how to wait for someone to buckle the waist belt and fasten the handcuffs. He'd been in jail now eight months.

"Are you from Linwood Police?" Jim asked. The officer shackling him was wearing a bulletproof police vest over a jacket and hoodie.

"I'm from the Prosecutors office," he responded. Patrolman Jarred Levenson spoke up, saying "I'm from Linwood."

Jim's orange shirt, pant combo had cuffed his too-long orange pants, and he wore Adidas slide flip-flops over his sock-covered feet. The belt around his waist connecting to his handcuffs hung low on his whittled-down frame, below his waist and hitting his rear end in the back. He thanked the Linwood Officer for helping Kauffman into the back seat of the police car. Then the same officer struggled with the trash bag containing Jim's worldly possessions, carefully making room for it in the trunk. Jim didn't realize that it was moving day for him—he wouldn't see The Atlantic County Jail again.

The two officers were tasked with taking Jim first to the FBI office to meet with Garrabrant and Levy, and then to be processed on the new charges at the Linwood Police Department. He had tried to make conversation with the Linwood cop while he waited in the FBI room, but the officer respectfully declined to speak with him, until they were leaving the FBI office.

"You understand everything going on?" the cop asked.

"Unfortunately, yes. Are there any news media out there?" Kauffman responded. The ACPO officer assured him they were entering and exiting through a back entrance, that the FBI building was unmarked, and there was no media outside. The three waited for the elevator,

"Now are you allowed to answer anything?" Kauffman looked at Patrolman Levenson.

"Depends on what you ask," Levenson responded.

"Did you go to Mainland [High School]?" Kauffman asked.

"No sir," the officer responded.

"So you're not related to the Levenson..." Jim had read the name on his name tag. The doors of the elevator opened and Sgt. Jim Scoppa walked out.

"No sir," the officer replied to Jim's question. Scoppa, exiting the elevator, realized the man in orange was Jim. Jim nodded at Scoppa, but it wasn't clear he even recognized him.

"Have a good trip," Scoppa said as they passed him. Kauffman didn't seem particularly distressed, even having been charged with murder, even having been told he was being protected from Fred Augello and the Pagans.

Kauffman had to go to Linwood PD first to be officially processed, before heading to the Hudson County Correctional Facility. Jim was being transferred to Hudson County, in northern New Jersey just outside of Manhattan, because of the threat Levy said was posed against him in Atlantic County. The ACPO believed the threat came from the Pagans, and moving Kauffman to North Jersey they thought would be a safer option.

When they shuffled Kauffman toward the back doors of the Linwood PD, Capt. John Hamilton swung the door open to let them in. Hamilton had been promoted to captain in 2015. Back in 2012, it was Hamilton who had interviewed Jim on the day April's body was discovered. Hamilton took the meticulous notes about Jim's demeanor that morning, noting "...at no point were any tears observed" when Jim was "crying out" on the lawn. Hamilton had scribbled down Kauffman's brash comment when asked whether he had touched April's body for a pulse: "Detective, I am a doctor, and I know a dead body when I see one."

Now, six years later, and an hour after Kauffman learned he was charged with his wife's murder, Capt. Hamilton ushered the doctor into the Linwood Police Department.

"How've you been?" the captain asked, and reached out to shake the doctor's hand.

"Just waiting for the summer," the doctor replied. Kauffman sat on a bench inside Linwood PD, his hands in his lap, his knees knocked together, his shoulders hunched as if protecting himself from the cold coming in through the door. After they processed his fingerprints and took his photo, Kauffman sat silently for nearly an hour, only asking to use the bathroom and inquiring if the press was waiting for him outside. He seemed relaxed and was pleasant to the officers handling the paperwork.

When it was time to go, Patrolman Levenson helped Kauffman inside the patrol SUV.

"You all right?" Levenson asked. Kauffman looked at him and answered, "Yes, well as

good as I can be." Levenson put on Kauffman's seatbelt. At 3:40 p.m., with The ACPO officer in the passenger seat, Levenson pulled out en route to Kauffman's new jail which was housed inside the Hudson County Correctional Facility in Kearney, New Jersey, 120 miles north of Linwood. As they drove off, the media converged on nearby Mays Landing for a scheduled press conference at four p.m., where Prosecutor Damon Tyner would address the media about the arrests. Kauffman would return one more time to South Jersey, when he appeared in court for his arraignment on Thursday, January 18th.

That day was the first time Kim Pack had seen her stepfather in person in years. Kim had not gone to any of Jim's court appearances on the gun charges. She didn't feel it was appropriate, even though her mother's friends had made sure to sit in the front row and tell the media how happy they were that Jim was behind bars, if only on gun charges. Once the murder charges came down and Kim heard the details, she decided she needed to sit in the courtroom. She dreaded being in the spotlight again, but she knew her mom would have done it for her.

Since there was no jury, members of the press filled the jury box, sitting only a few feet away from Kim. She sat surrounded by longtime girlfriends, friends from work, and her mother's closest companions. With her resemblance to her mother, Kim stood out. She radiated strength in a navy wrap dress and a triple strand of pearls, and was polite and patient with the press and everyone around her, even smiling at times. But she was nervous.

Once Jim entered the courtroom, her body language changed entirely: in that moment she became April's little girl, trembling at the sight of the man who had taken her mother from her. Kim had mentally prepared for months of Jim's court appearances, even as she dreaded the thought of a drawn-out trial, and having to hear the things Jim would say about her mother and their marriage in order to clear his name. She had even begun saving up vacation days from work. But that January day in court was the last time she would ever see Jim Kauffman again.

Chapter 24

DOA

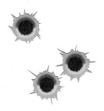

It began as a Code White at 9:34 am on January 26th, 2018. Hudson County Jail officials rushed to Charlie 500 East. In cell 513, Inmate #32229 was unresponsive. The other cells went on lockdown. A nurse and corrections officer worked to performed CPR. The nurse gave chest compressions, while the officer did mouth-to-mouth on the prisoner. They secured the scene, not knowing what they were dealing with. The call escalated to a Code Orange. More members of the medical and custody staff raced to help, bringing an automated external defibrillator as paramedics arrived to the 911 call.

Dr. James Kauffman was pronounced dead at 10:06 a.m., an apparent suicide.

The doctor had taken a bedsheet, twisted it tightly, then tied it to the bedpost and around his neck and looped it around the bedpost of the upper bunk. He then lay on the ground, face first, cutting off the flow of oxygen, creating just enough pressure for him to suffocate himself. The medical examiner ruled the immediate cause of death as hanging, and the manner of death as suicide. A source within the jail said the act was done with medical precision and was carefully planned.

Kauffman's wife Carole was his next of kin. She arranged for his body to be taken to Ivy Hill Crematory in Philadelphia, where it was cremated. A Trevose, Pennsylvania funeral home handled the arrangements. Carole held a small memorial for Jim, with friends and family and neighbors, in the multi-purpose room in the building where he and Carole had lived. A rabbi performed a quiet service.

At the time of his death, Kauffman had been alone in his cell because his cellmate was out that day for a court appearance. He left a lengthy suicide note. ABC's "20/20" obtained a copy for its June special on the case, and showed excerpts from it in the show.

His six-page letter gave a glimpse into his own version of what happened and he painted himself as a victim.

Those closest to April ripped apart Jim's final words. Yes, April had sent people to Jim who didn't have insurance from time to time to see if he could help them out. And Jim failed to mention in his letter that he had been operating two other illegal schemes that had nothing to do with the Pagans. Nor did any of this exculpate him of April's murder.

Damon Tyner was shocked at his suicide. When asked by ABC News correspondent Deborah Roberts if investigators questioned whether April was involved in Kauffman's illegal schemes, Tyner responded, "Our investigation at the time did not lead us to believe she had any involvement. I believe that at some point she became aware of it. I believe ultimately that's why she was killed." If Jim had lived to appear in court, he would have heard how even the people who flipped on Fred Augello and pinned the crime on him, made clear it was Dr. Kauffman who was relentless in his mission to have April killed. Kauffman's death was major news. It was a blow to the investigators who had hoped to prove his guilt in court.

For Kim, there was nothing positive in this turn of events; she was devastated. It was all just too much to handle in a short span of time. Patrick D'Arcy, Kim's attorney, commented, "He certainly, I think, knew the evidence was mounting. I'm sure he listened to what the prosecutor had to say and he made another choice." In the end, D'Arcy was the only attorney who ever got to question Kauffman under oath. D'Arcy believes Kauffman was devoid of emotion, a psychopath. In reference to this, he offered an astute observation: each time Kauffman tried to demonstrate emotion, he would attach a physical component to it. On the day of April's murder, for example, he said he was "throwing up" outside.

Dan Garrabrant was not surprised in the least that Kauffman chose suicide. He felt it fit with his narcissistic personality. The morning Jim took his life, Garrabrant happened to place a call to an ACPO detective about another matter, and the detective answered the agent's call with, "How did you know already?" Garrabrant hadn't heard the news yet, but without hesitation he responded, "Kauffman's dead?" He just knew it was a matter of time, and took a guess.

The public had become invested in the Kauffman story. With his suicide following on the heels of the announcement of the charges, interest in the case peaked. Online, comments on the stories carried by local news stations the comments proliferated.

"good hope his wife greeted him and kicked him to HELL"

"Coward! Hope he rots in hell. Although Kim will never find complete peace with the loss of her mother, at least his death will preclude her from having to attend a lengthy trial and have to look at his evil face."

"Took the easy way out. A hanging. He probably wouldn't last anyway. His biker buds would've most likely gutted him from the inside out. Coward. May he rot in hell."

"Smart man. Jail with likely fellow pagans probably wouldn't have worked out for him."

"Looks like they're gonna have to let Freddy go!"

"Ain't no one left to testify"

Yet Jim Kauffman had people who loved and cared about him too. Besides the friends who had visited and called him in jail, he had friends and patients who couldn't fathom that he could harm anyone. For them, his suicide confirmed his victimization as part of a tragic story.

Chapter 25

HOUSE OF CARDS

In the six years since April Kauffman's murder, Joseph Mulholland had given the most vivid picture of what had actually happened to April the morning she was killed. Joseph had heard the chilling details from Francis Mulholland on the morning he killed her. Joseph had then shared the information with investigators over several interviews.

Joseph told investigators and later testified that he had driven Francis Mulholland to the Kauffman home on the morning of May 10, 2012. Francis entered the house through the unlocked front door. Dr. Kauffman was waiting inside and gave Francis a gun. Then the doctor directed him to the upstairs bedroom. The doctor then left the house. Joseph reported, "He [Francis Mulholland] said [the doctor] got in his car and drove away."

The Wednesday night before the early Thursday morning murder, Joseph said that Dr. Kauffman received calls from Fred Augello, and then from Francis Mulholland. Those calls set the prearranged murder for hire in motion. Joseph picked Francis up around 4 or 4:30 that morning at his Villas home, and took the estimated 40-minute drive toward the Kauffman house. He dropped Francis off on Route 9, by the Mainland High School baseball fields. The surveillance video from Mainland High School showed Joseph's white Chevy Silverado with an extended cab near the bike path in Linwood at 5:16 AM that morning. Joseph identified the pick-up as his own.

Detectives believe the dark SUV that drove by three minutes later was Jim Kauffman's Ford Explorer. The man seen walking by on the same footage six minutes later, according to Joseph, was Francis, leaving the murder scene. He was headed south on the Linwood bike path. Presumably, he took the 6.5-mile path that ran parallel to Shore Road, and then he walked an extra three-quarters of a mile or so to the Point Diner, at MacArthur Boulevard and Mays Landing Road in Somers Point. There he would eventually meet up with Joseph. Francis had called Joe when he was finished, and Joseph said they met in the parking lot of the diner an hour later. Francis had a small brown or black gun in his hand, and he gave Joseph $1,000 cash out of $10,000 that he had in his sweat pants. Francis asked Joseph to drive him to Fred's to get the rest of his money, but Joseph said he wouldn't do that, and instead drove Francis back to his house in the Villas. Francis said he was going to get rid of the gun. He believed the money Fred had waiting for him was getting picked up by Beverly at the doctor's office that morning.

Joseph told the story to investigators during multiple interviews. During the first interview on the day of the sweep of arrests, January 9, 2018, he did not admit to driving Francis. But Rauch said something to Mulholland that day that must have stuck.

"Your past always comes back to haunt you. Hopefully, hopefully, in your case this is the last ghost you get visited by." After Mulholland left that interview, he spilled a lot more. Months later, after a plea agreement in exchange for testimony, he admitted to having driven Francis, after he claimed Augello threatened to kill him if he didn't drop Francis off and pick him up that morning. Mulholland said Kauffman originally offered to pay Fred $30,000, and Fred would give Joseph $10,000 from the total to pull the trigger. But Kauffman had then come to Joe separately and offered him $100,000, twice. Both times Joseph said he declined. Mulholland spilled more details during his confession to authorities March 23, before the grand jury met.

On the morning of the killing, Joseph said he dropped Francis off and then waited, first by a paint store, and then a bagel shop, before getting the call from Francis reporting he was done. Even Scoppa was taken aback when Mulholland calmly reported how he went inside, bought a bagel, and ate it—all while waiting for Francis to kill April.

Once Francis had joined Joseph in the truck at the Somers Point Diner, the two men called Fred to say the job was done. Scoppa asked how Joseph had contacted Fred afterward, but Joseph couldn't say for sure if he'd called Fred's main phone line or a throwaway phone. If the investigators were trying to nail down a record of the calls and proof Joseph was at the bagel store, they were unsuccessful. Francis wanted to head to Fred's shop to get the rest of the money owed to him, money that Joseph says Beverly had picked up at Kauffman's office on the morning of May 10. Joseph said he protested—he was tired of driving and wanted just to drop Francis off at his Villas home.

Joseph, the big, burly biker who had several inches and about fifty pounds over Fred, said he gave in and drove Francis home because Fred threatened to kill him if he didn't. Joseph had turned down a $10,000 offer, and then a $100,000 offer to kill April Kauffman; instead, he drove the hitman—making him an accessory to murder. In the end, he received $1,000 cash from Francis as a thank-you gesture, since nothing had been agreed to in advance. The catalyst for Joseph to drive Francis, he claims, was fear.

Joseph said that after the murder Fred wanted a way to get rid of Francis, and would bring it up often. Kauffman called Augello, pissed off, about six months after April's murder. He reported that Francis, who had never been a patient of Kauffman's, barged into the doctor's office one day demanding scripts and more money.

Joseph, however, did not initially have suspicions about Francis' death. Francis had threatened suicide before, and according to Joe, Francis had nightmares about killing April—the murder was haunting him.

After the grand jury came back with indictments in April 2018, the house of cards began to collapse.

First Joseph Mulholland pled guilty in June to second-degree racketeering, amended from a first-degree charge. He could be sentenced to a maximum of ten years in state prison. Mulholland's plea agreement was open-ended, meaning he pled guilty before the court had decided on his sentencing. He agreed to testify against Augello.

Then in July, Glenn Seeler and Cheryl Pizza pled guilty to conspiracy. Additionally, Seeler pled to second-degree racketeering, and Pizza to drug possession. Both agreed to testify against Augello.

In August 2018, Beverly Augello and Tabitha Chapman became the fourth and fifth defendants in the case to take plea deals from the Atlantic County Prosecutor's Office. Both pleaded guilty to third-degree conspiracy to possess drugs, specifically OxyContin. In addition, Beverly Augello pleaded guilty to possession of cocaine during a traffic stop in April while she was awaiting trial.

While awaiting trial, the defendants had all been out of jail, and all hired private attorneys. In January, Judge DeLury ruled that Tabitha Chapman and Joseph Mulholland were free to go under certain conditions. In February Beverly Augello was allowed out of jail, as long as she stayed in Atlantic and Cape May Counties. Seeler had received a similar ruling by DeLury in February—his condition was he must stay with his mother in Marmora, Cape May County until trial.

Back in January, when the Prosecutor's Office released the charging documents for all seven defendants in the Kauffman case, there were two men listed among the names who were not charged. At first, this portion of the affidavit was a head-scratcher for those covering the case: "Solicited individuals include Andrew Glick, Glenn Seeler, Joseph Mulholland and other, as of yet unidentified individuals."

Who was Andrew Glick? There was no explanation for the media, except that he had been "solicited" to do the murder. Court records showed that Glick had been in jail briefly for a second drug charge in November, but he was released; months later, there was still no indictment, and all of his appearances had been postponed. To the greater public that might seem like an example of the slow-moving justice system, but to Glick's circle of friends, it screamed *Rat*. Back in

November, John "Egyptian" Kachbalian had met with Andrew to prove he wasn't flipping when his arrest seemed suspicious. Kachbalian warned Augello at the time that something didn't seem right. Unbeknownst to Kachbalian, on November 7, 2017, First Prosecutor Cary Shill "authorized consensual interceptions for any and all in person and telephone conversations between Andrew Glick and Ferdinand Augello, Stephen Wittenwiler, Glenn Seeler, John Kachbalian and any other individuals involved in or [having] knowledge of the murder of April Kauffman."

Kachbalian's name was on the list because both Glick and law enforcement had given investigators intel that Kachbalian was a member of the Cape May Chapter of the Pagans at the time of April's murder.

The only defendant besides Fred who continued to stick with a not guilty plea was Paul Pagano. Pagano had an intimidating look with his slicked-back hair, intense light brown eyes, chiseled cheekbones, and strong face framed by sideburns and a goatee. Glick had told investigators that Pagano was a former president of the Atlantic County Chapter, but had left after a dispute to join the Cumberland Chapter in 2010. Pagano pled not guilty to second-degree racketeering, and hired high-profile Philadelphia defense attorney Chuck Peruto Jr. Peruto, known for his flair in the courtroom, gave an impassioned plea to DeLury to release his client from jail. Peruto said Pagano had been a Pagan years ago but left that life behind him.

"There's nothing in the discovery that says he did anything criminal," Peruto argued. Pagano was a patient of Kauffman's; he not only suffered from diabetes, but also had been involved in four major motorcycle accidents, including a horrific crash fifteen years earlier resulting in severe back injuries. Peruto told the judge that Pagano did receive pills from Kauffman with a legitimate prescription, but that he never re-sold them—he took them himself for his severe back pain. After getting his client released, Peruto successfully argued for Pagano to be tried separately from the other alleged associates in the case.

For media covering the case, interest began to wane from the moment Kauffman killed himself. It was still a story for local television stations, but the interest in gavel-to-gavel coverage for a murder trial of Dr. James Kauffman just wasn't there for a trial with Fred Augello. It still had all the allure of a sensational story: a beautiful woman, pills, a doctor, a quiet upscale community, and a motorcycle gang. But as each court appearance progressed throughout the spring, less attention was paid. However, ABC's 20/20 produced an hour-long piece on the story, interviewing Kim, April's friends, the D'Arcys, Damon Tyner, and Jim Scoppa.

Fred, following this from his jail cell, wanted his voice heard. Videotaped interviews are not allowed in the Atlantic County Jail. Fred did a brief interview with the Press of Atlantic City, but found the best forum for his side of the story was on Facebook. Through an intermediary, Fred began posting his thoughts and comments. Although he did not threaten anyone on his page, authorities started to notice. They did not like the fact that the person maintaining Fred's page also posted information from the discovery, including portions of the grand jury report, even though posting discovery is not actually illegal.

Support for Fred grew. His page was public, and comments began pouring in with support from old friends, Pagans, the wider bike community, new friends, and people drawn by curiosity who began to follow the case closely. The Prosecutor's office argued before Judge DeLury in July that the postings could taint a jury pool. DeLury agreed, but also gave a slap on the wrist to the Prosecutor's office for participating in the 20/20 episode. The gag order was imposed for everyone involved. Judge DeLury wanted everything from the 20/20 episode removed from the ACPO's website and social media accounts.

> ...[T]he parties shall take immediate steps to remove to the greatest extent possible any materials and information that the parties have posted concerning this case that remains under their control, such as personal social media sites, and organizational or business websites, within 48 hours..."

Around the same time, Kachbalian was also posting on his Facebook page. Kachbalian frequently posted updates on Pagan news, on motorcycle gatherings or recent deaths of club members. He was a "ride or die" Pagan who had served time, and followed the old-school maxim, "Snitches get stitches." Kachbalian began posting about Glick, labeling him as a rat and outing him for his role, and his Facebook friends reposted his claims.

When Beverly Augello was released in February, she went to see Kachbalian as Glick had. But she claims she went because she needed someone to talk to. Months later, when it was reported she had agreed to cooperate with the prosecution, Kachbalian added her to his public "rat list." The comment section on his posts started filling up, with bickering between some of the seven defendants' friends and some family members. Kachbalian also listed Wittenwiler as a rat even though he wasn't a defendant and wasn't even cooperating with police.

Glick was so upset with Kachbalian's public attacks that he actually broke out of pseudo-hiding and called reporter at the Toronto Star, Peter Edwards (Glick had read Edwards' articles on motorcycle gangs in the past). "I preached never to do this (cooperate with authorities) but I never thought I'd be looking at 40 years," Glick opined to the reporter. "It would basically be life for me." When the story ran in March 2018, Glick outed himself to the world as the number-one witness in the case. Glick's handlers at ACPO were pissed when they found out he had initiated the article. Kachbalian's followers also began posting, not just about Glick, but about the others as they began to flip, accusing them all of being rats.

Kachbalian reposted from another Facebook page a witness list for the prosecution. He and his followers skewered the people on the list, which included many who were not cooperating, and some who didn't even know they were on it. Pagano was one of them. His attorney took to Facebook to set the record straight—his client was not a rat, and had not flipped. Other people feared they would be hurt over the misinformation. But Kachbalian's Facebook postings continued. He had recently posted that Beverly Augello had decided to take the plea agreement and testify against Fred, and moreover, that she had made the agreement with prosecutors on their wedding anniversary, August 23rd. After that he went a step further: he posted what looked like an artistically done nude photograph of a woman's back. He didn't identify the woman, but it was later learned to be Beverly Augello.

"Guess which 'Lying Rat' this is," he wrote. "Hint, this [expletive] while out on bail for Murder Conspiracy and Drug Racketeering Case and after she agreed to snitch on her ex-husband, got arrested in April for cocaine, but through the help of her handlers at ACPO & FBI no mention in local news. In and out of confinement nice and quiet. Even the one-sided judge had no issue with her bail. Street justice at its best."

That took the postings too far for law enforcement. Kachbalian was charged with first-degree witness tampering, cyber harassment, posting obscene material and invasion of privacy/disclosing sex act without consent.

Police went to his home and arrested him. When they searched his home, they discovered letters that Fred Augello wrote to Kachbalian while in jail. Those letters would end up having an impact on the case.

Chapter 26

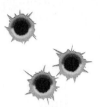

THE TRIAL

"You might think there's no more two different people: the wealthy doctor who wants to be part of high society and the Pagan president. In their mutual greed, they found common ground. They came together to silence April, to make sure their empires of easy money would last forever." In opening arguments, Chief Assistant Prosecutor Seth Levy aligned the two men who might seem like unlikely partners: Fred Augello and Dr. James Kauffman.

Levy began his opening statements to the jury on Monday, September 17, 2018, in the case of the State of New Jersey versus Ferdinand Augello. Even though Dr. Kauffman was dead and therefore would not be on trial, the State believed Jim Kauffman did seek a hitman to kill his wife; with this case, the prosecutors set out to prove that Augello was equally evil and culpable for arranging to kill April. Levy explained to jurors that April had learned of the criminal dealings her husband was involved in, and that she threatened to divorce him and bankrupt him, or to use what she had learned as leverage.

"His medical practice was thriving on diabetes patients, the elderly," Levy said. "He was married to a beautiful, vivacious, and successful wife, a woman who increased not only his practice but his fortune. This was Jim Kauffman's empire, and he loved it more than anything in the entire world."

Levy and his second-chair prosecutor, Christopher D'Esposito, had to prove in court that Ferdinand "Freddy" Augello was guilty beyond a reasonable doubt of first-degree racketeering—in the course of which he unlawfully distributed prescription pills, acting as a financier, organizer or supervisor of at least one other person through the Pagan Outlaw Motorcycle Gang. They also had to prove that he arranged the killing of April Kauffman, and that he attempted to arrange the murder of James Kauffman while he was in jail.

Levy and D'Esposito squared off against Augello's attorneys, Mary Linehan and Omar Aguilar, both career public defenders in Atlantic County for several decades. Augello sat with them at the defense table, his freedom on the line. Each day he wore a suit and tie and his hair tied back in a ponytail. He would adjust it throughout the day, and would shift his reading glasses from his nose to the top of his head. He would get animated when certain things were said, leaning over and whispering to his counsel like they were coaches on the sideline. Each time the attorneys had a sidebar in front of the judge, Augello would dutifully put on the headphones so he could hear the conversation, which was otherwise blocked to the jury and courtroom.

During opening statements, Augello's defense team dropped what at first seemed like a bombshell. Linehan said that, according to a confidential informant, the Atlantic County Prosecutor's Office might have known about the doctor's search for a hitman prior to the murder. Linehan also said the ACPO had known about the drug ring for years after the murder, yet allowed it to continue. She described the investigation as "too big to fail" after the ACPO went on 20/20 and widely publicized the arrests in the case before the trial.

The State declared its belief that April had been killed around 5:30 a.m. on May 10, 2012 by Francis Mulholland, who was hired by Fred Augello at the direction of Jim Kauffman, and that Joseph Mulholland had acted as the driver.

Fifty-three-year-old Andrew Glick was considered the star witness. He remained on the stand for three days, reviewing the hours of recordings from the wire he had worn from November 2017 through January 2018. Each day he was escorted in and out by detectives from the Atlantic County Prosecutors Office. Each day he sat wearing a button-down short-sleeve shirt, looking noticeably thinner, and visibly uncomfortable to be sitting across from his former friend, who stared directly at him.

At some points, as the recorded conversations played in open court, baring personal moments between the two men, Glick seemed to cringe. "I've lost every friend I ever had," Glick told Levy about his decision to cooperate. But Glick did not hold back describing Augello as manipulative and powerful, someone who could get dirty work done without getting his hands dirty. He explained how, in plotting to kill April, Fred was fueled by greed, desperate to keep his generous stream of cash going from the drug ring.

"Fred was not afraid of anybody," Glick said of Augello. "It was the money. [Augello's] sign shop didn't pay the bills. The doc's money paid the bills. He was just concerned of losing that cash flow."

Glick spoke openly about his dealings with the notorious Sinaloa cartel. This had some wondering, if Glick were to get prison time, whether he should be more concerned about the Pagans or the cartel. Glick was still waiting to see what he would be charged with since his drug charges had to be amended to hide his cooperation. Linehan tried to prove in court that the plot to take out James Kauffman in jail was not only fictitious but created by the prosecutor's office.

"That was me flying by the seat of my pants...," Glick told Linehan. She responded with a question phrased like a statement, "Supervised by Scoppa."

Glick responded, "There was no script or anything to go by; I just wung it..." Linehan questioned Glick about how Detective Scoppa had approached Glick to keep the conversation about killing Kauffman going. "He said to bring it up, but it was only brought up more so if Fred and "Irish" [Joseph Mulholland] found anybody... but yo... I took it upon myself when their avenues were closed just to run with....It would be something good to get discussion out of...." Linehan responded, "So Fred and "Irish" didn't have any avenues...?" Glick answered, "Well, their avenues didn't provide any fruit."

Glick, Seeler, Drinhouser, and Mulholland all testified that they were approached about killing April, and described the varying amounts they were offered. The original sum Kauffman had offered to Augello was $50,000 for the job; depending on who Augello asked, he would offer $20,000 or $30,000 of that to the potential shooter. The men described how the prescription arrangement between Kauffman and Augello worked. All four said that they feared for their lives.

Seeler sat composed, still sporting his shaved head and goatee, wearing black-rimmed glasses and a long-sleeved blue button-down shirt that did not completely cover his tattoos. He wore multiple thick plugs and hoops in his earlobes. "I was told we had a doctor in our back pocket," is how Seeler described the arrangement with Kauffman to the court. Seeler said the drug ring was not a sanctioned Pagan activity, but that Fred was the boss. It was a message prosecutors made sure was brought up over and over in court—Fred was the boss.

Levy quizzed Seeler about the proposition to kill April. "Did you take it seriously?" Seeler clasped his hands together and gave a goofy laugh as he chuckled, "To murder somebody?"

"Were you shocked when you found out she had been killed?" Seth continued.

"Absolutely," Seeler stated without hesitation.

"Did you offer the job to anyone else?" Levy asked. Seeler paused, his eyes darted, he pursed his lips and gulped as he responded, "I don't recall if I did or not," his voice sounding froggy. Then Levy asked about what Fred had told him about the hit beforehand,

"He said he was in contact with the doctor and the doctor would leave his house around 5 or 6 am every morning, walk out the door, walk up the steps and handle business." Seeler surmised the job would be done with a "throwaway gun." On cross -examination, Aguilar mentioned Seeler's tattoos and asked whether he was a Nazi sympathizer. Seeler admitted to having white supremacist tattoos.

When Joseph Mulholland took the stand in September 2018 and told the courtroom the details of the murder plot, he was the only person still alive among the people in and around 2 Woodstock Drive that morning who were directly involved with the murder. April Kauffman, the murder target, was dead. Dr.

Kauffman was dead. So was Francis Mulholland, the man authorities said was the hitman. But, according to Joseph, all of it had been done at the direction of Fred Augello. And Augello was alive and sitting in the courtroom on trial for arranging April's murder, for the attempted murder of James Kauffman, and charges stemming from the drug ring.

Fifty-two-year-old Mulholland walked calmly into the courtroom. He had a big presence—tall, and carrying his weight around his middle. He wore dark khakis and a cream-colored checked button-down shirt and. His hair was now dark gray and his goatee white, and reading glasses hung from his neck. Even sitting down in the witness box, you could see his broad shoulders, and the tattoos peeking out of his cuffs onto the tops of his hands.

His testimony as to the day of the murder was chilling. He recounted what he said Francis told him about April's final moments, "He said she let out a scream, and then he did what he did. He shot and then he left. He walked down the steps and walked out... "

Joseph detailed how, after Kauffman's June arrest and Andrew Glick's subsequent November 2017 arrest, Fred became paranoid. Joseph told Fred not to trust Andrew. Then in November, Joseph said Fred accused him of planting information that made its way to the infamous letter that Glick had shown Fred. Joseph had been a client of the Jacobs Barbone law firm in the past on a separate matter.

"[Fred] had called me, 'cause his girlfriend wanted me to paint the house, He slid a letter over to me, like that, and he had a gun pointed at me. I read the letter. He said to me, you know, that was your attorney. I said, what the fuck? What are you pointing a gun at me for? He thought I was setting him up. He thought I did it."

Mary Linehan questioned how he could be scared of Fred. Mulholland leaned his head into the microphone, squinted, and replied, "Because I was afraid for my life." Linehan paced and continued, "If you were afraid for your life, why in 2017 were you up at Fred's girlfriend's house looking to do a paint job?" The two went back and forth:

JM: Because Fred is the type of guy that will intimidate you when he's got
     something on you... he's got something on you and I was afraid for
     my life and I still am ...and I will be for many years after this."
ML: So it's your testimony that Mr. Augello had such control over you
     that he could call you and you would respond?
JM: (without hesitation, leaning into the mic) Yes.
ML: You'd speak to him on the phone even if you didn't want to.
JM: Yes.
ML: Because he has some control over you.
JM: (voice going a little higher) Yes.

Linehan then questioned Joseph about Francis Mulholland's death. Joseph described how he had gone to Philadelphia that morning, an hour and forty-minute drive, and had stopped by Francis's house to take him along to the doctor's appointment. Joseph stated that he had not only gone all the way to Philadelphia for a doctor's appointment that morning, but after that went to his sister's in South Jersey, and returned to his home in the Villas around 1 or 2:30 in the afternoon.

This was not what he told police on the day Francis died, nor was it what he had told investigators since his arrest on January 9. The day Francis was discovered dead, Joseph told police he went to pick up his friend at 6:30 in the morning for a doctor's appointment, but Francis did not answer. That day, Joseph stated that he returned to check on Francis later in the morning, around 10:30 a.m., but Francis still wasn't answering. The police report described Joseph as saying he returned around 12:30 p.m. with a friend, Henry Van Colln, and that's when Van Colln went through the window and found Francis dead inside.

All of Mulholland's accounts differed from that of Henry Van Colln. He said Joseph had picked him up that day twice, once in the morning and once before 12:30 p.m. to go to AA meetings together. Joseph said Francis wasn't answering the door for the first meeting that Francis planned to attend with them. The second time, Joseph picked up Van Colln and asked him to come with him to look through a window and see if Francis was okay. Van Colln found Francis dead inside.

But Van Colln's account was never included in court testimony or the police report about Francis's death investigation. Even though Van Colln was the one who found Francis, authorities never asked him his account of what transpired that morning. If investigators had questioned him, Mulholland's testimony could have been called into question.

Cheryl Pizza and Beverly Augello also took the stand; both had deals in exchange for their testimony. Beverly Augello wore her blonde hair long and curly. She avoided looking at Fred except when Levy asked her to point out the defendant. She detailed how she set up the burner phone for Fred, using the bogus name Harry Johnson and a fake address. Beverly also testified how Fred told her to make a last-minute doctor's appointment the morning of April's murder, and that she picked up the envelope with Fred's name on it at Dr. Kauffman's office. The State said that envelope was payment to Augello from the doctor for April's murder. It allegedly included cash and extra scripts, although Beverly said she never looked inside.

Pizza no longer had the shocking cherry-red dye job as in her mug shot; now her hair was a muted blond. Dressed conservatively, she testified that Seeler, who was legally still her husband, had begun to see Kauffman before she did. He received pain pills from Kauffman, and had introduced her to the doctor. She reported starting to get narcotics herself from Kauffman after a few months of seeing him. She would give the drugs to her husband, and they would then bring them to Fred's shop while she waited in the car.

The defense questioned Pizza about the drug bust in 2013 at Pizza's and Seeler's home in Ocean City. Authorities had questioned her about her prescription drugs, and she told them it was Kauffman who prescribed them. Now they asked: was it Detective Scoppa who had questioned her? Pizza explained that though she remembered being questioned, she was high at the time and in pain from a car accident, and couldn't remember who questioned her.

Also called to the stand was Kauffman's former nurse practitioner, Barb Greenling, who testified how had she warned the doctor not to get them into trouble, and described the string of new "biker-looking patients." She also testified about the day of Francis Mulholland's death: how officers had called the practice after finding pills near the body prescribed by Kauffman; how she was asked to come to pronounce Francis Mulholland dead; and how, seeing the dead man on the floor, she had no idea who he was.

An FBI agent testified to the location of the Harry Johnson burner phone, citing the towers it bounced off as likely being from the area where Fred Augello lived. Fred's defense pointed out to the jury that Seeler often stayed at his mother's house, which was also in the vicinity of the cell towers.

Scoppa spent several days taking Levy through the investigation from the spring of 2017 through all of the meetings Glick had with Augello. He also explained Dr. Kauffman's various lies, even showing his fake Green Beret hat that they had confiscated as evidence. And he showed Fred's Pagan denim vest with its various patches. While Scoppa held up the vest, an increasingly agitated Fred—angry with his legal team and the entire process—shouted, "Stolen!" Scoppa and Glick's testimony, and the recordings from the wires he wore, carried the prosecution's case against Fred.

It was while Scoppa was on the stand that Levy handed him two letters Fred had sent to Kachbalian, the letters confiscated from Kachbalian's home. Fred had written them while in jail, signing them "1%er." Immediately, Mary Linehan moved for a mistrial, citing a conflict: Augello had written something about Linehan in the letters. Levy argued that they could redact her name. It's not clear if the letters mentioned anything misogynistic or embarrassing, or if they might put Linehan in a legal situation in which the court might remove her from the case, and possibly put Augello's case in jeopardy. Whatever was written didn't call Linehan's ethics into question, or she would have been removed. DeLury denied the motion for a mistrial, but would not allow them to be read in open court. He did, however, allow the letters to stay in the folder jurors would look through when making their decision.

April's time of death was never brought into question during the trial, but in fact, it had been questioned behind the scenes. In the prosecution's narrative, April was killed around 5:30 a.m. By the time of the trial the medical examiner, Dr. Hydow Park, had died, and his unwritten memories were lost. Right after April's death, the Atlantic County Prosecutor's Office under Jim McClain had questions about the time of death and had requested an expert opinion from well-known forensic pathologist Dr. Michael Baden. Baden placed April's death around 2 a.m. Five years later, when April's case began to gain momentum, the ACPO asked several more pathologists to give their opinions on the time of death. Those results came back with a range of different time estimates, varying between 10 p.m. to 10:48 in the morning.

In spite of all this, in the end, questions about the time of death didn't play a major role in the trial. Investigators would later say about the varying results that estimating time of death is not an exact science, and can only provide a window; in addition, different doctors may use different methods and techniques. Only Delaware's State Medical Examiner, Gary Collins, who was also asked to review the report, was called to testify. Omar Aguilar, Augello's second attorney, asked Collins if he knew he was the fourth doctor to render an opinion, and the doctor said he did not. And that was that.

Kim Pack ended the testimony for the prosecution, describing her mother's tumultuous and terrifying marriage. During cross-examination, Omar Aguilar asked Pack whether Kauffman was abusive and controlling, and whether she thought Kauffman could have been capable of killing April himself.

"Yes, sir," Pack said. "I think anything is possible." Aguilar followed up with a last-ditch effort to insinuate reasonable doubt into juror's minds: "This guy was volatile, wasn't he?"

Augello did not take the stand in his own defense.

The defense called one witness, Jessica Bonner, an investigator with the New Jersey Office of the Public Defender. Bonner testified that hundreds of phone calls between Kauffman and the Harry Johnson phone could have been made by Glenn Seeler, not Augello.

As both sides rested, the State asked for a change to the charges on which the jury would deliberate. The judge responded by ruling that the prosecution no longer had to prove that Francis Mulholland was the killer, as the State had contended in the charges on January 9. Judge DeLury made changes to the charges that included expanding who might have killed April Kauffman for Augello to still be found guilty of murder.

Specifically, rather than allege that Augello had hired Mulholland, Chief Assistant Prosecutor Seth Levy asked that Mulholland's name be replaced with "by another." It was a big blow to the defense.

Everyone thought it would take days for jurors to come to a decision. The wire recording testimony alone had taken three days. In Levy's closing arguments, he made a highlight reel of the wire recordings and gave jurors transcripts to read along while the audio played, since parts of it were hard to understand.

Mary Linehan told jurors in her closing arguments that the State's case was "prosecution by multiple choice." She pointed to the paucity of evidence such as ballistic reports, controlled buys, or even pills. She attacked the witnesses' credibility, pointing out that Glick was paid by the prosecution. "The only pills found were in Joseph Mulholland's name. Glick had his people lined up and they're telling the story that the prosecutor paid for."

It took just two hours for jurors to come to a decision in the case of Fred Augello. Inside the jury room, two jurors had some reservations at first, but they came around to consensus with the others rather quickly.

The jurors made sure to review everything, including what was in the evidence box. The letters from Fred Augello in Atlantic County Jail to John Kachbalian had a major impact on their decision. Jurors said the contents of those letters and the wire conversations that played for three days in court are what led to their unanimous decision to find Fred guilty on all counts. One juror said that they also agreed that Seth Levy's compelling presentation made a huge difference. He helped them understand the case, and to keep in mind that they didn't have to like the defendants testifying against Fred. Simply put, there was nothing the defense said that made them think that Fred did not do it.

The verdict came so quickly that some members of the media missed it—they'd left the courthouse, assuming the jury's deliberations would take at least a day. Kim and her husband were on their way out of the courthouse when someone ran after them to say a decision had been made. When Superior Court Judge Bernard DeLury read the verdict, Kim sobbed with her head in her hands. She then embraced Damon Tyner in the courtroom for several long minutes.

Augello, visibly upset, yelled, "This is for the media: I did not kill Mrs. Kauffman, nor did I pay anyone to kill Mrs. Kauffman."

Even though it was Augello's trial, for some it was a trial by proxy for Dr. James Kauffman. After the jury's decision, Tyner made a statement.

"Ultimately Dr. Kauffman was tried by a higher jury," Tyner said. "It cost him his life. He couldn't live with the weight of the evidence that would have been presented against him on this date. I don't think much of Jim Kauffman. I think of the victim, April Kauffman, all the family members that were affected by his actions. I think of his role in flooding the market with Oxycodone. His legacy is all of the tragedy he left behind, the lives that were lost, and the people who were affected by his misprace of medicine."

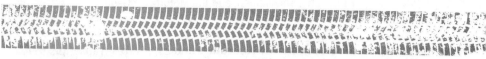

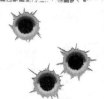

Chapter 27

READY FOR
FREDDY

"Let's go, I'm ready for Freddy." —John Gotti

"...Basically why I'm talking to you is because I didn't murder this woman, and people keep calling me the murderer of this woman... but it's bizarre and it ruined my life and I'm not ready to shut up about it...."

Sitting across from Fred Augello in person, he doesn't look evil. He has big eyes and a contagious smile that highlights his dimples. Fred is charming, and today his demeanor doesn't match his nickname, "Miserable." At 62, he seems like he has a younger outlook on life, although weary from spending nearly nine months in jail at this point. There is, however, still a spark in his eye, and his hands are animated when he starts talking about something that excites or irritates him. Fred also has "the stare" that defendants like Andrew Glick described. Either when he's processing something, or just listening, his big eyes fix on you and betray no emotion, either good or bad; it's actually his own poker face.

His long hair is white and fluffy at the crown and falls down to his back with a natural balayage that gradually becomes darker, ending in a deep gray. His orange V-neck jail uniform looks too big on his slim frame, and he manages to look tan for someone locked up inside for most of the day, thanks to his natural Sicilian skin tone. He has tattoos on his arms including the Italian flag and a diamond with a one-percent sign in the middle. He walked in with a large, clear Ziploc bag that held documents from his case and his own notes scribbled on various pages. He was staying fit inside the Atlantic County Jail facility thanks to Tai-Chi, a martial art he began practicing. Fred said he was getting respect since he is one of the older inmates; people left him alone. But he was getting frustrated, stuck inside, watching the world outside pass him by.

On one of the days we met in June of 2018, he was particularly upset that the Hard Rock Casino was set to open in Atlantic City. It was a stage he wished he could play with his band one day. Fred and I met again a few weeks after his trial, prior to his sentencing date, inside the Atlantic County Jail. Immediately Fred asked, "If I'm a drug kingpin, where is the money?" He was a guy, he said, who drove a van, and whose girlfriend paid all the bills. He couldn't even afford a private defense attorney. Fred had never even been arrested before January 9, 2018. "I think April Kauffman was a wonderful person," he said, staring at me. "She didn't deserve to die." Fred admitted he knew April, though not well. They had met at a biker event in Smithville. She knew Fred's uncle through her veterans' work, and she inquired about getting a sign for her shop through Fred's business.

Augello asserts that Glick and Mulholland were working together to frame him. "I think Mulholland contacted Glick....It just seems too much of a coincidence, in a two-day time period, that both these guys were pitching killing the doctor in here....I didn't think about killing the doctor in the county jail....I wasn't there; it wasn't in my head. I'm convinced Mulholland came and talked to Glick and they were like, this is the plan....We're going to make this up... to kill the doctor in here....We're dragging Fred into this plan. He [Glick] even talks to Seeler; this is going to be all about Fred."

After he learned that both his and Francis Mulholland's names were mentioned in the letter written by Ed Jacobs, he said he called Joe Mulholland to ask him if Francis was his real name and perhaps Joe was his nickname. Fred said that over the years he had met Francis Mulholland briefly in passing, but not as Francis—Joseph always referred to Francis as "my cousin Frank." After his call to Mulholland, Augello says it was Mulholland who set an attempt on the doctor's life in motion.

On the wiretaps, Fred talks with Glick about wanting Doctor Kauffman dead. His explanation, "Maybe that makes me an awful person. I didn't care about this guy I saw he gave a letter and implicated me in a murder I didn't commit. I thought, fuck this guy, I don't care if he gets run over by a truck. I don't care if you guys want to kill him, go for it."

The meeting with the two men at the Borgata and the subsequent phone calls, he says, were about them hiring Freddymade Signs to create large real estate signs, and one of the men at the meeting was a developer. It was not about the Mafia or killing anyone. As for the surveillance video that shows him displaying what looked like "the Jacobs letter" to them, Fred did not admit to doing that but said, "If I did, it was to be like, why is Joey Merlino's lawyer writing this? I never asked this gentleman or anyone to harm Kauffman in jail. We were talking about work.... the situation is I never asked anyone to kill anyone...."

Augello did not take the stand in his own defense, on the advice of his lawyers. He is consistent in saying that he believes Joseph Mulholland and Francis Mulholland committed the crimes, and that Francis was killed by Joseph. Augello wants to sit side by side with Mulholland and take a lie detector test. He posted a longer explanation on his Facebook page.

The conversations between Andrew Glick and I are but snippets of our relationship over the last 15 years or better. Absolutely nowhere on any of these recordings or any recordings, do I take responsibility or claim for the murder of April Kauffman. What I do is discuss details of situations pertaining to such that were told to me by Joseph Mulholland in November 2013, as he described to me details of Francis Mulholland's death along with his and Francis's participation in the murder of April Kauffman and finally his attempt to clean up evidence of the murder. I explained this over and over to my court-appointed attorneys as they blatantly refused to cross examine Mr. Mulholland and put him on the spot with this information. Mr. Mulholland's conversation with me in 2013 explains all my personal knowledge of this awful situation while I am talking to Andrew Glick. Joseph Mulholland's perjury on the stand was never challenged by my defense attorneys, and was probably one of the greatest factors in the case against me. Because not only was his perjury the key to unlocking my and Glick's conversations, it is THE key to the knowledge that April Kauffman was murdered by the murderous duo of Francis and Joseph Mulholland without any assistance from myself whatsoever.

The Free Freddy movement, as Fred calls it, continues to grow on his Facebook page. He embraces his followers and their support. He regularly updates the page through an intermediary and appreciates the assistance. The number of supporters continues to grow as his case receives more attention. He posts articles pertinent to his case, as well as some criticizing Damon Tyner's office. He also posted a music video he made prior to his arrest. In it, Fred stands in the snow singing over photos from his childhood, of him with his girlfriend and with his band, and photos of his ancestors. "Where've you been? All my life?" Fred croons in the video, backed up by vocals, saxophone, drums, and guitars. Below the post he typed a message for his loyal followers: "This is for all of you, thank you, from Me. I wrote this song about the love of my life - I hope you enjoy it."

Fred says he continues to seek a lawyer to handle his appeal. He hoped upon sentencing that he would be moved to Trenton's maximum-security prison. "I have friends there, they are playing music there, guitar there."

On December 5, 2018, the day of Augello's sentencing date, Judge DeLury denied a motion by the defense for a new trial. A letter authored by three current and former employees of the Atlantic County Prosecutor's Office made several allegations about Tyner and the office. The first alleged that the prosecutor's office withheld evidence from the defense. DeLury ruled that the letter could not be included in the argument without some sort of certification, which the defense was ultimately unable to obtain.

Chief Assistant Prosecutor Seth Levy said that his office looked into their records and found nothing missing in what was turned over to the defense.

Kim Pack's nerves were getting to her as she prepared to read her victim-witness impact statement. She had carefully written it over several weeks, pouring years of hurt into just a few paragraphs.

Never in a million years, did I imagine finding myself where I am today. Six years ago, on May 9, 2012, would be the last time I would hear my mother's voice. It was the last time I was able to say "I love you." My earliest memories of my mom were instilling kindness, compassion, integrity, and being the best you could be. She always gave people second chances and rooted for the underdog.

Just because there is justice, I don't get to have her come back. My children don't get their Mimi back. If someone would have anonymously tipped off authorities that something like this was going to occur, I would not be here now and my mom would be here with us. One choice, one phone call and none of this would be happening.

Kim sat at the prosecutors' table, her blonde hair slightly curled, wearing a simply styled black wrap dress. Her natural beauty shone through, and she looked every bit like her mother. At 36 years old, she was a year shy of April's age when she married Jim. "What most do not realize," Kim went on, "is the darkness that James Kauffman brought into our lives. He was evil, manipulative, abusive, abrasive, and narcissistic. We dealt with that for over ten years. She was trying to escape, trying to leave; it was too late."

Kim, a private person juggling a family and a job at a Fortune 500 company, had been forced to become a public figure, putting herself out there after year, begging for people to come forward with information. She had to open her life up to the media, while constantly jockeying for privacy. She was conscious of her need to maintain a relationship with the press so they wouldn't forget her when she would call with a story or idea, any way to keep the quest for her mother's killer alive. Sentencing day hopefully could mean a new beginning for Kim and her family.

My life has changed so much. I've had people criticize me, whisper, point, stare at me. The conspiracy theories, lies, rumors and fabrications have brought me to my knees...

I think where I am now in life is that I want peace. I want to move on. I don't want this to define me. I am done with arguing with people or justifying this case to nay-sayers. I'm done with banter from defendants who continue to victimize me after everything I have endured. I have been very respectful to all defendants in this case, never speaking ill of them or stating my feelings. Everyone in this case had choices. Choices of loyalty, the choice to tell the truth, the choice to refrain from committing such heinous acts, and the choice to say no and not get involved with this in the first place. I did not have a choice. My mother was ripped from my life, shot to death in her home... I've had to sit back and watch my mother's life be put up for auction, had to stand by a headstone that read "beloved wife"...No matter what sentence anyone will serve in this case, it doesn't bring her back to us. I've decided the best way for me to heal is to forgive. I need to do this to live, to be happy, and enjoy what I have left of this beautiful life God has given me.

The courtroom stayed silent as Kim read her statement. Some parts she read through tears, but when she was done she did have the look of a woman at some sort of peace—maybe not completely there, but further along than she had been before.

Fred Augello never took the stand during the trial, but now, prior to his sentencing, he was allowed to address the court after Kim Pack's victim impact statement. However, Kim left the room when Augello began to speak.

"I'm no John Gotti," Augello began. He continued speaking for at least a half-hour. "I didn't murder Mrs. Kauffman," he said. "I didn't send anyone to murder Mrs. Kauffman. This whole thing is a farce. There's no justice for April until you can dig Francis Mulholland out of his grave."

When Augello was done, Kim re-entered the courtroom to hear Augello's sentencing, bracing herself for yet another wave of emotions.

DeLury listened and then gave Augello life in prison for his role in leading the drug ring, plus thirty years for murder. Augello will not be eligible for parole unless he lives until he is 117 years old.

EPILOGUE

In late fall of 2018, the front lawn of 2 Woodstock Drive lay matted with leaves that no one had raked. Trees were overgrown. A "No Trespassing" sign hung on the front door. The once vibrant house, the nucleus of April's community of friends and family, where memories were made at holidays and parties, was now dark, cold and eerie.

Inside was worse. Years of neglect had left leaks and cracks in the walls and foundation. The only portion of the house that looked frozen in time was a bed with the sheets thrown off, a pair of men's boxers on the floor, as if someone had just jumped out of bed. Most likely this was the last place Jim slept before he was arrested at his office on June 13, 2017, never to return home again. In the bathroom were toothbrushes and medication, and in a downstairs sink, there were bottles of hair dye, with residue in the sink as if he'd just done a touch-up. The remnants of Jim's once extensive weapons collection included a small "trigger trainer," a gun-shaped plastic device meant to train the hand to pull the trigger better and faster. Dozens of hollow-point bullets were in boxes and strewn about.

The property had gone into foreclosure, and was set to be auctioned in a Sheriff's sale in November 2018, but was pulled off the auction block. As of now, the home sits at the end of the cul-de-sac unoccupied and unsold, ultimately a tear-down where someone can start fresh. A creepy landmark of a sinister act that marred a peaceful town.

* * *

In the Rodef Sholom Cemetery, April Kauffman's grave is never short of visitors—you can tell by the keepsakes left behind. There's a Tinkerbell figurine, and small stones left on top of the headstone, as is custom in Jewish faith. Kim often comes by and cleans up the flowers left behind. The one thing that never felt right to Kim was the headstone itself. Jim had ordered it and chosen the inscription. Underneath April Kauffman's name, it read BELOVED WIFE. In her heart, Kim always knew she would have to change those words. She ordered a new one and waited until the timing was just right to unveil it. After Fred Augello's trial was over, it felt right.

Kim and Randy visited the cemetery on October 22, a few weeks after the trial concluded and five days before April's birthday. As they looked at the newly carved headstone, Kim finally felt she was liberating her mom from Jim Kauffman's grip. The original Hebrew remained at the top and bottom. Kim had dropped "Kauffman" from April's name, and the word "wife." Instead, she used her mother's middle name. An American flag was added, delicately carved into the stone next to the words:

April Christine
Loving Mother and Best Friend
beloved Grandmother and Friend to all

CODA

People still talk about the April Kauffman murder around Linwood in hushed tones. It seems to have touched everyone to some degree: someone knew someone who was a patient of Jim's, a volunteer with April, or a former customer of hers; someone has a cousin in law enforcement who was there the morning her body was found, or the day of the standoff at Kauffman's medical practice. The theories about who killed April continue to swirl even after Augello's conviction. The varying estimated times of death for April from the multiple autopsy results spanned between ten p.m. on May 9 to ten a.m. on May 10. This leaves room for the question many still ask—could Jim Kauffman have been the one who really pulled the trigger? The other rumor circulating prior to the trial suggested that Jim did not commit suicide, but rather was killed, or even more far-fetched, is still alive and in witness protection. The prosecution still asserts that April was killed at the direction of Jim Kauffman and Fred Augello, and that Augello's conviction is just.

There were also questions about Francis Mulholland's death. Mulholland's family questioned the circumstances among themselves, but never knew they could ask investigators to re-open the case. On December 5th, 2018, Cape May County Prosecutor Jeffrey Sutherland confirmed to Action News, WPVI-TV that his office had received a referral from The Atlantic County Prosecutor's Office to re-open the investigation into Francis Mulholland's death. Mulholland's family now wonders if the overdose he appeared to die of was in fact a homicide.

Fred Augello is incarcerated at Trenton's maximum-security prison, sentenced to life. It is the same prison where Rabbi Fred Neulander is serving his term of thirty years to life in the murder-for-hire of his wife.

Andrew Glick has, to this date, never been charged. In court he said he hopes to move on with his life, move and get a new job, although the publicity has made it hard for him to secure a job in the restaurant industry.

Glenn Seeler was sentenced to three years in prison.

Joseph Mulholland received four years in prison.

Beverly Augello was given a suspended sentence. DeLury gave her concurrent five-year sentences. Those sentences will only be served if Augello re-offends during the next five years.

Tabitha Chapman also dodged prison time and was accepted into the court's pretrial intervention program. Pretrial intervention lets eligible defendants avoid trial and provides rehabilitative services to deter future criminal behavior.

Cheryl Pizza received a suspended sentence of three years. If she avoids any criminal activity she will not have to serve prison time.

Paul Pagano's felony charges were dropped. His attorney, Chuck Peruto, was able to avoid trial and argue Pagano's charge down to a misdemeanor, failure to turn over controlled dangerous substances. He pled guilty and received fines and no jail time.

Stephen "Little Stevie" a.k.a. "Billboard" Wittenwiler died in March of 2019. Wittenwiler's estranged wife posted a message on social media that he had died of a heart attack, and that his death was not Pagan-related.

ACKNOWLEDGMENTS

First and foremost, thank you Kim Pack, for letting me see firsthand your relentless pursuit for justice. I have learned so much from you since we first connected in 2013. I will always look up to you, and I wish I had an ounce of your strength and grace.

A.J., thank you for all your support from day one, when I first had the idea to write this book. You gave me the tools to make this happen and you never doubted that I could do this. Also, your grammar will always be better than mine.

Mom, thank you for all of your grammar checks. I know you always wanted to be a copy editor, and you got your chance thanks to me!

To my lawyer, Jim Leonard: you are a true crime muse. You believed in me from day one on this project, and you've become a true friend, a sounding board and the best lawyer a girl could ask for. Without you, this would not have been possible.

To my publisher, Edward Jutkowitz: you took a chance on me when Jim and I first reached out to you. Thank you for believing in me.

To my editor Miriam Seidel: I knew when I met you that you understood what a passion project truly meant. Thank you for your patience, insight, and talent. For a first-time author, it is a daunting task to hand over your manuscript to a seasoned editor. I learned invaluable lessons from you that I never could have gained in a classroom.

To 6abc President and General Manager Bernie Prazenica and 6abc Vice President of News and News Director Tom Davis. Thank you for your patience and encouragement, and for giving me the time and space to allow me to tackle this challenge.

To Amy Morris: you were my mentor when I returned to Philadelphia to report for 6abc and you always supported April's story and my connection to the case.

To my second family at 6abc: I am so lucky to have the best colleagues, who have been a major support system since I announced I was doing this.

To the dozens of people who helped me, but I can't publicly thank because they don't want their names used. You know who you are. Thank you for trusting me.